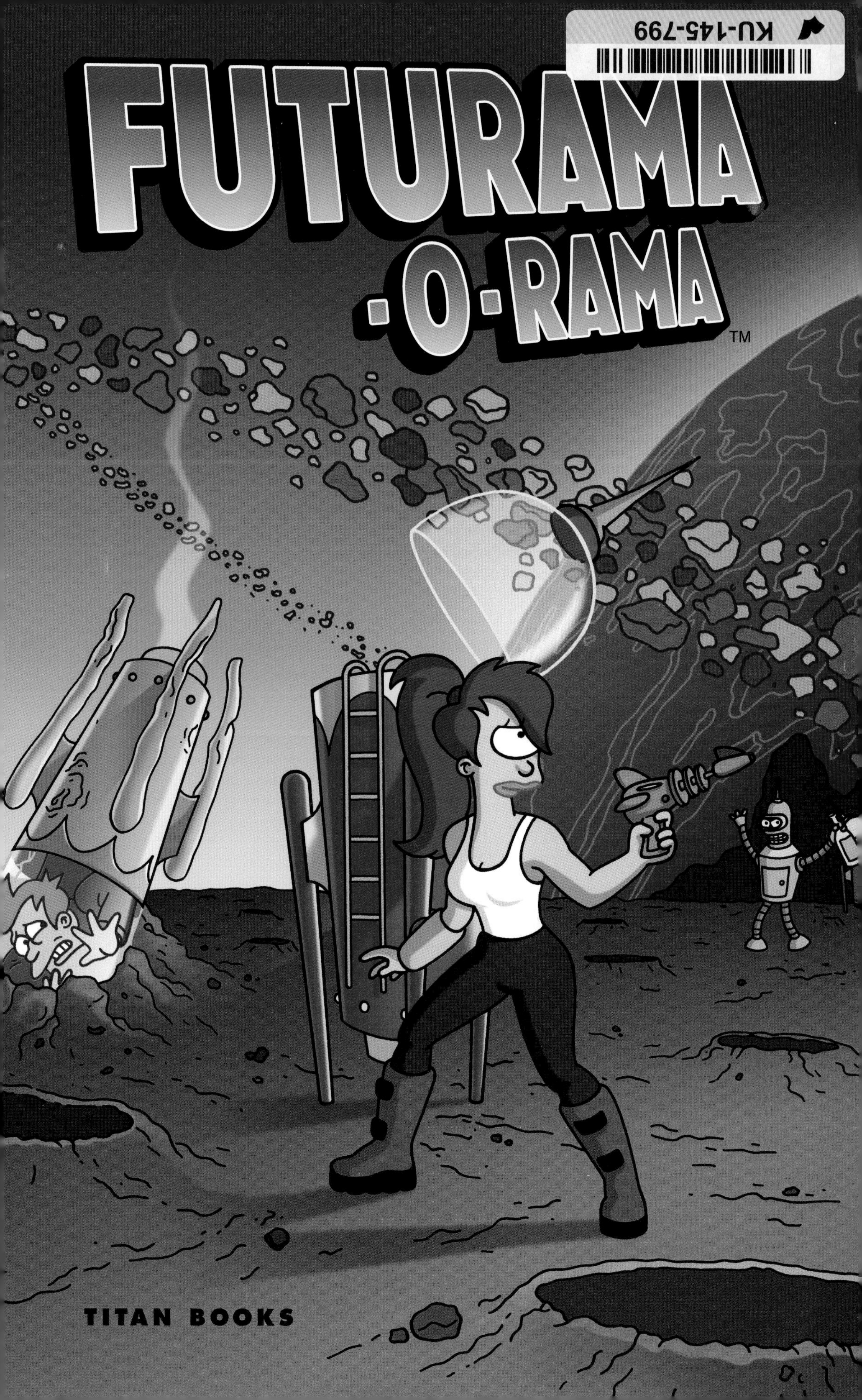
FUTURAMA
-O-RAMA
TM
TITAN BOOKS

FUTURAMA-O-RAMA

Copyright ©2000, 2001 & 2002 by
Bongo Entertainment, Inc. All rights reserved.
No part of this book may be used or reproduced in any manner whatsoever
without written permission except in the case of brief quotations
embodied in critical articles and reviews. For information address:
Bongo Comics Group c/o Titan Books
P.O. Box 1963, Santa Monica, CA 90406-1963

Published in the UK by Titan Books, a division of Titan Publishing Group,
144 Southwark St., London SE1 0UP, under licence from Bongo Entertainment, Inc.

FIRST EDITION: SEPTEMBER 2002

ISBN 1-84023-434-2
ISBN-13: 9781840234343

2 4 6 8 10 9 7 5 3

Publisher: MATT GROENING
Creative Director: BILL MORRISON
Managing Editor: TERRY DELEGEANE
Director of Operations: ROBERT ZAUGH
Art Director: NATHAN KANE
Production Manager: CHRISTOPHER UNGAR
Administration: SHERRI SMITH
Legal Guardian: SUSAN GRODE

Trade Paperback Concepts & Design: SERBAN CRISTESCU

Contributing Artists:
KAREN BATES, PAM COOKE, SERBAN CRISTESCU, PETER GOMEZ, CHIA-HSIEN JASON HO,
NATHAN KANE, TOM KING, JAMES LLOYD, BILL MORRISON, PHYLLIS NOVIN, RICK REESE,
MIKE ROTE, STEVE STEERE, JR., CHRIS UNGAR, ART VILLANUEVA

Contributing Writers:
ERIC ROGERS, BILL MORRISON

PRINTED IN ITALY

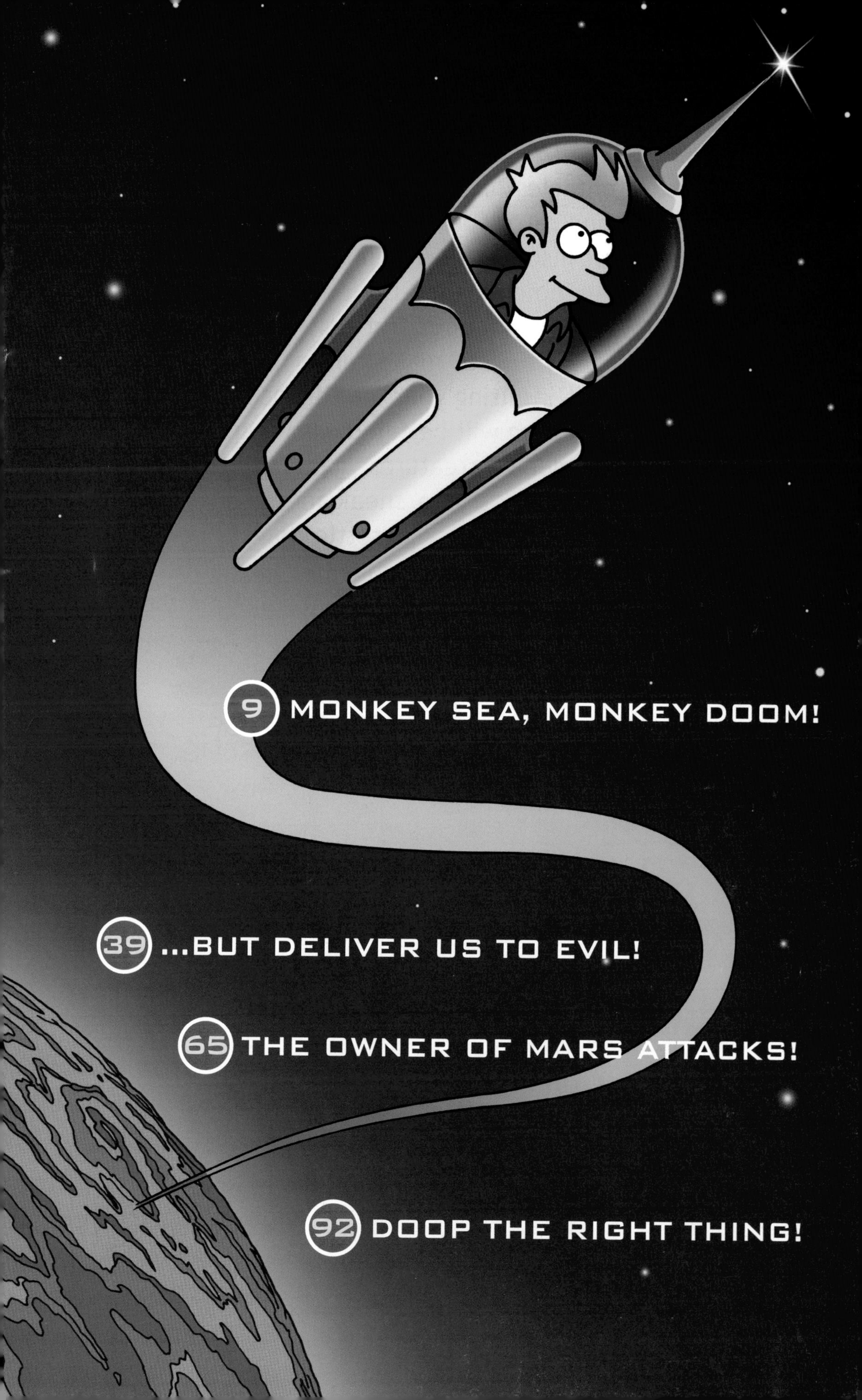

Aliens, Robots, Mutants, and the Rest of You:

Welcome to *Futurama-O-Rama*! The thing you're holding in your hot little tentacles (or claws, clamps, tendrils, whatever) is not just another retro-futuristic, space-opera, sci-fi comic book, but the first installment of a mindbending, intergalactic, multi-dimensional, epic science-fiction history that we think you might just find downright spiffy! Our humble aim is to both honor science fiction and to make fun of the genre's built-in absurdities, without insulting your intelligence too much or too little. So, yes, *Futurama* will be filled with bug-eyed monsters, cyborgs, assorted oddball creatures, gadgets, and death rays, but we're also going to try to sneak in some actual human emotion along with the laughs. So settle down, open up a cold can of Slurm, and get ready to laugh with us, or at us. We don't care, as long as you're snickering in one form or another.

Yours Till the Brain Slugs Take Over Earth,

MATT GROENING

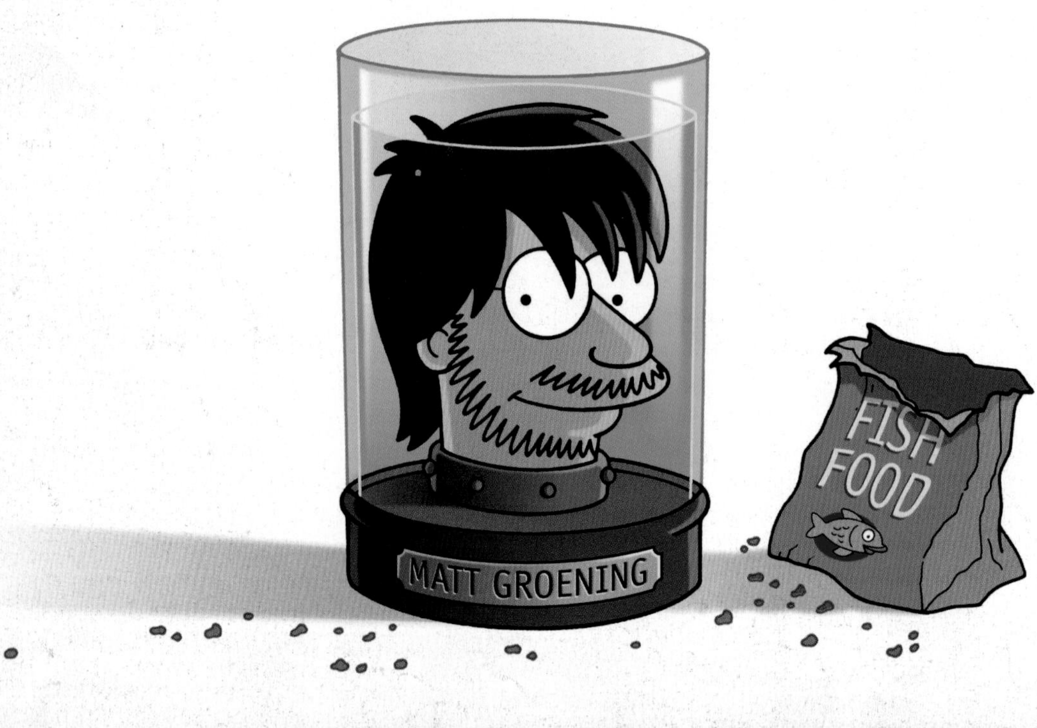
MATT GROENING
FISH FOOD

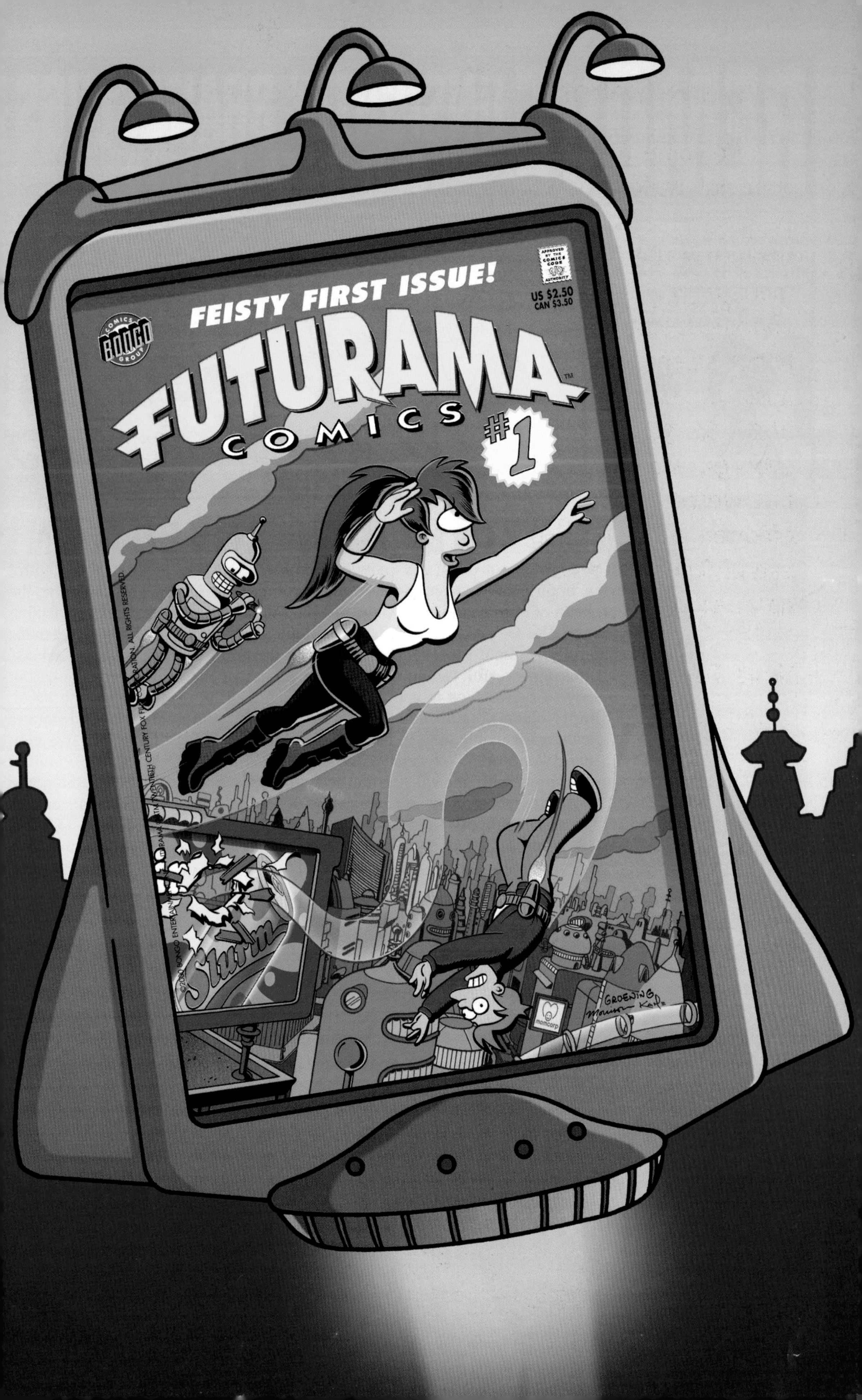

FEISTY FIRST ISSUE!
APPROVED BY THE COMICS CODE AUTHORITY
US $2.50
CAN $3.50
COMICS BONGO GROUP
FUTURAMA™
COMICS
#1
ALL RIGHTS RESERVED
Slurm
momcorp
GROENING

REMOVE UNSIGHTLY BRAIN SLUGS OR NO COST

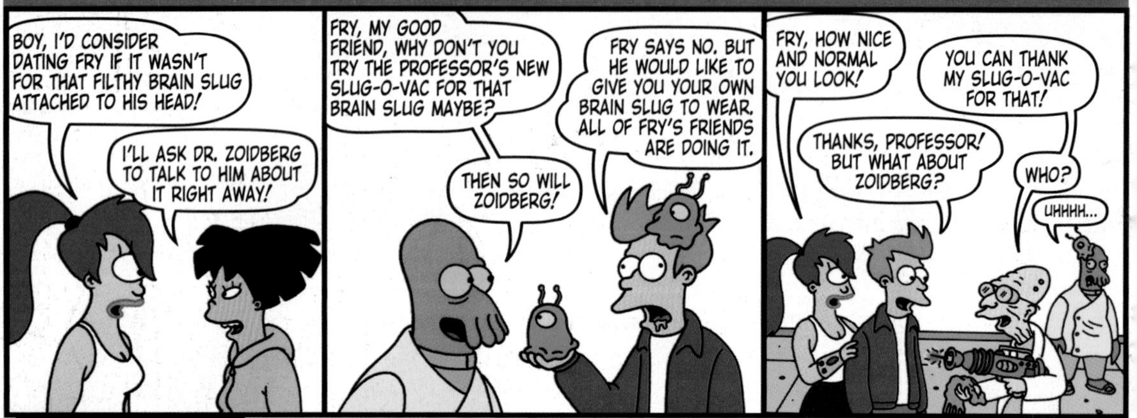
BOY, I'D CONSIDER DATING FRY IF IT WASN'T FOR THAT FILTHY BRAIN SLUG ATTACHED TO HIS HEAD!
I'LL ASK DR. ZOIDBERG TO TALK TO HIM ABOUT IT RIGHT AWAY!
FRY, MY GOOD FRIEND, WHY DON'T YOU TRY THE PROFESSOR'S NEW SLUG-O-VAC FOR THAT BRAIN SLUG MAYBE?
THEN SO WILL ZOIDBERG!
FRY SAYS NO. BUT HE WOULD LIKE TO GIVE YOU YOUR OWN BRAIN SLUG TO WEAR. ALL OF FRY'S FRIENDS ARE DOING IT.
FRY, HOW NICE AND NORMAL YOU LOOK!
YOU CAN THANK MY SLUG-O-VAC FOR THAT!
THANKS, PROFESSOR! BUT WHAT ABOUT ZOIDBERG?
WHO?
UHHHH...

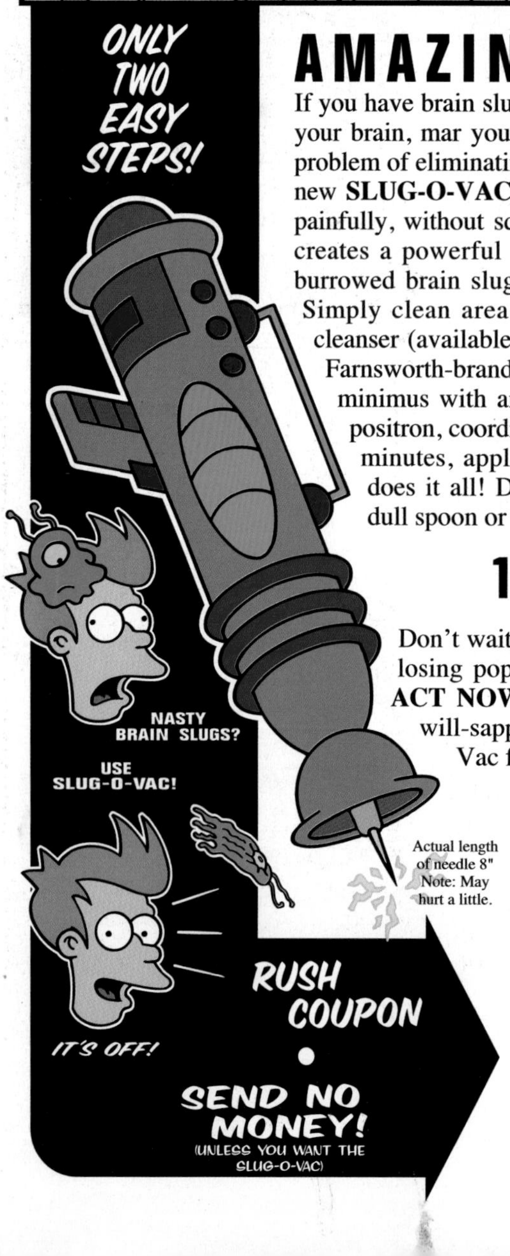
ONLY TWO EASY STEPS!
NASTY BRAIN SLUGS?
USE SLUG-O-VAC!
IT'S OFF!
Actual length of needle 8" Note: May hurt a little.
RUSH COUPON
•
SEND NO MONEY!
(UNLESS YOU WANT THE SLUG-O-VAC)

AMAZING NEW INVENTION!

If you have brain slugs, you know how embarrassing they are, how they control your brain, mar your appearance, and invite criticism. Now you can solve the problem of eliminating brain slugs forever with Professor Farnsworth's amazing new **SLUG-O-VAC**. It extracts filthy brain slugs from your brain in seconds, painfully, without squeezing or bashing in the brain or skull. **SLUG-O-VAC** creates a powerful vacuum around the mouth of the brain slug! Sucks out burrowed brain slugs in a jiffy. Germ-laden drill bits never touch the brain. Simply clean area around brain slug's mouth with synthesized ammonia cleanser (available only in Nevada), apply suction plates to temple-area with Farnsworth-brand oxygenator (no longer sold), massage brain slug's gluteus minimus with ancient Martian technique, fluctuate the needle's diametric positron, coordinate intake valve with timer setting, wait five hours and 24 minutes, apply searing needle to skull... and it's off! **SLUG-O-VAC** does it all! Don't risk infection with old-fashioned methods, such as a dull spoon or fireworks. Order TODAY!

10-DAY TRIAL OFFER

Don't wait for embarrassing criticism or brain-death to act. Don't risk losing popularity and success because of ugly, brain-starved slugs. **ACT NOW!** Enjoy the thrill of having your own thoughts, free of will-sapping, soul-sucking, embarrassing brain slugs. Try Slug-O-Vac for 10 days. We guarantee it to do all we claim.*

*No actual claims were made in this advertisement, only strongly-worded suggestions

GOOD NEWS INNOVATIONS, Dept. 8.273
P.O. Box 793, New New York, NY 10101.793

☐ Ship C.O.D. I will pay postman $100 plus postal beak-wetting, if any. If I am not delighted, the brain slug will most likely still be attached to my brain and I won't know the difference!

☐ I prefer to enclose $100 now and save postage and hassle. Same guarantee as above.

NAME ____________________
ADDRESS ____________________
CITY ____________________ STATE ________
COUNTRY ______ PLANET ________ GALAXY _______ ZIP ______

(Sorry, no deliveries to Island of Canada or Omicron Persei 9)
Offer not valid before Aug. 3000

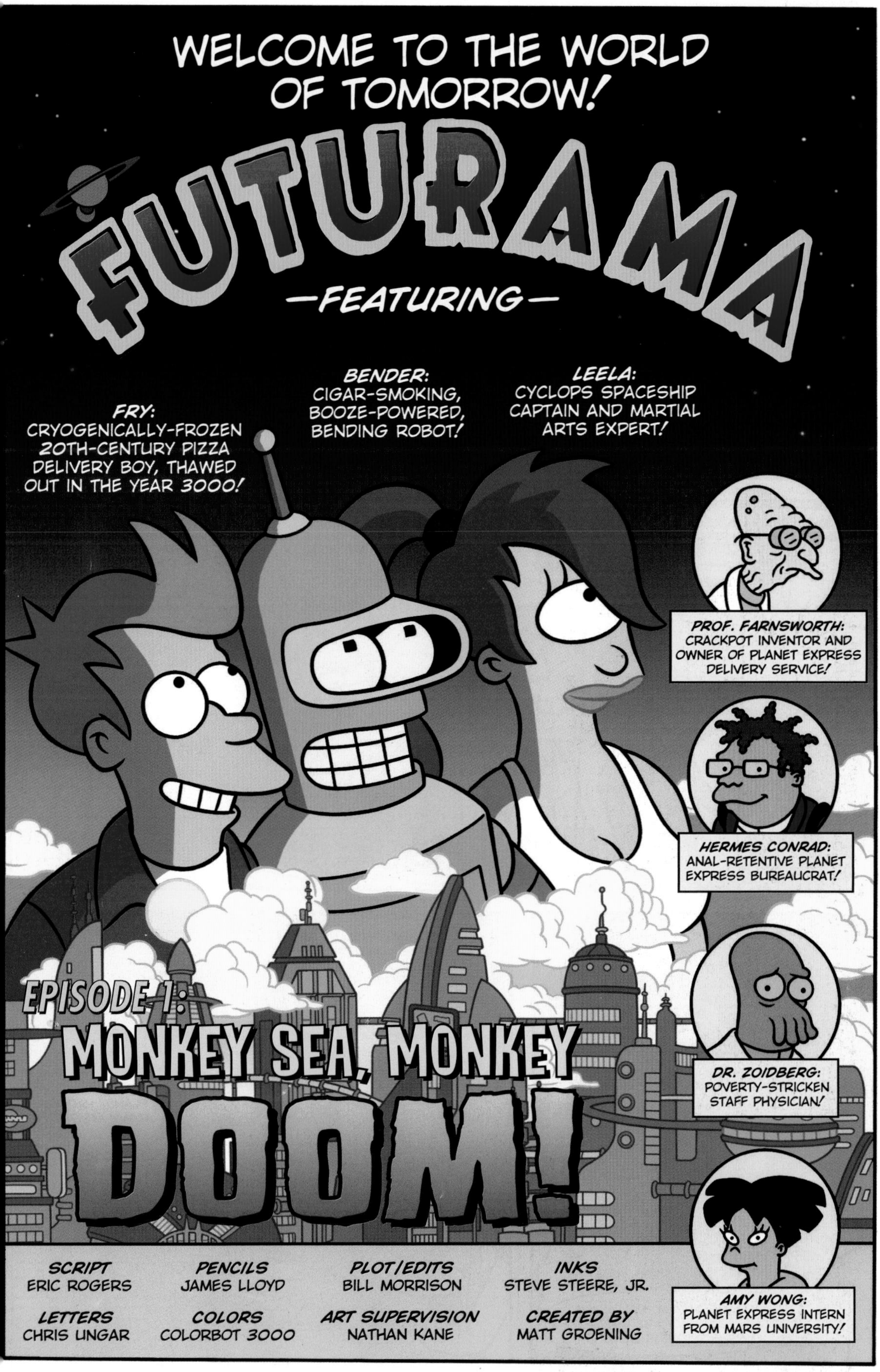

WELCOME TO THE WORLD OF TOMORROW!
FUTURAMA
—FEATURING—
FRY: CRYOGENICALLY-FROZEN 20TH-CENTURY PIZZA DELIVERY BOY, THAWED OUT IN THE YEAR 3000!
BENDER: CIGAR-SMOKING, BOOZE-POWERED, BENDING ROBOT!
LEELA: CYCLOPS SPACESHIP CAPTAIN AND MARTIAL ARTS EXPERT!
PROF. FARNSWORTH: CRACKPOT INVENTOR AND OWNER OF PLANET EXPRESS DELIVERY SERVICE!
HERMES CONRAD: ANAL-RETENTIVE PLANET EXPRESS BUREAUCRAT!
DR. ZOIDBERG: POVERTY-STRICKEN STAFF PHYSICIAN!
EPISODE 1:
MONKEY SEA, MONKEY DOOM!
AMY WONG: PLANET EXPRESS INTERN FROM MARS UNIVERSITY!
SCRIPT ERIC ROGERS
PENCILS JAMES LLOYD
PLOT/EDITS BILL MORRISON
INKS STEVE STEERE, JR.
LETTERS CHRIS UNGAR
COLORS COLORBOT 3000
ART SUPERVISION NATHAN KANE
CREATED BY MATT GROENING

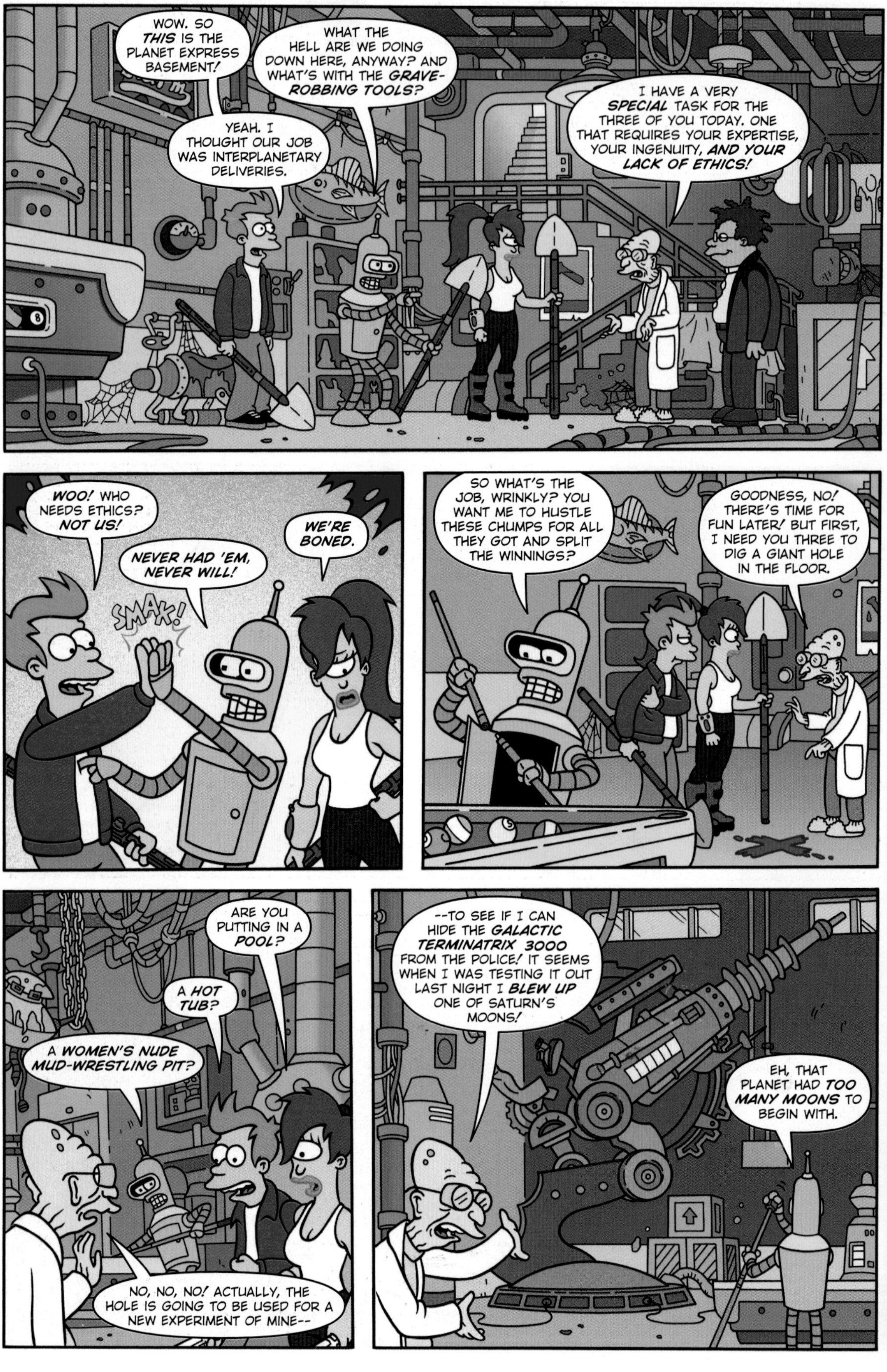
WOW. SO THIS IS THE PLANET EXPRESS BASEMENT!
YEAH. I THOUGHT OUR JOB WAS INTERPLANETARY DELIVERIES.
WHAT THE HELL ARE WE DOING DOWN HERE, ANYWAY? AND WHAT'S WITH THE GRAVE-ROBBING TOOLS?
I HAVE A VERY SPECIAL TASK FOR THE THREE OF YOU TODAY. ONE THAT REQUIRES YOUR EXPERTISE, YOUR INGENUITY, AND YOUR LACK OF ETHICS!
WOO! WHO NEEDS ETHICS? NOT US!
NEVER HAD 'EM, NEVER WILL!
SMAK!
WE'RE BONED.
SO WHAT'S THE JOB, WRINKLY? YOU WANT ME TO HUSTLE THESE CHUMPS FOR ALL THEY GOT AND SPLIT THE WINNINGS?
GOODNESS, NO! THERE'S TIME FOR FUN LATER! BUT FIRST, I NEED YOU THREE TO DIG A GIANT HOLE IN THE FLOOR.
ARE YOU PUTTING IN A POOL?
A HOT TUB?
A WOMEN'S NUDE MUD-WRESTLING PIT?
NO, NO, NO! ACTUALLY, THE HOLE IS GOING TO BE USED FOR A NEW EXPERIMENT OF MINE--
--TO SEE IF I CAN HIDE THE GALACTIC TERMINATRIX 3000 FROM THE POLICE! IT SEEMS WHEN I WAS TESTING IT OUT LAST NIGHT I BLEW UP ONE OF SATURN'S MOONS!
EH, THAT PLANET HAD TOO MANY MOONS TO BEGIN WITH.

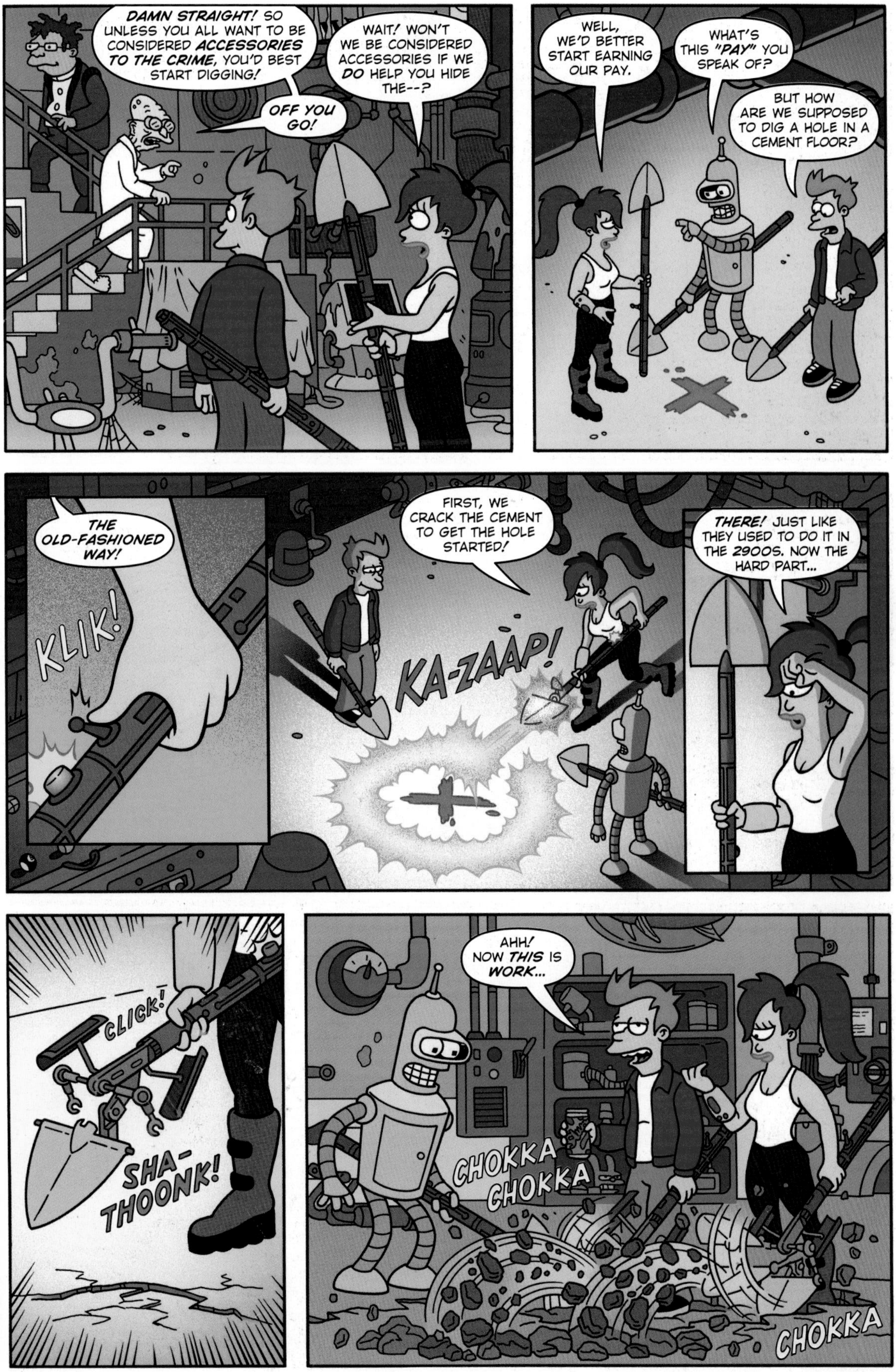
DAMN STRAIGHT! SO UNLESS YOU ALL WANT TO BE CONSIDERED ACCESSORIES TO THE CRIME, YOU'D BEST START DIGGING!
OFF YOU GO!
WAIT! WON'T WE BE CONSIDERED ACCESSORIES IF WE DO HELP YOU HIDE THE--?
WELL, WE'D BETTER START EARNING OUR PAY.
WHAT'S THIS "PAY" YOU SPEAK OF?
BUT HOW ARE WE SUPPOSED TO DIG A HOLE IN A CEMENT FLOOR?
THE OLD-FASHIONED WAY!
KLIK!
FIRST, WE CRACK THE CEMENT TO GET THE HOLE STARTED!
KA-ZAAP!
THERE! JUST LIKE THEY USED TO DO IT IN THE 2900S. NOW THE HARD PART...
CLICK!
SHA-THOONK!
AHH! NOW THIS IS WORK...
CHOKKA
CHOKKA
CHOKKA

SECONDS LATER...

I CAN'T TAKE IT ANYMORE! *THIS IS TOO HARD!*

FRY, YOUR SHOVEL'S BEEN SHOVELING FOR LESS THAN A MINUTE!

YEAH, WELL, THERE MUST BE SOMETHING DIFFERENT ABOUT THE DIRT IN THE FUTURE, LIKE IT'S MADE OUT OF *STEEL* OR *PLEXIGLAS* OR SOMETHING.

WHAT HAVE YOU DONE TO MY PRECIOUS SOIL?

CHOKKA

CHOKKA

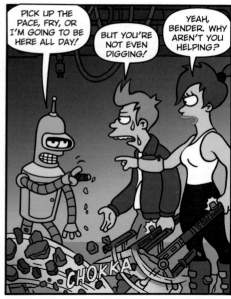

PICK UP THE PACE, FRY, OR I'M GOING TO BE HERE ALL DAY!

BUT YOU'RE NOT EVEN DIGGING!

YEAH, BENDER. WHY AREN'T YOU HELPING?

CHOKKA

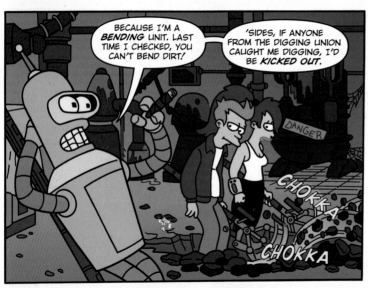

BECAUSE I'M A *BENDING* UNIT. LAST TIME I CHECKED, YOU CAN'T BEND DIRT!

'SIDES, IF ANYONE FROM THE DIGGING UNION CAUGHT ME DIGGING, I'D BE *KICKED OUT.*

DANGER

CHOKKA

CHOKKA

THOSE GUYS HAVE STRONG TIES TO THE *ROBOT MAFIA!*

EUHH!

KLANK!

YOU'VE HIT SOMETHING!

HEY, IT'S A *PARTRIDGE FAMILY LUNCHBOX!*

OHH! I GOT DIBS! GIMME!

the partridge family

WHAT DO YOU THINK COULD BE IN THERE?

PERHAPS THE *ANSWER* TO THE *MEANING* OF LIFE!

MAYBE THE *SECRET* INGREDIENTS OF *WHITE-OUT!*

PIRATE'S BOOTY!

OR MAYBE BEST OF ALL... *FOOD!*

THINK AGAIN, YOU *POVERTY-STRICKEN PRAWN!* WHATEVER *GOLD* OR *PORN* OR *ILLEGAL SUBSTANCES* WE FIND IN HERE GOES TO THE MAN WHO FOUND THE LUNCHBOX IN THE FIRST PLACE.

AW, THANKS, BEND--

SWIPE!

YOU GO ALONG WITH THE STORY--WHATEVER SMUT THERE IS, I'LL SPLIT WITH YOU 70-30.

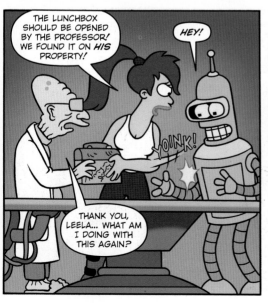

THE LUNCHBOX SHOULD BE OPENED BY THE PROFESSOR! WE FOUND IT ON *HIS* PROPERTY!

HEY!

YOINK!

THANK YOU, LEELA... WHAT AM I DOING WITH THIS AGAIN?

OPEN IT AND SEE WHAT'S INSIDE, FOR JAH'S SAKES.

OOH, YES, RIGHT, OF COURSE. WELL, HERE WE GO...

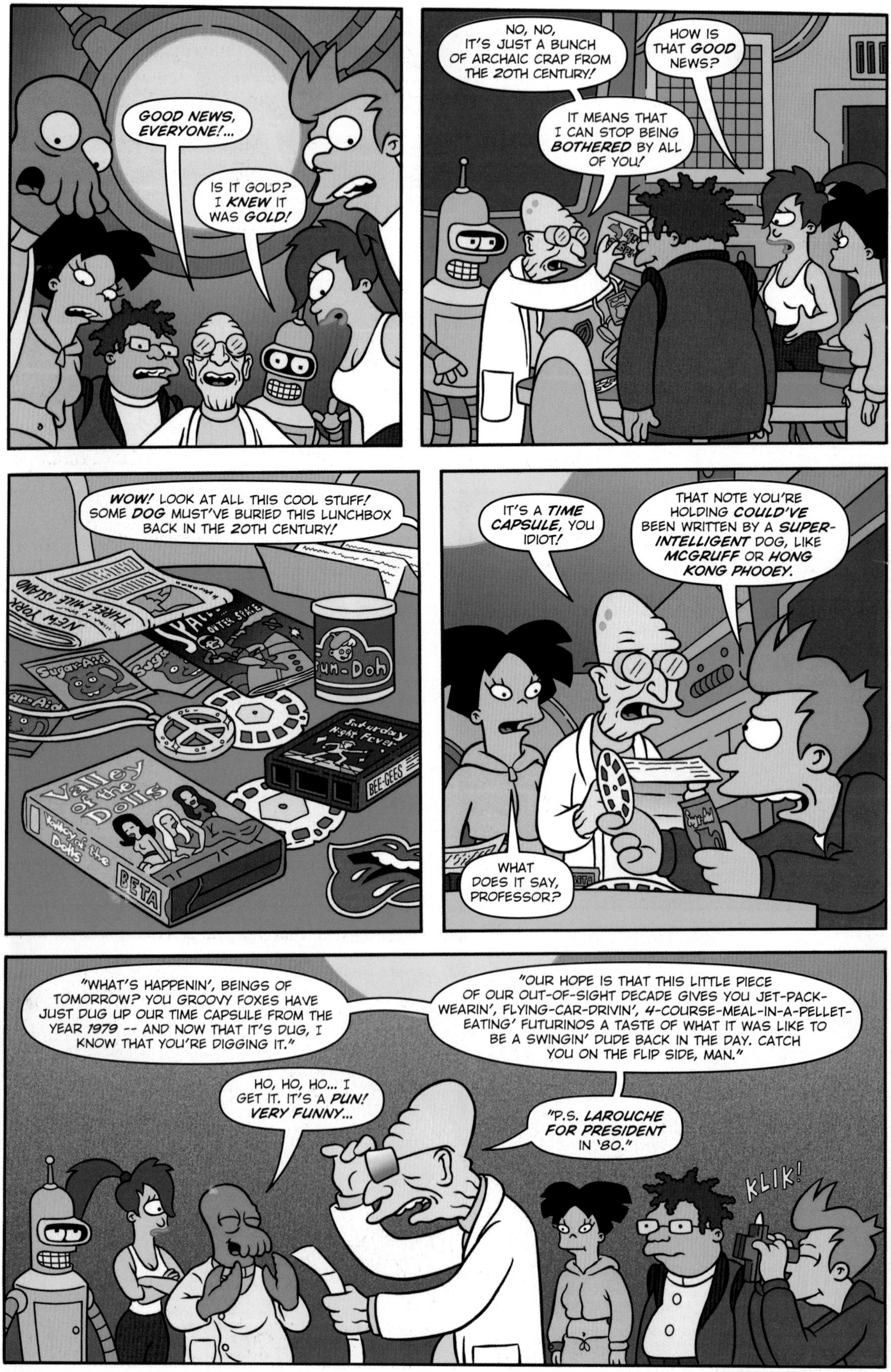
GOOD NEWS, EVERYONE!...
IS IT GOLD? I KNEW IT WAS GOLD!
NO, NO, IT'S JUST A BUNCH OF ARCHAIC CRAP FROM THE 20TH CENTURY!
HOW IS THAT GOOD NEWS?
IT MEANS THAT I CAN STOP BEING BOTHERED BY ALL OF YOU!
WOW! LOOK AT ALL THIS COOL STUFF! SOME DOG MUST'VE BURIED THIS LUNCHBOX BACK IN THE 20TH CENTURY!
NEW YORK
THREE MILE ISLAND
Sugar-Aid
Sun-Doh
Saturday Night Fever
BEE-GEES
Valley of the Dolls
BETA
IT'S A TIME CAPSULE, YOU IDIOT!
THAT NOTE YOU'RE HOLDING COULD'VE BEEN WRITTEN BY A SUPER-INTELLIGENT DOG, LIKE MCGRUFF OR HONG KONG PHOOEY.
WHAT DOES IT SAY, PROFESSOR?
"WHAT'S HAPPENIN', BEINGS OF TOMORROW? YOU GROOVY FOXES HAVE JUST DUG UP OUR TIME CAPSULE FROM THE YEAR 1979 -- AND NOW THAT IT'S DUG, I KNOW THAT YOU'RE DIGGING IT."
"OUR HOPE IS THAT THIS LITTLE PIECE OF OUR OUT-OF-SIGHT DECADE GIVES YOU JET-PACK-WEARIN', FLYING-CAR-DRIVIN', 4-COURSE-MEAL-IN-A-PELLET-EATING' FUTURINOS A TASTE OF WHAT IT WAS LIKE TO BE A SWINGIN' DUDE BACK IN THE DAY. CATCH YOU ON THE FLIP SIDE, MAN."
HO, HO, HO... I GET IT. IT'S A PUN! VERY FUNNY...
"P.S. LAROUCHE FOR PRESIDENT IN '80."
KLIK!

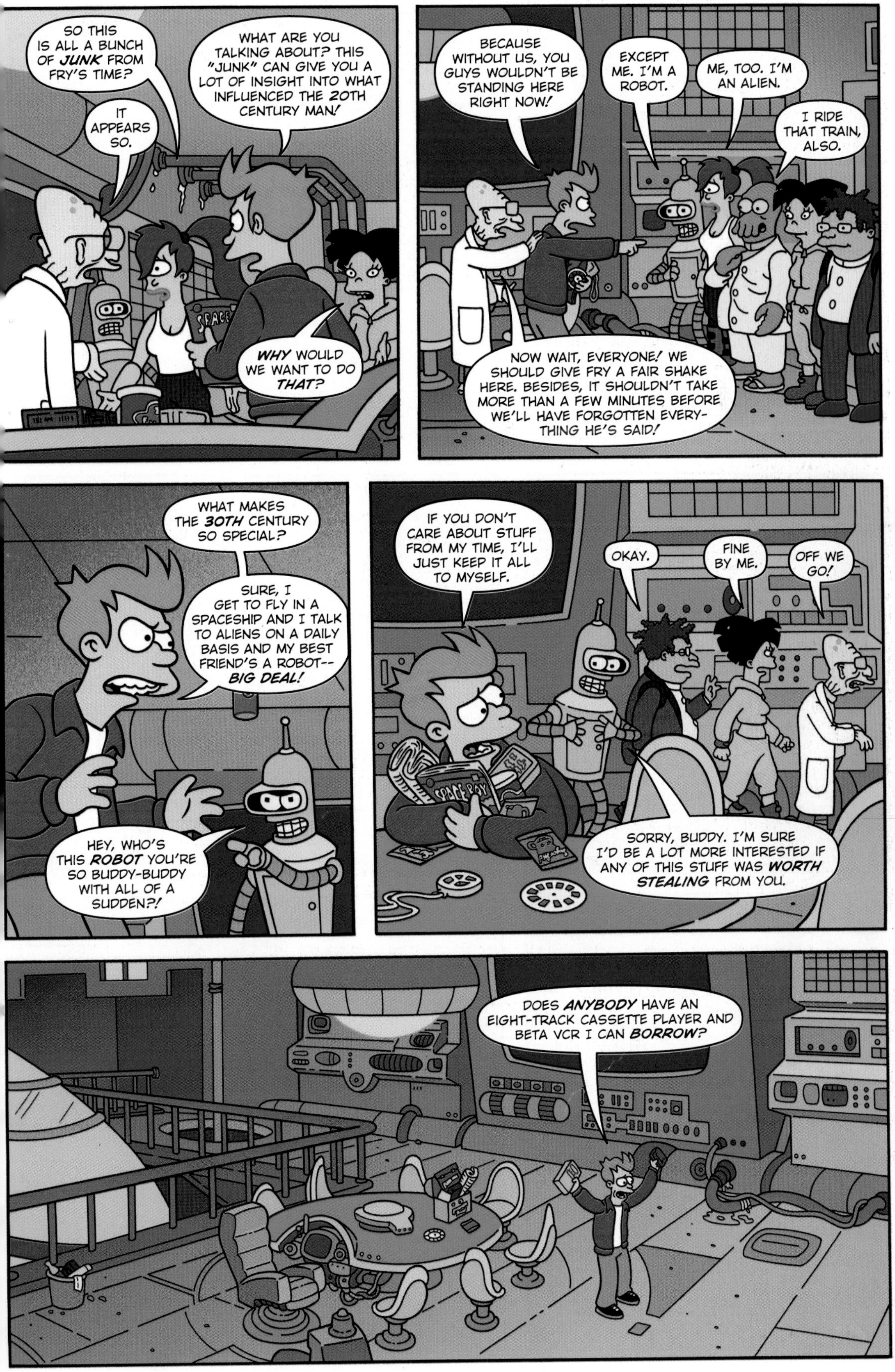
SO THIS IS ALL A BUNCH OF JUNK FROM FRY'S TIME?
IT APPEARS SO.
WHAT ARE YOU TALKING ABOUT? THIS "JUNK" CAN GIVE YOU A LOT OF INSIGHT INTO WHAT INFLUENCED THE 20TH CENTURY MAN!
WHY WOULD WE WANT TO DO THAT?
BECAUSE WITHOUT US, YOU GUYS WOULDN'T BE STANDING HERE RIGHT NOW!
EXCEPT ME. I'M A ROBOT.
ME, TOO. I'M AN ALIEN.
I RIDE THAT TRAIN, ALSO.
NOW WAIT, EVERYONE! WE SHOULD GIVE FRY A FAIR SHAKE HERE. BESIDES, IT SHOULDN'T TAKE MORE THAN A FEW MINUTES BEFORE WE'LL HAVE FORGOTTEN EVERYTHING HE'S SAID!
WHAT MAKES THE 30TH CENTURY SO SPECIAL?
SURE, I GET TO FLY IN A SPACESHIP AND I TALK TO ALIENS ON A DAILY BASIS AND MY BEST FRIEND'S A ROBOT-- BIG DEAL!
HEY, WHO'S THIS ROBOT YOU'RE SO BUDDY-BUDDY WITH ALL OF A SUDDEN?!
IF YOU DON'T CARE ABOUT STUFF FROM MY TIME, I'LL JUST KEEP IT ALL TO MYSELF.
OKAY.
FINE BY ME.
OFF WE GO!
SORRY, BUDDY. I'M SURE I'D BE A LOT MORE INTERESTED IF ANY OF THIS STUFF WAS WORTH STEALING FROM YOU.
DOES ANYBODY HAVE AN EIGHT-TRACK CASSETTE PLAYER AND BETA VCR I CAN BORROW?

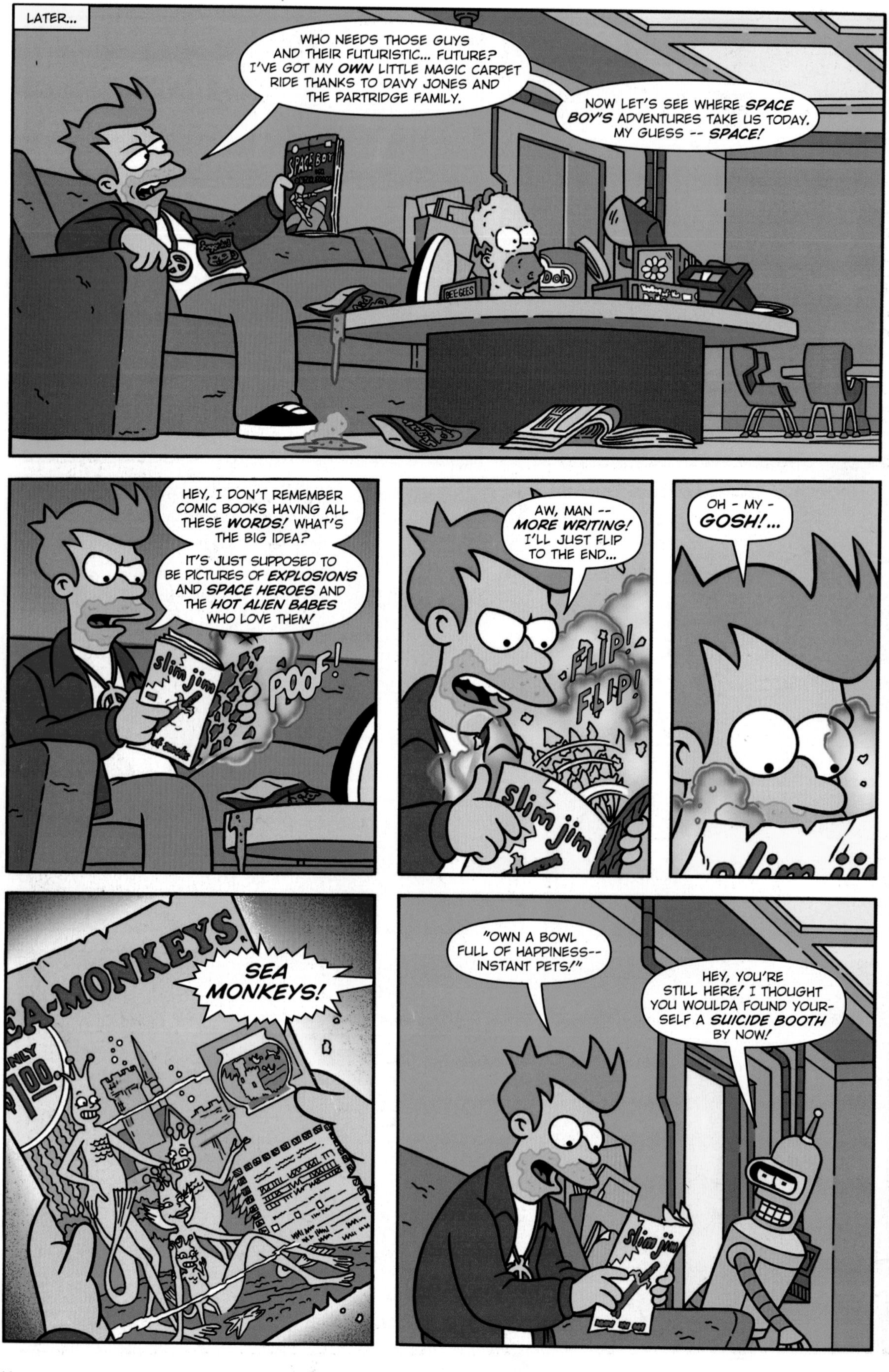
LATER...
WHO NEEDS THOSE GUYS AND THEIR FUTURISTIC... FUTURE? I'VE GOT MY OWN LITTLE MAGIC CARPET RIDE THANKS TO DAVY JONES AND THE PARTRIDGE FAMILY.
NOW LET'S SEE WHERE SPACE BOY'S ADVENTURES TAKE US TODAY. MY GUESS -- SPACE!
SPACE BOY
BEE GEES
HEY, I DON'T REMEMBER COMIC BOOKS HAVING ALL THESE WORDS! WHAT'S THE BIG IDEA?
IT'S JUST SUPPOSED TO BE PICTURES OF EXPLOSIONS AND SPACE HEROES AND THE HOT ALIEN BABES WHO LOVE THEM!
slim jim
POOF!
AW, MAN -- MORE WRITING! I'LL JUST FLIP TO THE END...
FLIP! FLIP!
slim jim
OH - MY - GOSH!...
SEA-MONKEYS
SEA MONKEYS!
"OWN A BOWL FULL OF HAPPINESS-- INSTANT PETS!"
HEY, YOU'RE STILL HERE! I THOUGHT YOU WOULDA FOUND YOURSELF A SUICIDE BOOTH BY NOW!
slim jim

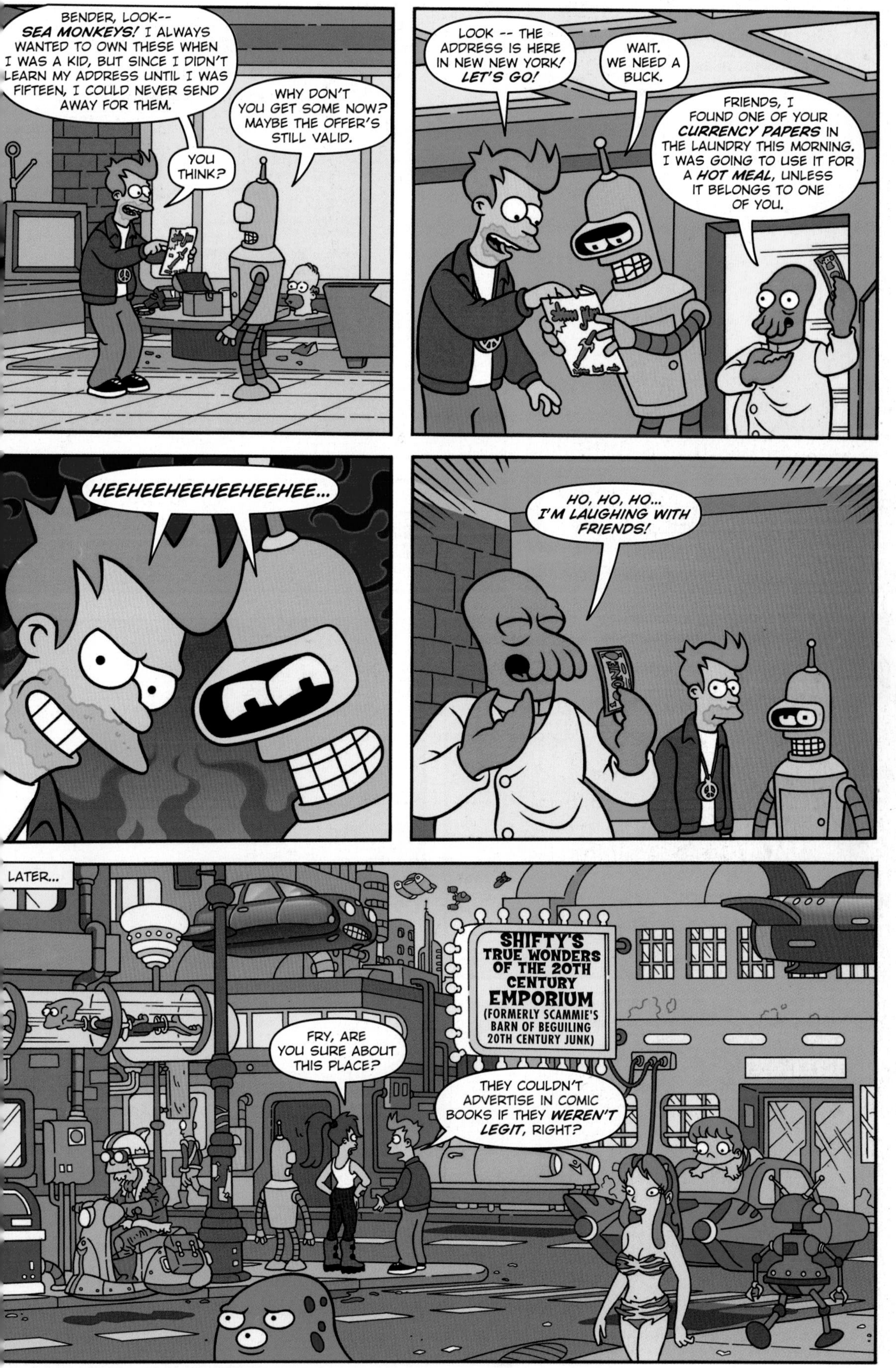
BENDER, LOOK-- SEA MONKEYS! I ALWAYS WANTED TO OWN THESE WHEN I WAS A KID, BUT SINCE I DIDN'T LEARN MY ADDRESS UNTIL I WAS FIFTEEN, I COULD NEVER SEND AWAY FOR THEM.
WHY DON'T YOU GET SOME NOW? MAYBE THE OFFER'S STILL VALID.
YOU THINK?
LOOK -- THE ADDRESS IS HERE IN NEW NEW YORK! LET'S GO!
WAIT. WE NEED A BUCK.
FRIENDS, I FOUND ONE OF YOUR CURRENCY PAPERS IN THE LAUNDRY THIS MORNING. I WAS GOING TO USE IT FOR A HOT MEAL, UNLESS IT BELONGS TO ONE OF YOU.
HEEHEEHEEHEEHEEHEE...
HO, HO, HO... I'M LAUGHING WITH FRIENDS!
LATER...
SHIFTY'S TRUE WONDERS OF THE 20TH CENTURY EMPORIUM (FORMERLY SCAMMIE'S BARN OF BEGUILING 20TH CENTURY JUNK)
FRY, ARE YOU SURE ABOUT THIS PLACE?
THEY COULDN'T ADVERTISE IN COMIC BOOKS IF THEY WEREN'T LEGIT, RIGHT?

WELL, I'LL KEEP AN EYE ON YOU JUST IN CASE. REMEMBER WHEN YOU TRIED TO SELL YOUR *KIDNEYS* FOR *SALSA* LAST WEEK?

HE *SHOULDA* DONE IT! I WAS OFFERING *BELOW MARKET VALUE!*

CAN I HELPS YOUSE?

YES, SIR! I'LL TAKE THREE OF YOUR BEST SEA MONKEYS!

HMM, I'LL SEES IF WE GOT THOSE IN STOCK--*RONNIE!*

YES SIR, MR. SAL!

WHILES YOU'RE WAITIN', FEEL FREES TO BROWSE AROUNDS.

THANKS!

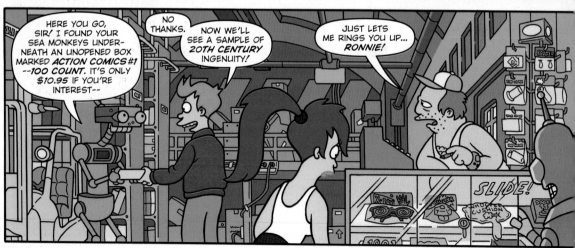

HERE YOU GO, SIR! I FOUND YOUR SEA MONKEYS UNDERNEATH AN UNOPENED BOX MARKED *ACTION COMICS #1 --100 COUNT.* IT'S ONLY *$10.95* IF YOU'RE INTEREST--

NO THANKS.

NOW WE'LL SEE A SAMPLE OF *20TH CENTURY* INGENUITY!

JUST LETS ME RINGS YOU UP... *RONNIE!*

SLIDE!

ONE DOLLARS, PLEASE.

DEE-DA LEET!

1.00

WAIT A SECOND-- SEA MONKEYS, X-RAY GLASSES, MIRACLE DIET KITS... FRY, THIS ALL SEEMS *VERY FISHY.*

WHY ARE YOU ALWAYS TRYING TO PUT DOWN COOL STUFF FROM MY TIME, LEELA?

I JUST DON'T WANT TO SEE YOU GET RIPPED OFF--

USUALLY THOSE IN THE *MOST NEEDS* FOR THE MIRACLE DIET KIT IS THE *MOST SKEPTICALS.*

WHAT'S *THAT* SUPPOSED TO MEAN?

INFERS WHAT YOU *WILLS.*

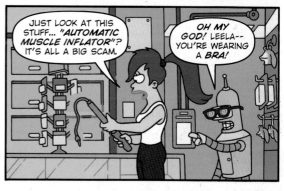

JUST LOOK AT THIS STUFF... *"AUTOMATIC MUSCLE INFLATOR"?* IT'S ALL A BIG SCAM.

OH MY GOD! LEELA-- YOU'RE WEARING A *BRA!*

I *ALWAYS* WEAR A BRA! THAT DOESN'T PROVE THAT THIS CRAP WORKS.

WAIT--THE *FAT GUY* ISN'T WEARING ANY *DEODORANT!*

YEAH, BUT YOUSE DON'T NEEDS X-RAY GLASSES TO *KNOW THAT.*

EWW!

ALL RIGHT THEN... *SWEET BABY JAMES!* FRY'S WEARING *LADIES UNDERPANTS!*

YEAH, RIGHT. NICE TRY, BENDER. YOU SEE, FRY?

UHH, CAN WE *GO* NOW?

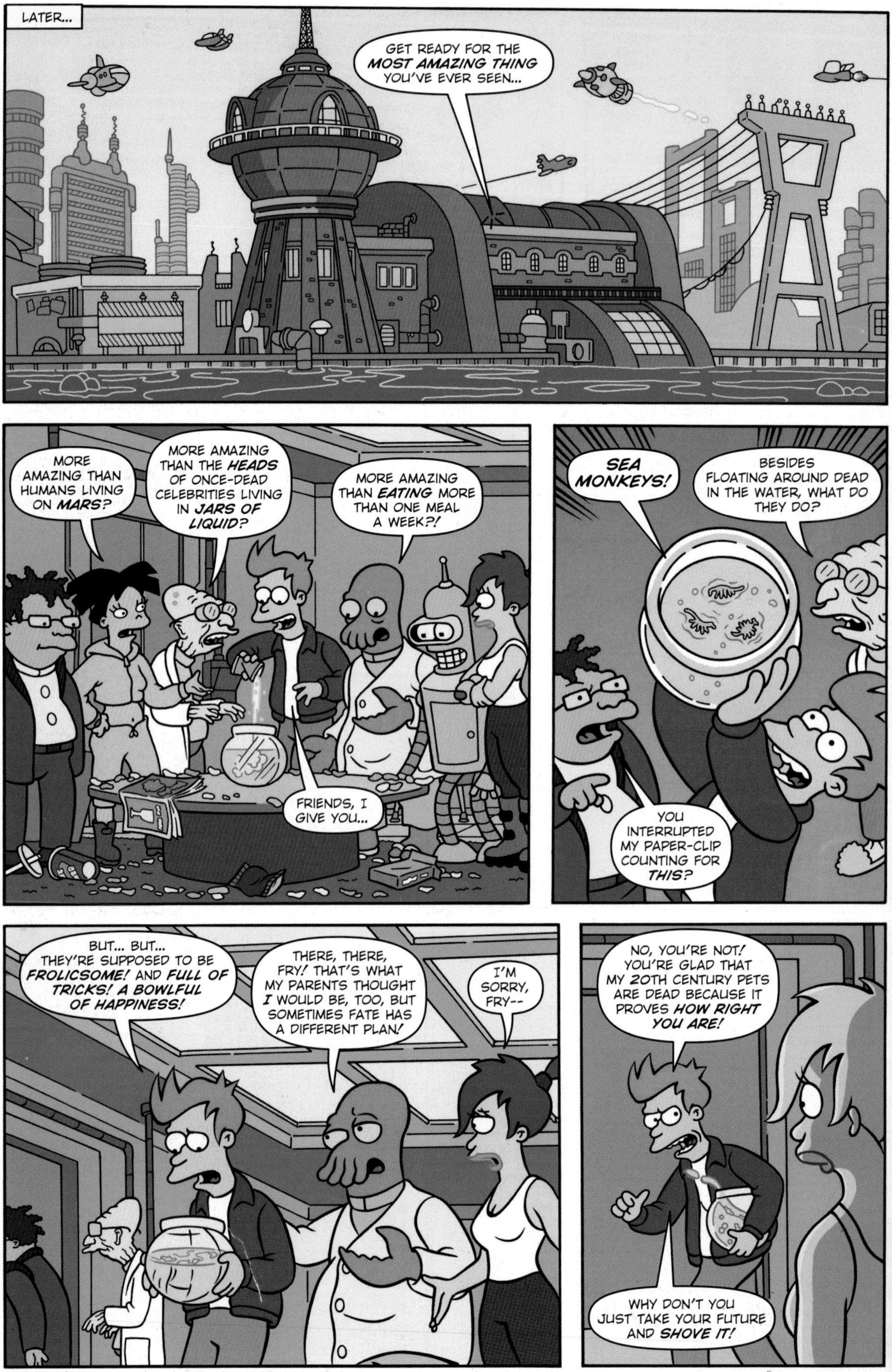
LATER...
GET READY FOR THE **MOST AMAZING THING** YOU'VE EVER SEEN...
MORE AMAZING THAN HUMANS LIVING ON **MARS?**
MORE AMAZING THAN THE **HEADS** OF ONCE-DEAD CELEBRITIES LIVING IN **JARS OF LIQUID?**
MORE AMAZING THAN **EATING** MORE THAN ONE MEAL A WEEK?!
FRIENDS, I GIVE YOU...
SEA MONKEYS!
BESIDES FLOATING AROUND DEAD IN THE WATER, WHAT DO THEY DO?
YOU INTERRUPTED MY PAPER-CLIP COUNTING FOR **THIS?**
BUT... BUT... THEY'RE SUPPOSED TO BE **FROLICSOME!** AND **FULL OF TRICKS! A BOWLFUL OF HAPPINESS!**
THERE, THERE, FRY! THAT'S WHAT MY PARENTS THOUGHT **I** WOULD BE, TOO, BUT SOMETIMES FATE HAS A DIFFERENT PLAN!
I'M SORRY, FRY--
NO, YOU'RE NOT! YOU'RE GLAD THAT MY **20TH** CENTURY PETS ARE DEAD BECAUSE IT PROVES **HOW RIGHT YOU ARE!**
WHY DON'T YOU JUST TAKE YOUR FUTURE AND **SHOVE IT!**

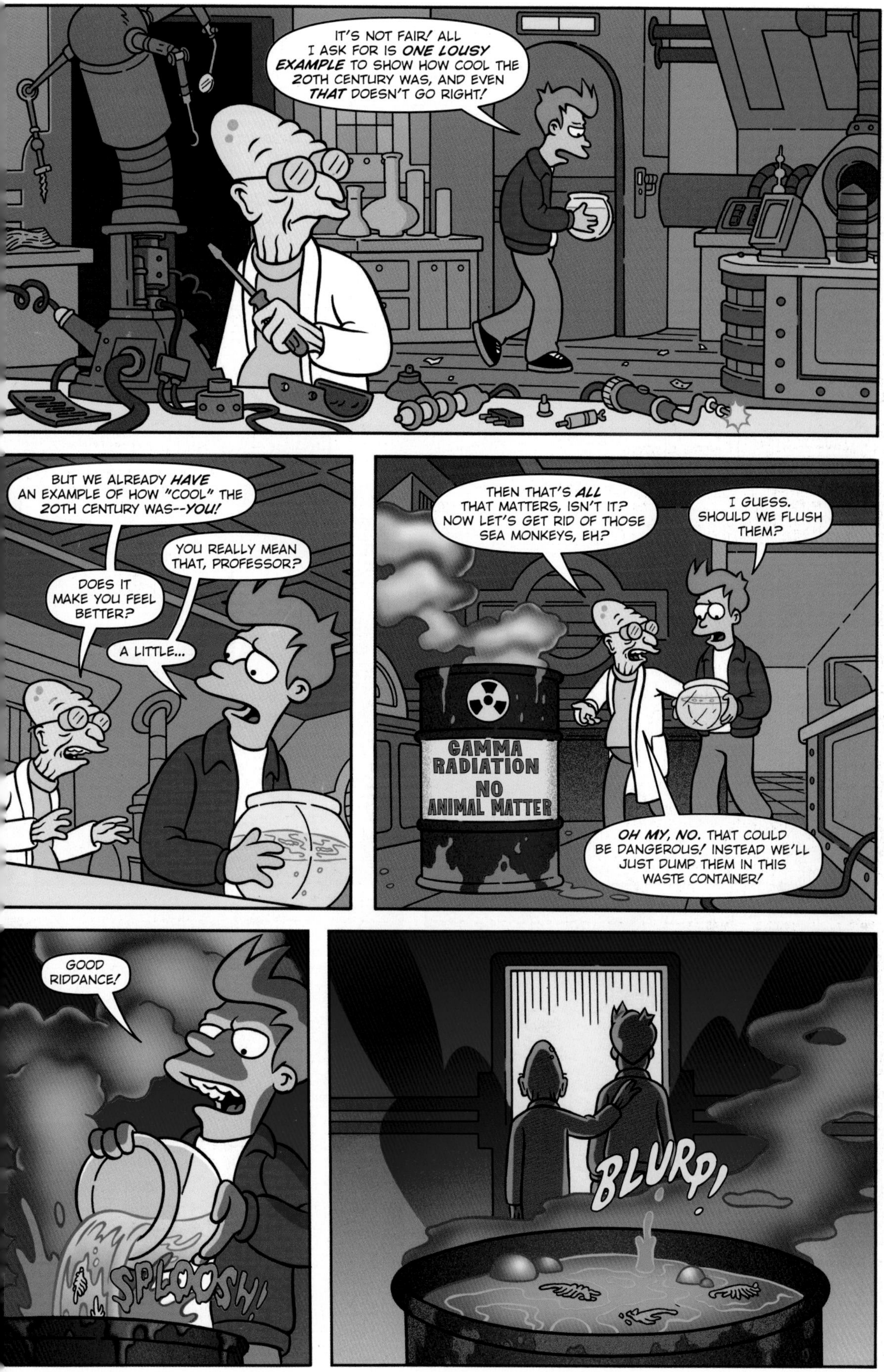
IT'S NOT FAIR! ALL I ASK FOR IS ONE LOUSY EXAMPLE TO SHOW HOW COOL THE 20TH CENTURY WAS, AND EVEN THAT DOESN'T GO RIGHT!
BUT WE ALREADY HAVE AN EXAMPLE OF HOW "COOL" THE 20TH CENTURY WAS--YOU!
YOU REALLY MEAN THAT, PROFESSOR?
DOES IT MAKE YOU FEEL BETTER?
A LITTLE...
THEN THAT'S ALL THAT MATTERS, ISN'T IT? NOW LET'S GET RID OF THOSE SEA MONKEYS, EH?
I GUESS. SHOULD WE FLUSH THEM?
GAMMA RADIATION
NO ANIMAL MATTER
OH MY, NO. THAT COULD BE DANGEROUS! INSTEAD WE'LL JUST DUMP THEM IN THIS WASTE CONTAINER!
GOOD RIDDANCE!
SPLOOSH!
BLURP!

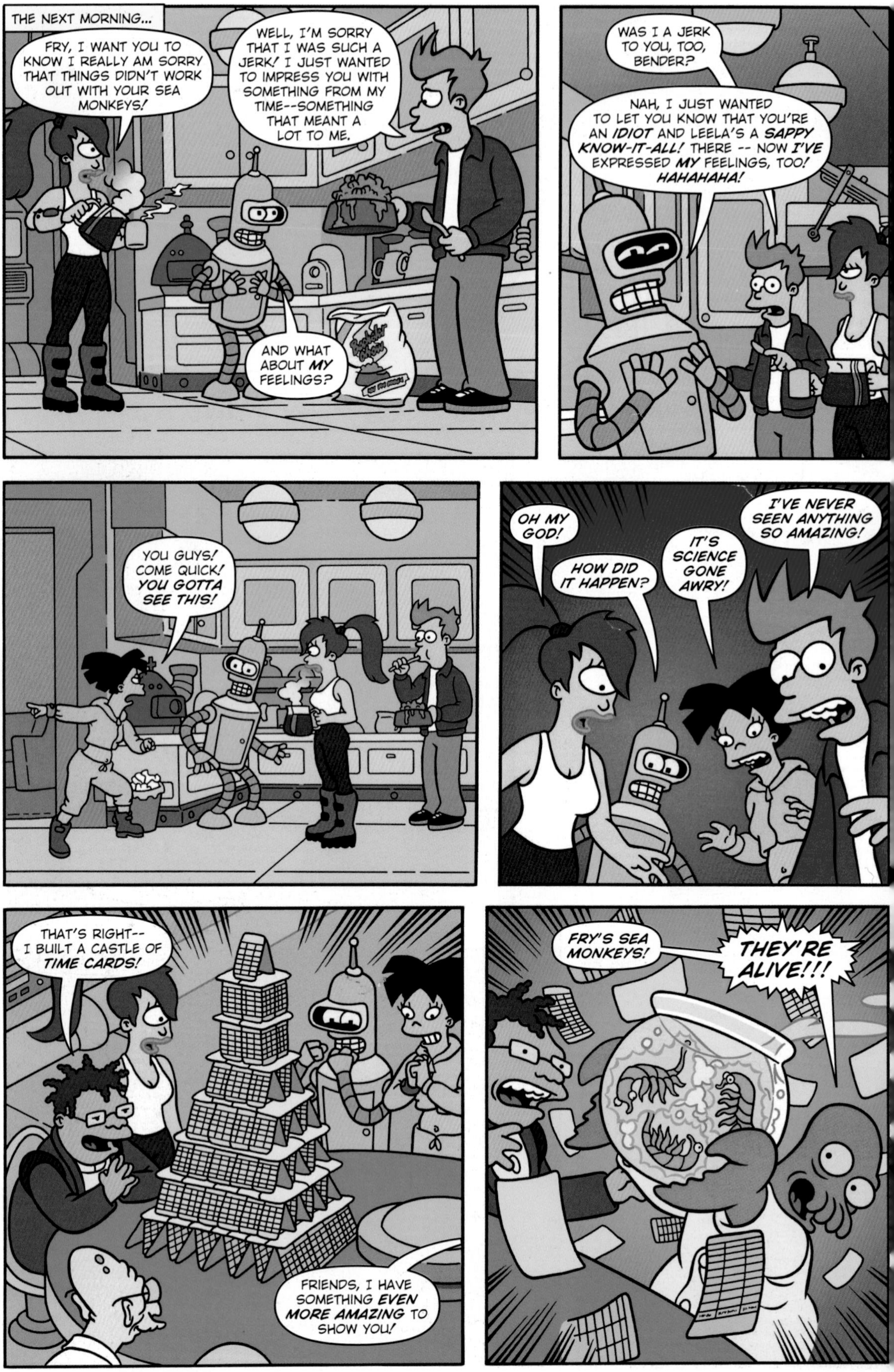
THE NEXT MORNING...
FRY, I WANT YOU TO KNOW I REALLY AM SORRY THAT THINGS DIDN'T WORK OUT WITH YOUR SEA MONKEYS!
WELL, I'M SORRY THAT I WAS SUCH A JERK! I JUST WANTED TO IMPRESS YOU WITH SOMETHING FROM MY TIME--SOMETHING THAT MEANT A LOT TO ME.
AND WHAT ABOUT MY FEELINGS?
WAS I A JERK TO YOU, TOO, BENDER?
NAH, I JUST WANTED TO LET YOU KNOW THAT YOU'RE AN IDIOT AND LEELA'S A SAPPY KNOW-IT-ALL! THERE -- NOW I'VE EXPRESSED MY FEELINGS, TOO! HAHAHAHA!
YOU GUYS! COME QUICK! YOU GOTTA SEE THIS!
OH MY GOD!
HOW DID IT HAPPEN?
IT'S SCIENCE GONE AWRY!
I'VE NEVER SEEN ANYTHING SO AMAZING!
THAT'S RIGHT-- I BUILT A CASTLE OF TIME CARDS!
FRIENDS, I HAVE SOMETHING EVEN MORE AMAZING TO SHOW YOU!
FRY'S SEA MONKEYS!
THEY'RE ALIVE!!!

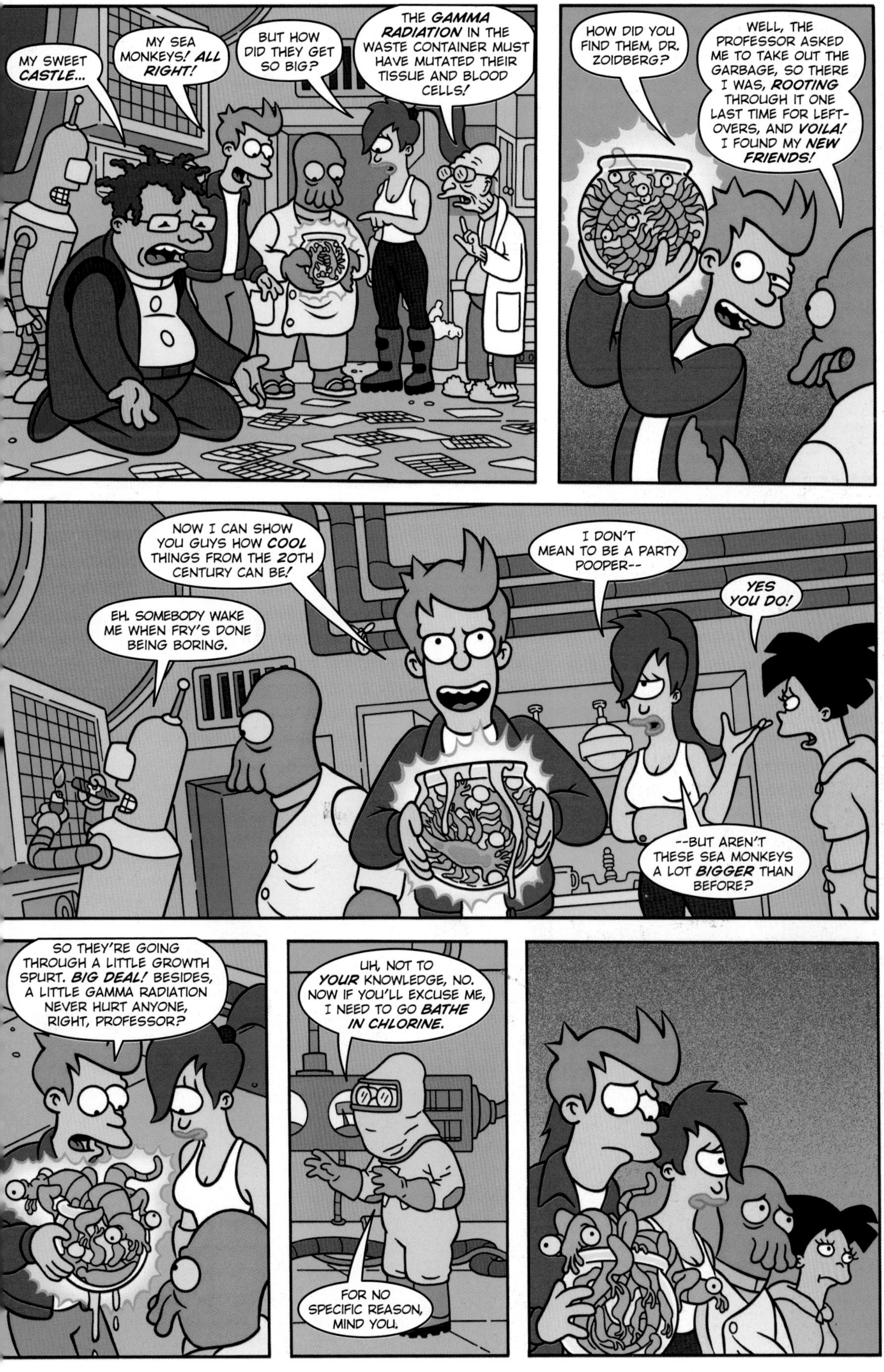
MY SWEET CASTLE...
MY SEA MONKEYS! ALL RIGHT!
BUT HOW DID THEY GET SO BIG?
THE GAMMA RADIATION IN THE WASTE CONTAINER MUST HAVE MUTATED THEIR TISSUE AND BLOOD CELLS!
HOW DID YOU FIND THEM, DR. ZOIDBERG?
WELL, THE PROFESSOR ASKED ME TO TAKE OUT THE GARBAGE, SO THERE I WAS, ROOTING THROUGH IT ONE LAST TIME FOR LEFT-OVERS, AND VOILA! I FOUND MY NEW FRIENDS!
NOW I CAN SHOW YOU GUYS HOW COOL THINGS FROM THE 20TH CENTURY CAN BE!
EH. SOMEBODY WAKE ME WHEN FRY'S DONE BEING BORING.
I DON'T MEAN TO BE A PARTY POOPER--
YES YOU DO!
--BUT AREN'T THESE SEA MONKEYS A LOT BIGGER THAN BEFORE?
SO THEY'RE GOING THROUGH A LITTLE GROWTH SPURT. BIG DEAL! BESIDES, A LITTLE GAMMA RADIATION NEVER HURT ANYONE, RIGHT, PROFESSOR?
UH, NOT TO YOUR KNOWLEDGE, NO. NOW IF YOU'LL EXCUSE ME, I NEED TO GO BATHE IN CHLORINE.
FOR NO SPECIFIC REASON, MIND YOU.

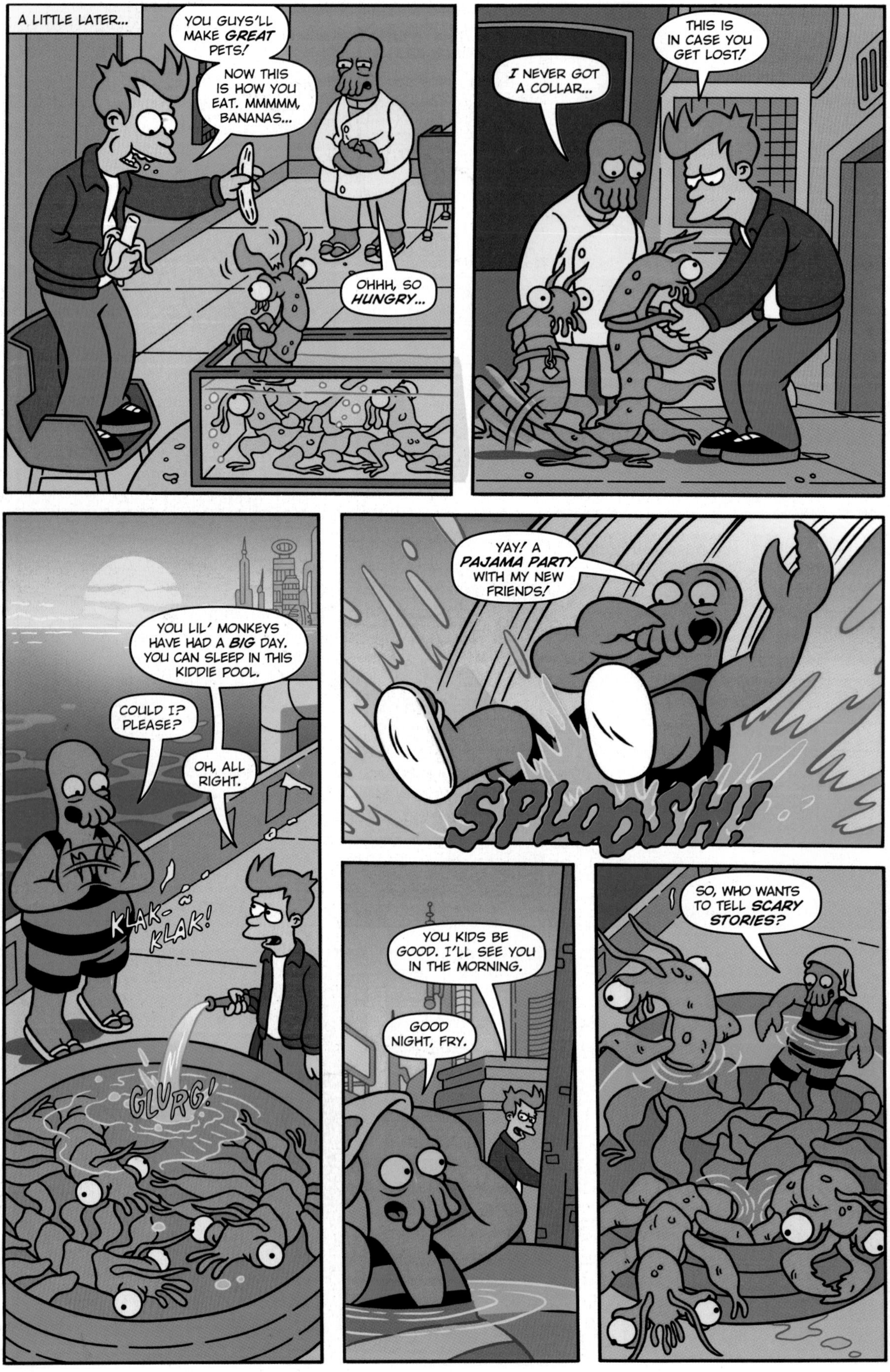
A LITTLE LATER...
YOU GUYS'LL MAKE **GREAT** PETS!
NOW THIS IS HOW YOU EAT. MMMMM, BANANAS...
OHHH, SO **HUNGRY**...
I NEVER GOT A COLLAR...
THIS IS IN CASE YOU GET LOST!
YOU LIL' MONKEYS HAVE HAD A **BIG** DAY. YOU CAN SLEEP IN THIS KIDDIE POOL.
COULD I? PLEASE?
OH, ALL RIGHT.
KLAK-KLAK!
GLURG!
YAY! A **PAJAMA PARTY** WITH MY NEW FRIENDS!
SPLOOSH!
YOU KIDS BE GOOD. I'LL SEE YOU IN THE MORNING.
GOOD NIGHT, FRY.
SO, WHO WANTS TO TELL **SCARY STORIES**?

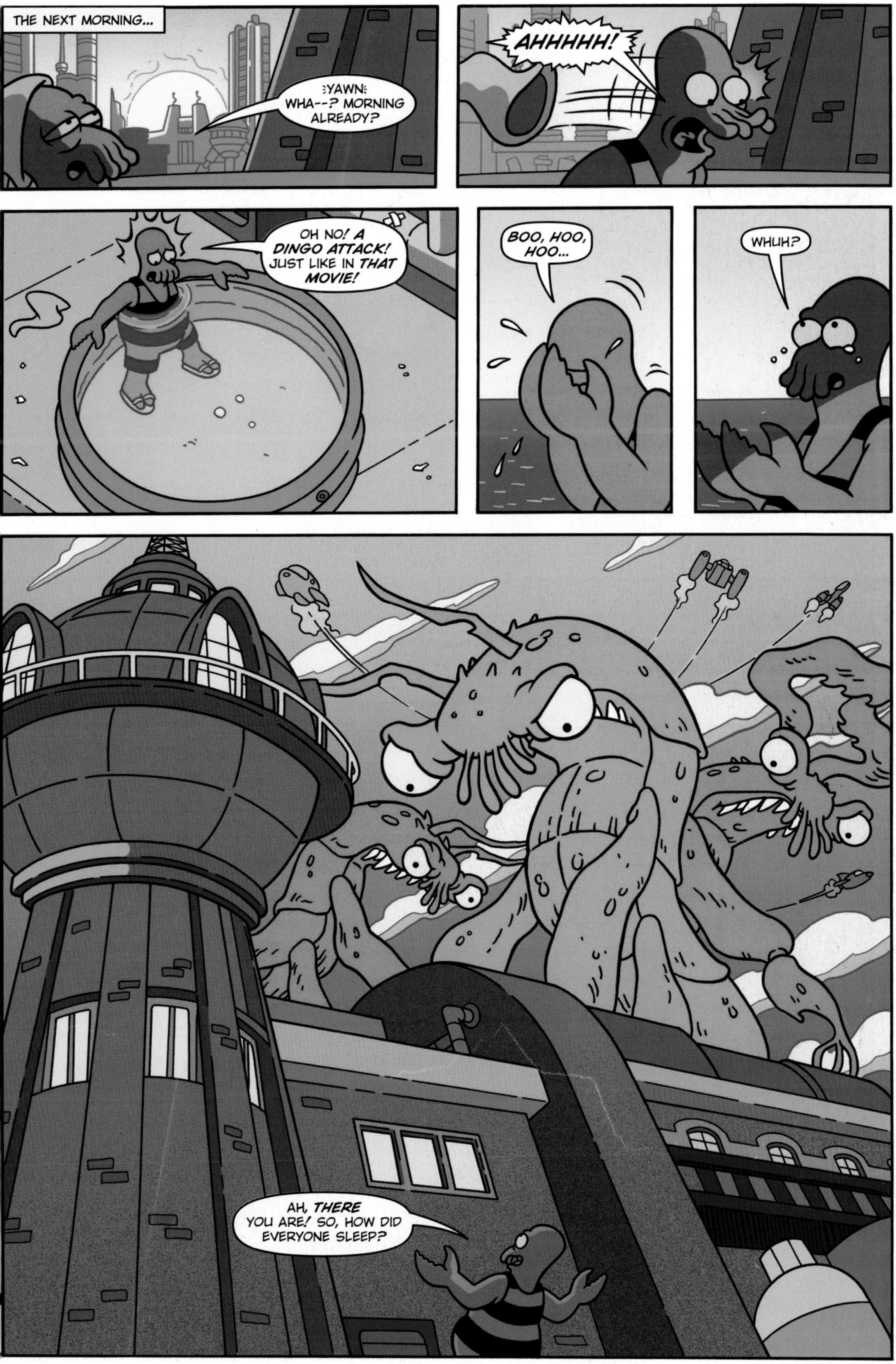

THE NEXT MORNING...
:YAWN: WHA--? MORNING ALREADY?
AHHHHH!
OH NO! A DINGO ATTACK! JUST LIKE IN THAT MOVIE!
BOO, HOO, HOO...
WHUH?
AH, THERE YOU ARE! SO, HOW DID EVERYONE SLEEP?

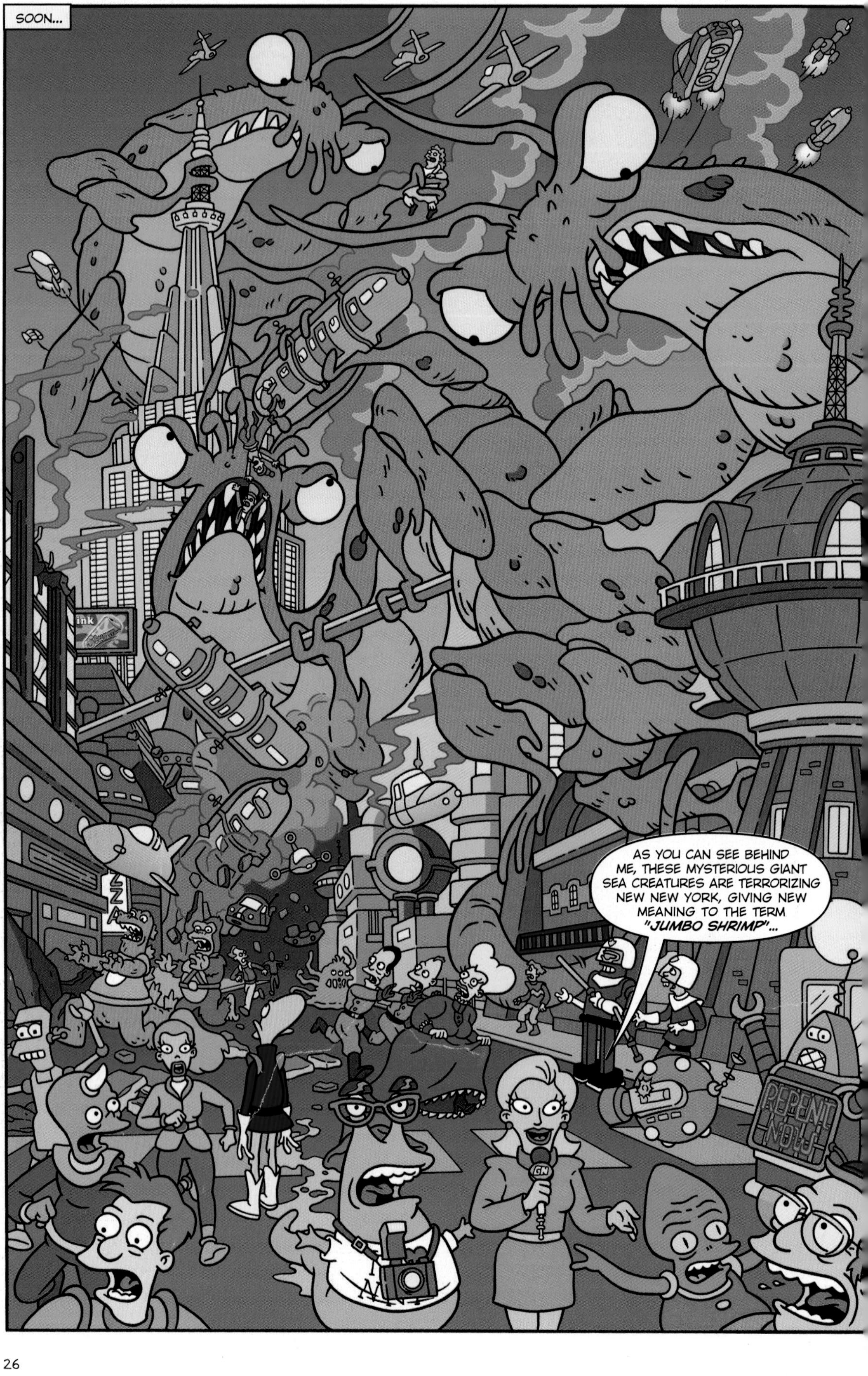
SOON...
AS YOU CAN SEE BEHIND ME, THESE MYSTERIOUS GIANT SEA CREATURES ARE TERRORIZING NEW NEW YORK, GIVING NEW MEANING TO THE TERM "JUMBO SHRIMP"...

...AND AT THIS POINT, MORBO, I THINK WE'D ALL BE HAPPY TO SEE THESE MONSTERS ON A GIANT PLATTER WITH A BAKED POTATO AND COLE SLAW!

MORBO WOULD PREFER HIS WITH FRIES, BUT SINCE THAT SEEMS UNLIKELY, MORBO WILL SETTLE FOR THE NEXT BEST THING--*THE DESTRUCTION OF THE HUMAN RACE!*

HA, HA, HA, HA...

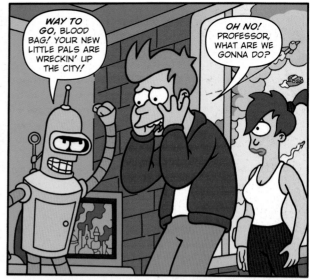

WAY TO GO, BLOOD BAG! YOUR NEW LITTLE PALS ARE WRECKIN' UP THE CITY!

OH NO! PROFESSOR, WHAT ARE WE GONNA DO?

DON'T WORRY. WE, BY WHICH I MEAN *"YOU,"* CAN USE THIS *INCREDIBLY POWERFUL* DE-RADIATION GUN!

HAS IT BEEN TESTED?

OH MY, NO! *THAT* WOULD BE *RISKY!*

COME ON -- *THERE'S NO TIME TO LOSE!*

NO! I WON'T LET YOU HARM MY NEW *BEST FRIENDS!*

BUT THEY'RE *EATING* THE CITY, ZOIDBERG!

SO, THEY'RE HUNGRY! YOU'RE GOING TO JUDGE THEM FOR ACTING ON INSTINCT?

GO BURY YOURSELF IN THE SAND, DOC LOBSTER. WE GOT *SHRIMP TO BARBIE!*

FINE! THEN I'M GOING ON A *HUNGER STRIKE* TO PROTEST YOUR BARBARIC WAYS!

I THOUGHT ONLY *PEOPLE WHO ATE ON A REGULAR BASIS* COULD GO ON HUNGER STRIKES! HAHAHAHAHA!!

27

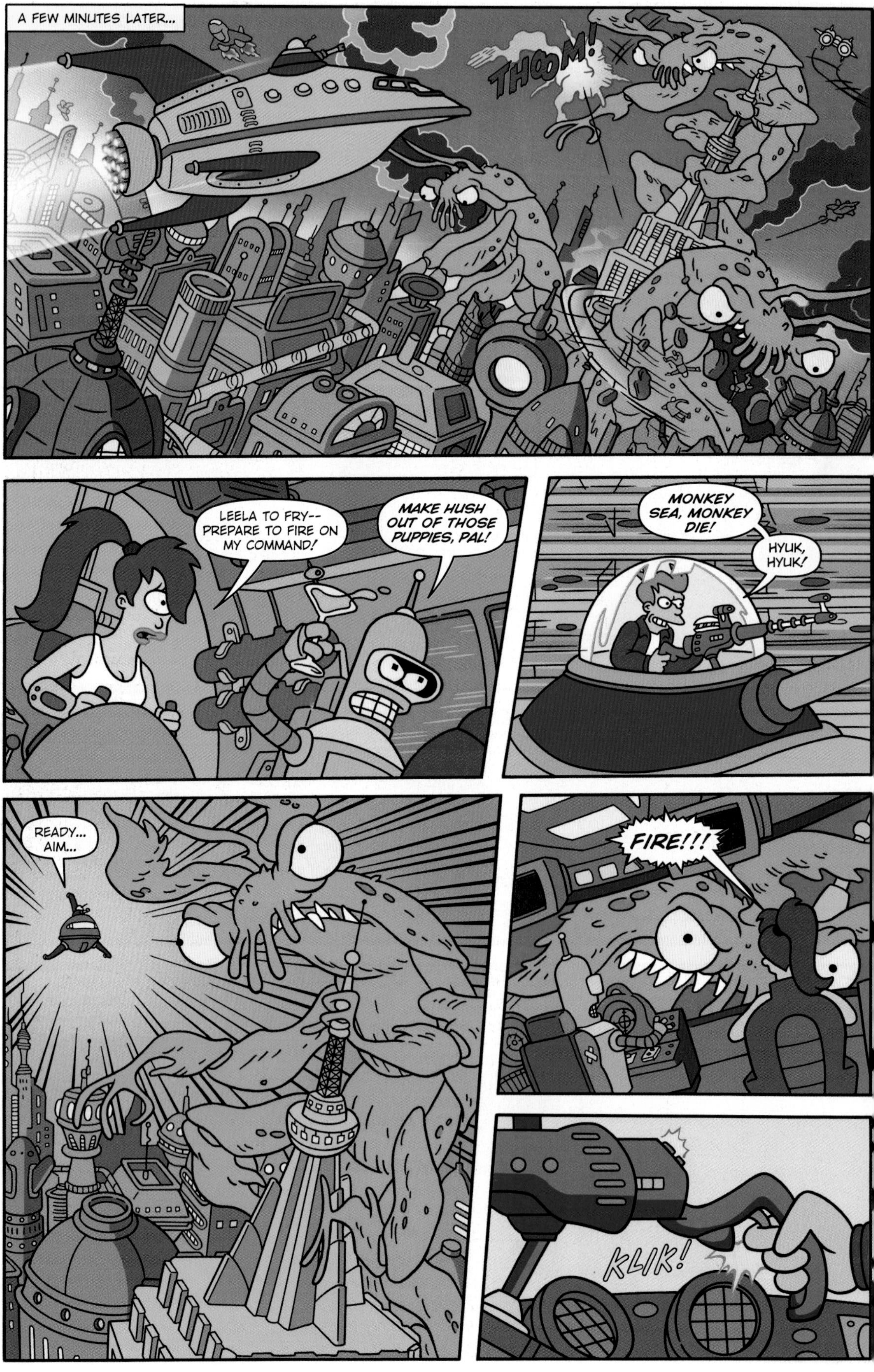
A FEW MINUTES LATER...
THOOM!
LEELA TO FRY-- PREPARE TO FIRE ON MY COMMAND!
MAKE HUSH OUT OF THOSE PUPPIES, PAL!
MONKEY SEA, MONKEY DIE!
HYUK, HYUK!
READY... AIM...
FIRE!!!
KLIK!

NOTHING HAPPENED!

ZOOOOM!

FRY, WHAT'S WRONG?

PULL THE TRIGGER HARDER!

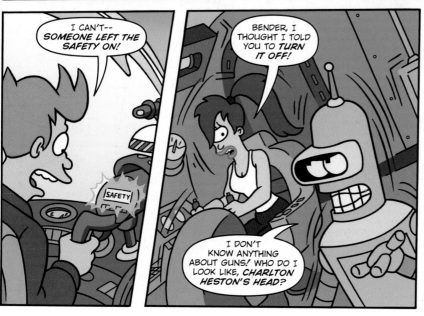

I CAN'T-- SOMEONE LEFT THE SAFETY ON!

SAFETY

BENDER, I THOUGHT I TOLD YOU TO TURN IT OFF!

I DON'T KNOW ANYTHING ABOUT GUNS! WHO DO I LOOK LIKE, CHARLTON HESTON'S HEAD?

TIME FOR EVASIVE ACTION!

YANK!

EJECT

AHHHHHH!

FOOM!

FOOM! FOOM!

NOW *THIS* IS WHAT I CALL FLEEING FOR OUR LIVES...

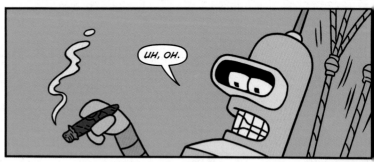

UH, OH.

OHHHHHH, LORDYYY

FRY!

AHH! LEELA-- HELP!

OOF! MAN, *PAIN* SUCKS!

KRUD!

BENDER! I'M NOT BREAKING MY *HUNGER STRIKE*, IF THAT'S WHAT YOU'RE THINKING!

CRAM IT, CRABBY! I HAVE TO SAVE MY BEST FRIEND FROM BECOMING A DRIVE-BY HORS'-D'OEUVRE!

OY, THE STORY OF MY LIFE!

WAIT A SECOND--*WHAT'S THAT?*

IF IT'S FOOD, I'M *SO* NOT INTERESTED!

NO, THE SEA MONKEYS AD-- LOOK AT THIS!

TIME TO SAVE THE DAY, ZOIDBERG!

100% SATISFACTION GUARANTEED OR WE'LL TAKE THE SHRIMP BACK AND REFUND YOUR MONEY!

Cash   Check   Money Order

Name
Address
City
State
Zip

HOORAY! I'M SAVING THE DAY WITH FRIENDS!

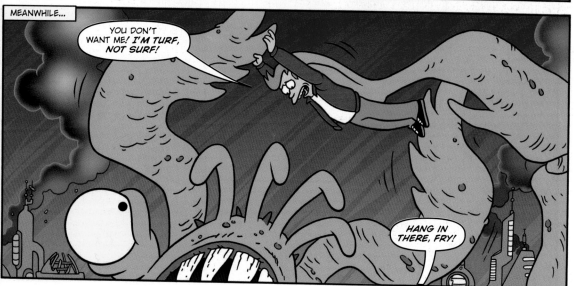

MEANWHILE...

YOU DON'T WANT ME! *I'M TURF, NOT SURF!*

HANG IN THERE, FRY!

31

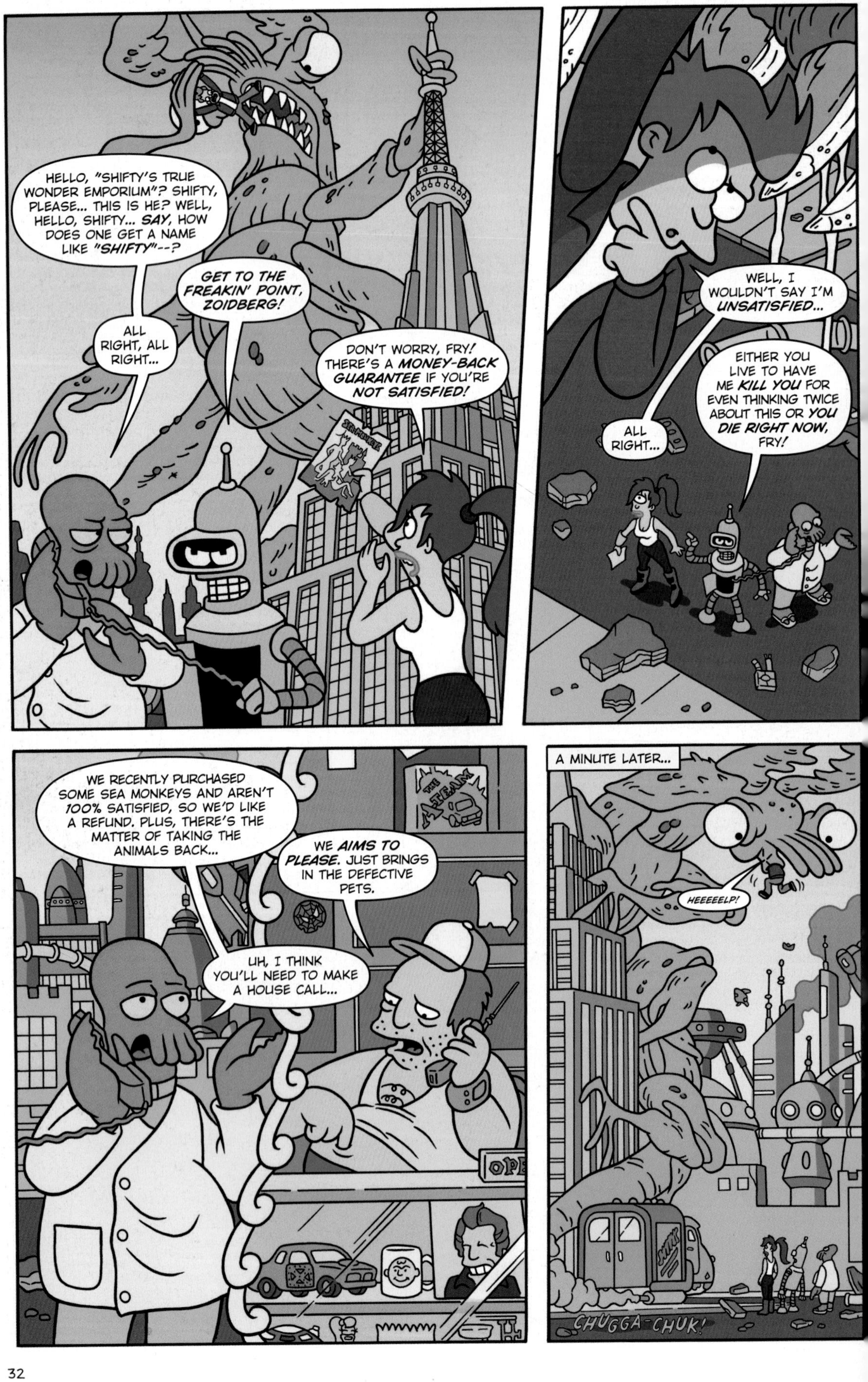

HELLO, "SHIFTY'S TRUE WONDER EMPORIUM"? SHIFTY, PLEASE... THIS IS HE? WELL, HELLO, SHIFTY... *SAY,* HOW DOES ONE GET A NAME LIKE *"SHIFTY"*--?
GET TO THE FREAKIN' POINT, ZOIDBERG!
ALL RIGHT, ALL RIGHT...
DON'T WORRY, FRY! THERE'S A ***MONEY-BACK GUARANTEE*** IF YOU'RE ***NOT SATISFIED!***
WELL, I WOULDN'T SAY I'M ***UNSATISFIED...***
ALL RIGHT...
EITHER YOU LIVE TO HAVE ME ***KILL YOU*** FOR EVEN THINKING TWICE ABOUT THIS OR ***YOU DIE RIGHT NOW,*** FRY!
WE RECENTLY PURCHASED SOME SEA MONKEYS AND AREN'T *100%* SATISFIED, SO WE'D LIKE A REFUND. PLUS, THERE'S THE MATTER OF TAKING THE ANIMALS BACK...
WE ***AIMS TO PLEASE.*** JUST BRINGS IN THE DEFECTIVE PETS.
UH, I THINK YOU'LL NEED TO MAKE A HOUSE CALL...
A MINUTE LATER...
HEEEEELP!
CHUGGA-CHUK!

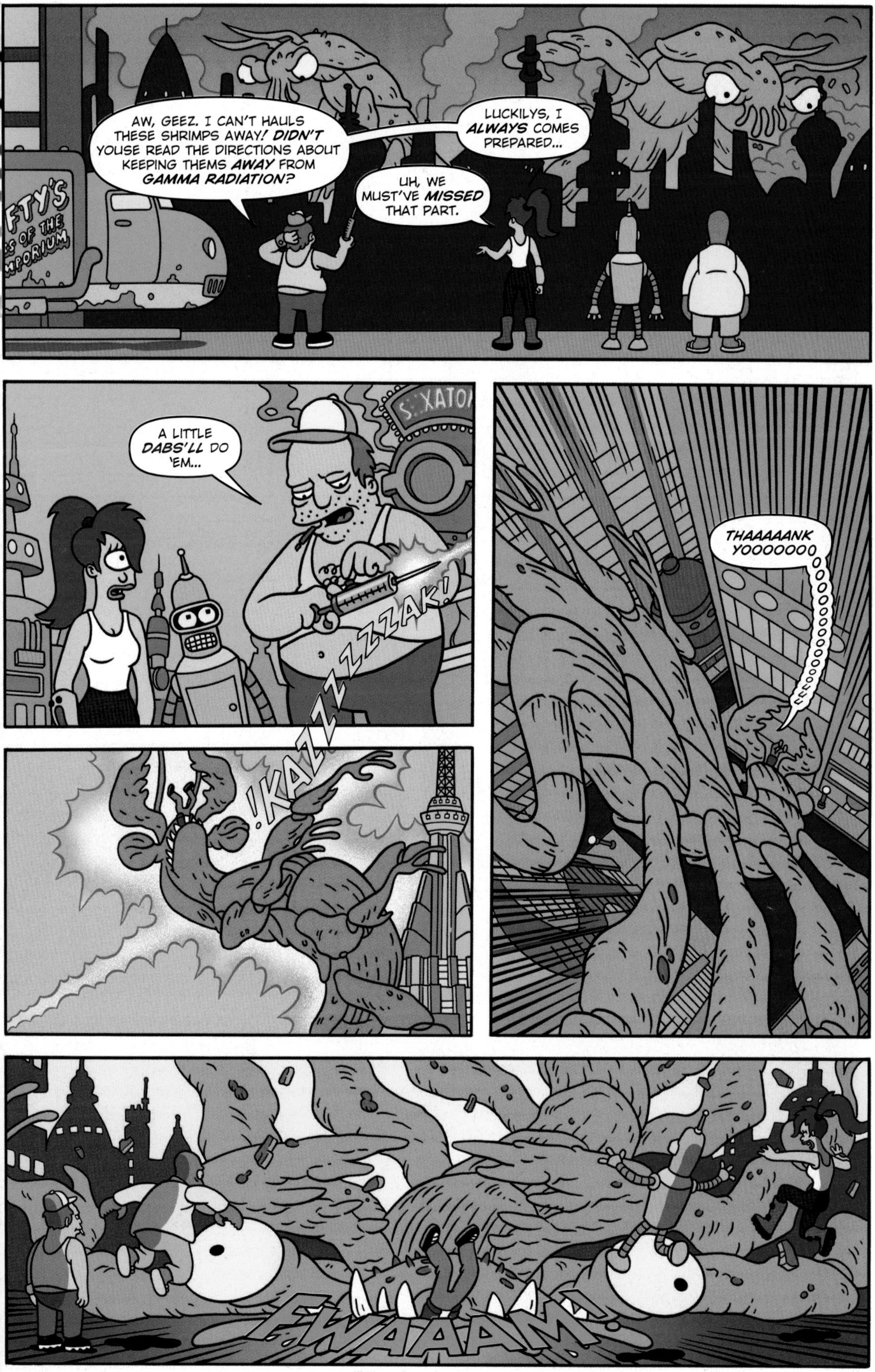
AW, GEEZ. I CAN'T HAULS THESE SHRIMPS AWAY! DIDN'T YOUSE READ THE DIRECTIONS ABOUT KEEPING THEMS AWAY FROM GAMMA RADIATION?
UH, WE MUST'VE MISSED THAT PART.
LUCKILYS, I ALWAYS COMES PREPARED...
A LITTLE DABS'LL DO 'EM...
!KAZZZZZZZZZZAK!
THAAAAANK YOOOOOOOOOOOOOOOOOOOOU!
FWAAAM!

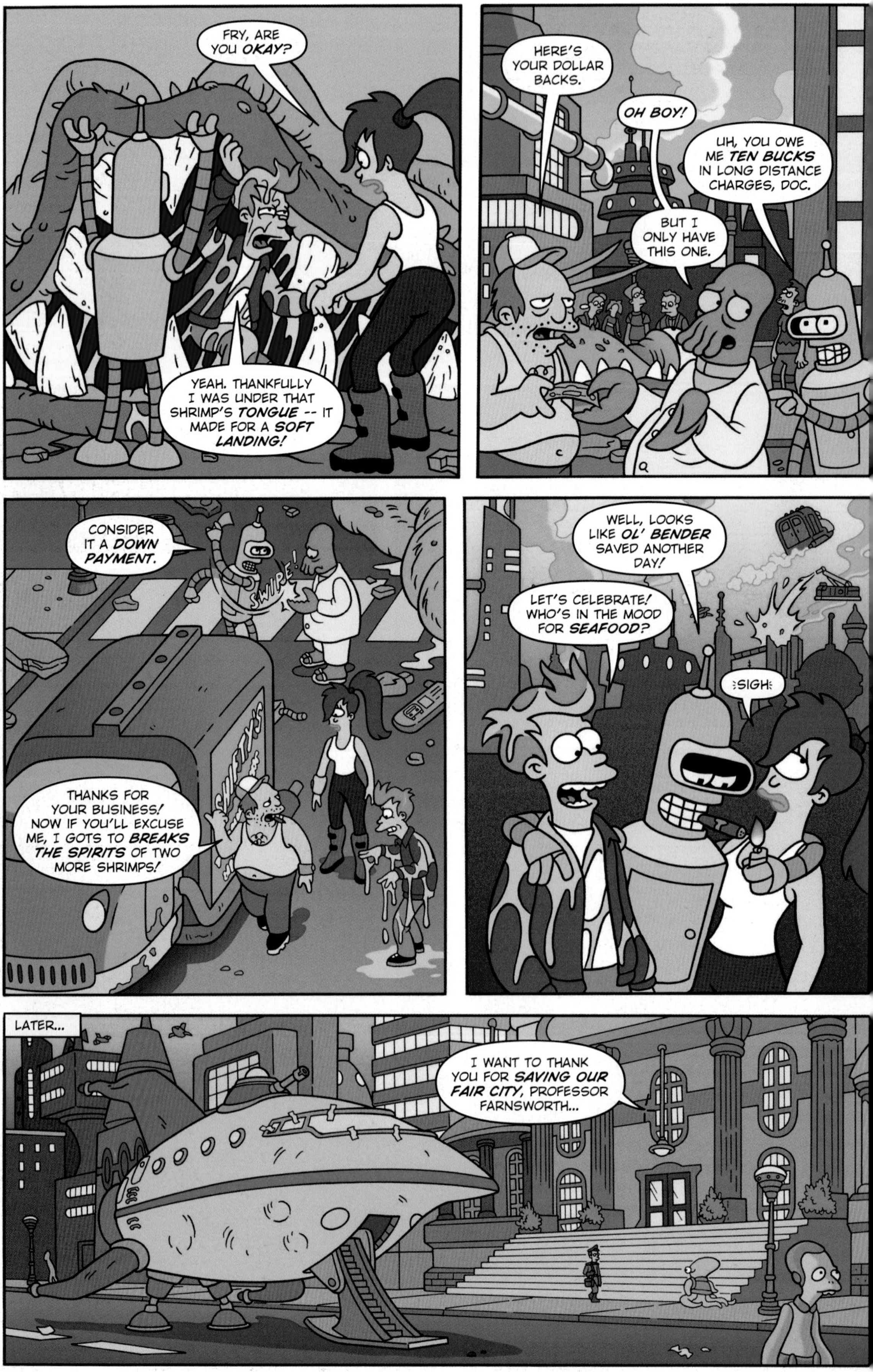
FRY, ARE YOU OKAY?
YEAH. THANKFULLY I WAS UNDER THAT SHRIMP'S TONGUE -- IT MADE FOR A SOFT LANDING!
HERE'S YOUR DOLLAR BACKS.
OH BOY!
UH, YOU OWE ME TEN BUCKS IN LONG DISTANCE CHARGES, DOC.
BUT I ONLY HAVE THIS ONE.
CONSIDER IT A DOWN PAYMENT.
SWIPE!
THANKS FOR YOUR BUSINESS! NOW IF YOU'LL EXCUSE ME, I GOTS TO BREAKS THE SPIRITS OF TWO MORE SHRIMPS!
WELL, LOOKS LIKE OL' BENDER SAVED ANOTHER DAY!
LET'S CELEBRATE! WHO'S IN THE MOOD FOR SEAFOOD?
SIGH
LATER...
I WANT TO THANK YOU FOR SAVING OUR FAIR CITY, PROFESSOR FARNSWORTH...

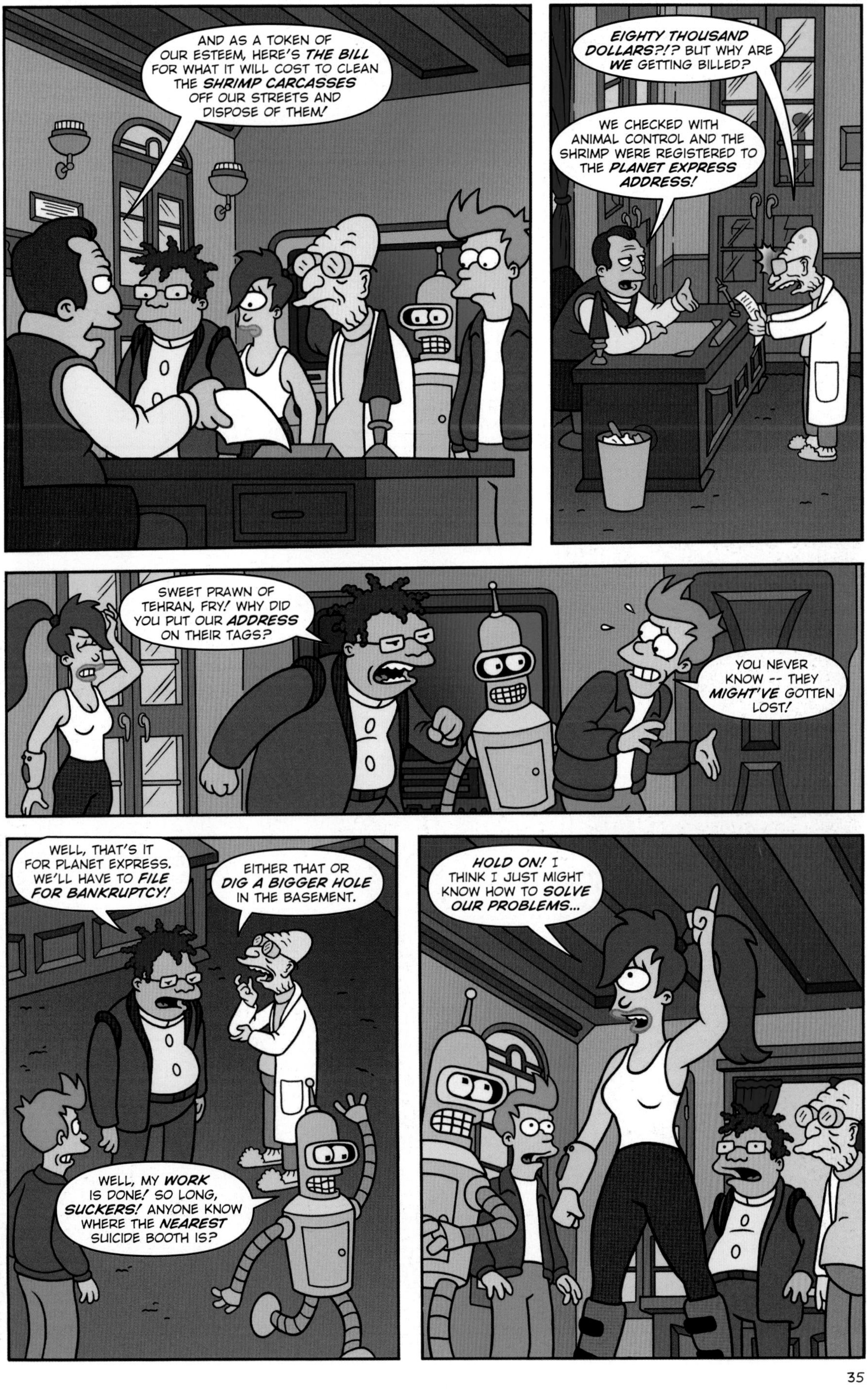
AND AS A TOKEN OF OUR ESTEEM, HERE'S THE BILL FOR WHAT IT WILL COST TO CLEAN THE SHRIMP CARCASSES OFF OUR STREETS AND DISPOSE OF THEM!
EIGHTY THOUSAND DOLLARS?!? BUT WHY ARE WE GETTING BILLED?
WE CHECKED WITH ANIMAL CONTROL AND THE SHRIMP WERE REGISTERED TO THE PLANET EXPRESS ADDRESS!
SWEET PRAWN OF TEHRAN, FRY! WHY DID YOU PUT OUR ADDRESS ON THEIR TAGS?
YOU NEVER KNOW -- THEY MIGHT'VE GOTTEN LOST!
WELL, THAT'S IT FOR PLANET EXPRESS. WE'LL HAVE TO FILE FOR BANKRUPTCY!
EITHER THAT OR DIG A BIGGER HOLE IN THE BASEMENT.
WELL, MY WORK IS DONE! SO LONG, SUCKERS! ANYONE KNOW WHERE THE NEAREST SUICIDE BOOTH IS?
HOLD ON! I THINK I JUST MIGHT KNOW HOW TO SOLVE OUR PROBLEMS...

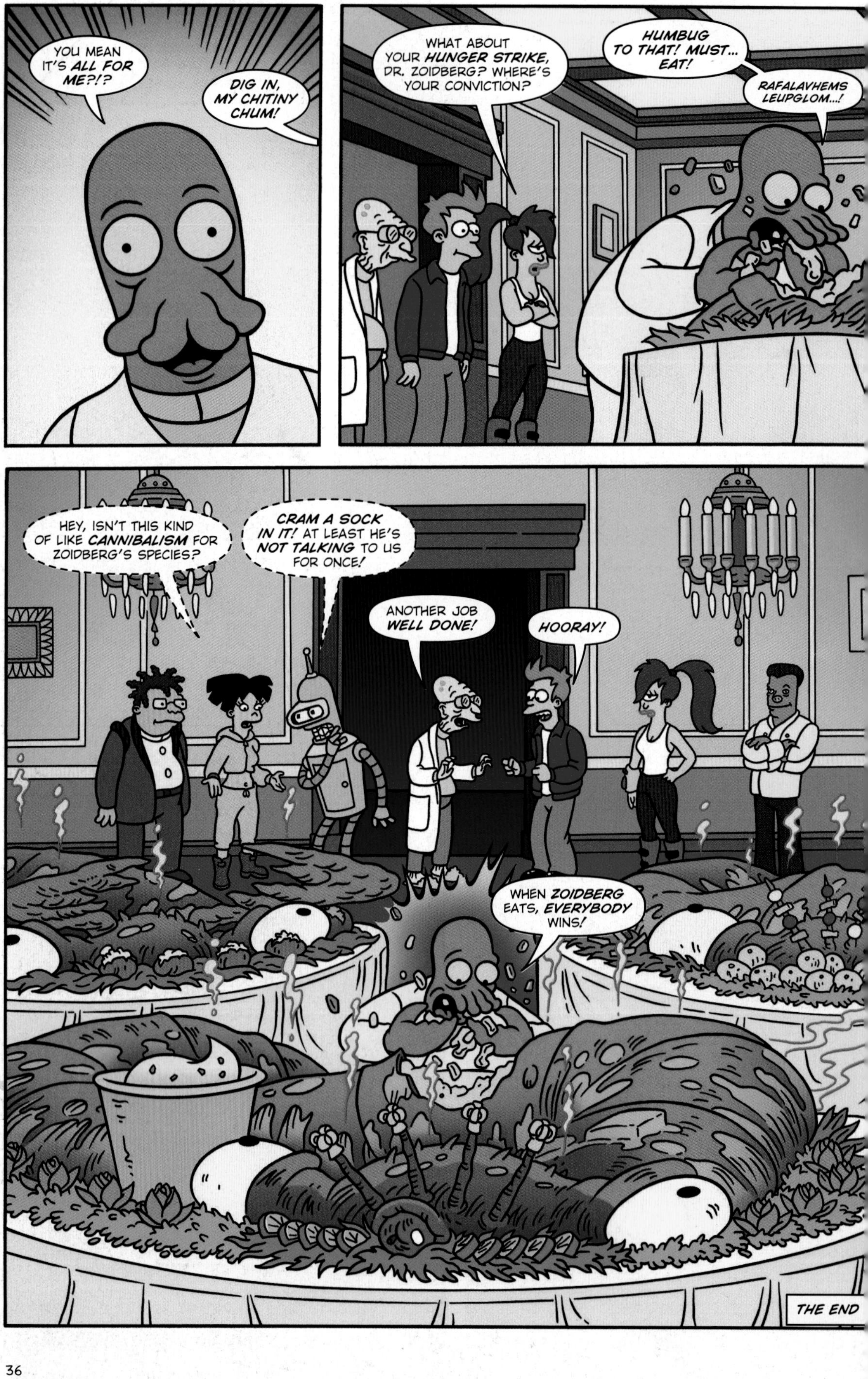
YOU MEAN IT'S ALL FOR ME?!?
DIG IN, MY CHITINY CHUM!
WHAT ABOUT YOUR HUNGER STRIKE, DR. ZOIDBERG? WHERE'S YOUR CONVICTION?
HUMBUG TO THAT! MUST... EAT!
RAFALAVHEMS LEUPGLOM...!
HEY, ISN'T THIS KIND OF LIKE CANNIBALISM FOR ZOIDBERG'S SPECIES?
CRAM A SOCK IN IT! AT LEAST HE'S NOT TALKING TO US FOR ONCE!
ANOTHER JOB WELL DONE!
HOORAY!
WHEN ZOIDBERG EATS, EVERYBODY WINS!
THE END

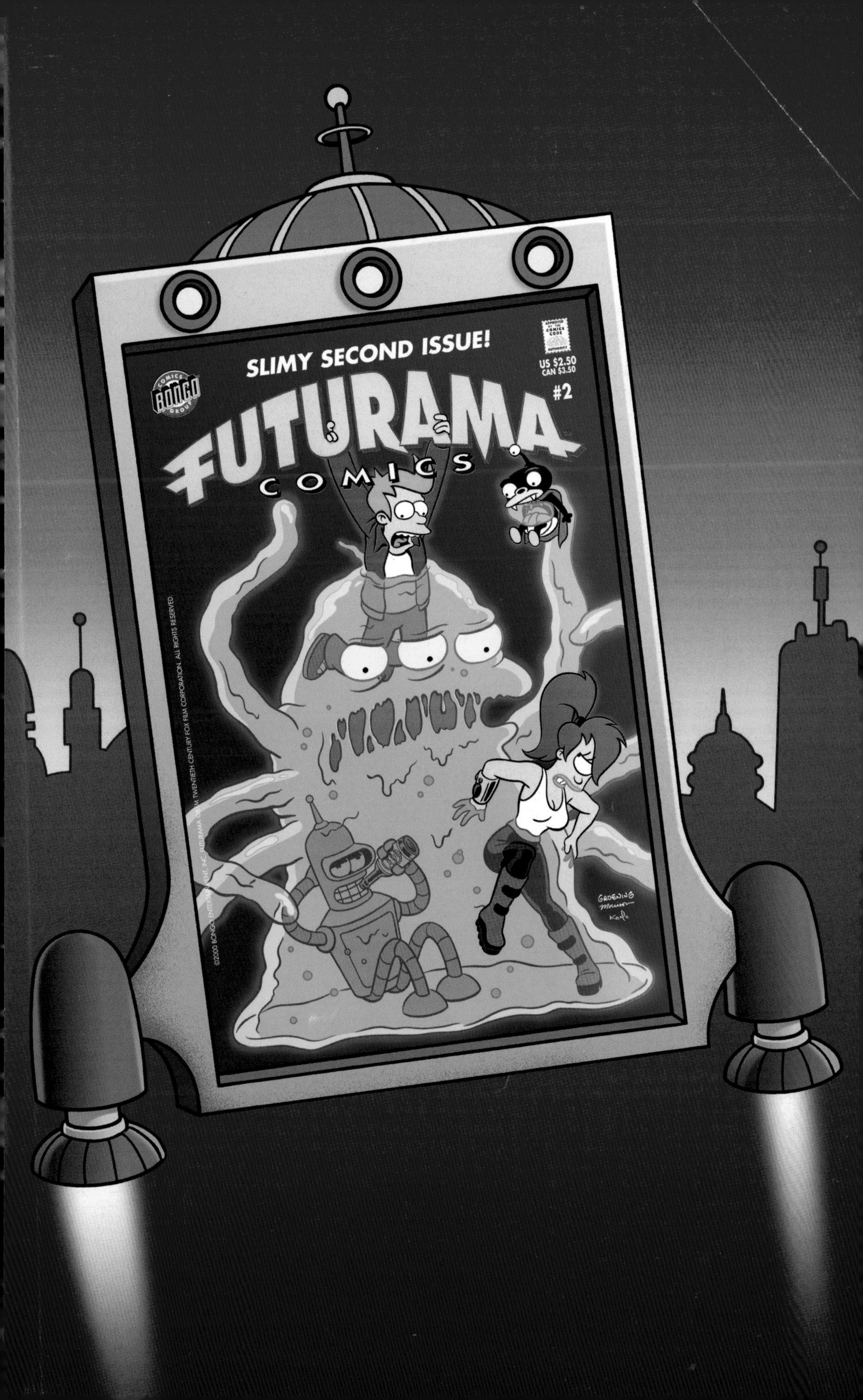
SLIMY SECOND ISSUE!
US $2.50
CAN $3.50
#2
FUTURAMA
COMICS

MOM'S GERIATRIC SUPPLIES-FOR-LESS

MAIL-ORDER FOR THE OVER-120 SET
PRESENTS:

The CLAPPER-CLAPPER®!

AS SEEN IN YOUR DREAMS!

TIRED OF CLAPPING THINGS ON AND OFF?
LET THE CLAPPER-CLAPPER® DO IT FOR YOU!
SIMPLY GIVE THE UNIT AUDIO COMMANDS AND SIT BACK AND RELAX.

IT'S THAT EASY!

- **THE CLAPPER CLAPPER CAN CONTROL LIGHTING UNITS, SECURITY SYSTEMS - - JUST ABOUT ANYTHING ACTIVATED BY CLAPPING!**
- **SAFE AND SECURE, THE UNIT REQUIRES A SECRET 20-DIGIT CODE BEFORE IT WILL DO ANYTHING.**
- **SO EASY TO USE, EVEN THE FEEBLE-MINDED ELDERLY CAN OPERATE IT!**

OPTIONAL WALL MOUNTING BRACKETS MADE OF SPACE AGE TIN INCLUDED AT NO ADDITIONAL COST -- A SPECIAL GIFT FROM MOM HERSELF!

BASIC UNIT IS ONLY
2
FEET TALL
FITS ALMOST ANYWHERE!

Only $499.99!!!*

HELP! I'VE CRASHED AND I CAN'T GET UP!
CLAPPER CLAPPER, ACTIVATE THE EMERGENCY RESCUE BEACON!
CERTAINLY, MADAM. PLEASE ENTER YOUR 20-DIGIT ACCESS CODE.

*MARS RESIDENTS PAY 20% NON-RED TAX. ALL ORDERS PLACED DURING THE FIRST FIVE DAYS OF EACH WEEK SUBJECT TO 10% SURCHARGE FOR RUSH. ORDERS NOT ACCEPTED ON WEEKENDS. NOT RESPONSIBLE FOR ACCIDENTAL DEATH, CHOKING, OR DISMEMBERMENT INFLICTED BY THE UNIT, ESPECIALLY DURING SOLAR FLARES. CASH AND CARRY, NO WARRANTIES OR REFUNDS. PLEASE CLAP RESPONSIBLY.

DON'T FORGET ABOUT THESE OTHER FINE PRODUCTS:

- SEEING EYE-TORPEDOES
- HOVER LUNG (BACK IN STOCK!)
- NANITE POWERED HEMORRHOID PILLOWS.

MAIL TODAY!

MOM'S Geriatric Supplies For Less
P.O. Box 693
New New York, NY 10101.71453

Dear Sirs:
Please rush my **Clapper-Clapper** to me.
I am enclosing **$499.99** in full for each Clapper-Clapper ordered.

Total Number of Units ______
Name_ _ _ _ _ _ _ _ _ _ _ _ _ _ _
Address_ _
City_ _ _ _ _ _ _ State_ _ Planet_ _ _ _ _ _ _ _ _
Galaxy_ _ _ _ _ _ _ _ _ _ _ _ _ _ Zip_ _ _ _ _ _

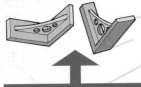

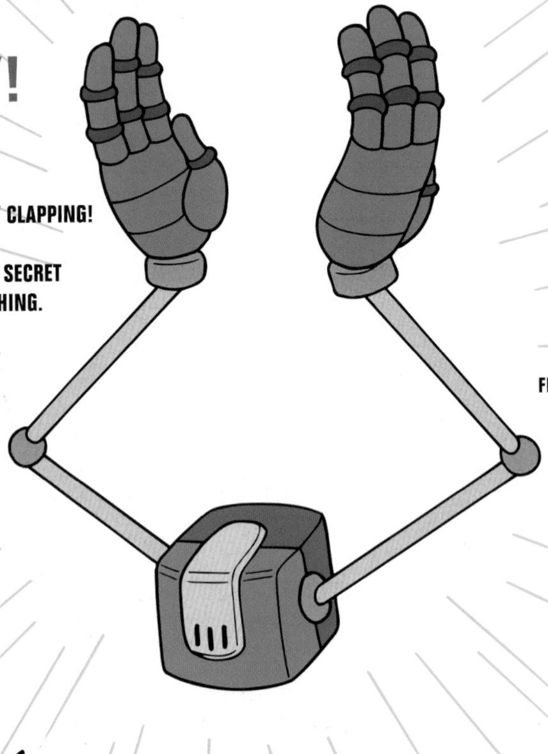

...BUT **DELIVER** US TO **EVIL!**

EXCELLENT HAPPENINGS, PEOPLE!

ERIC ROGERS	TOM KING	STEVE STEERE, JR.	CHRIS UNGAR
SCRIPT	PENCILS	INKS	LETTERS

NATHAN KANE	BILL MORRISON	MATT GROENING
COLORS	EDITS	SHIP STOWAWAY

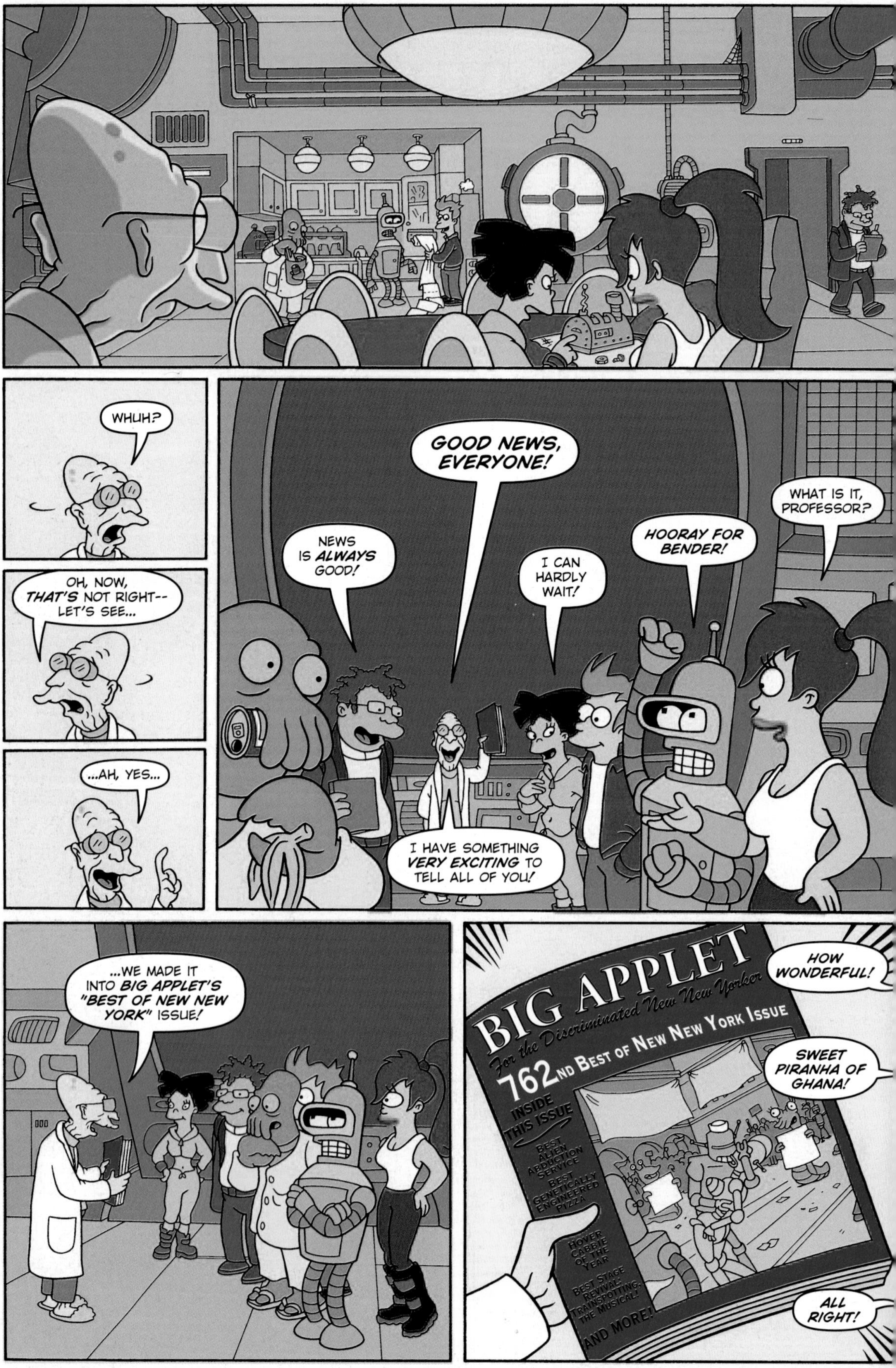
WHUH?
OH, NOW, THAT'S NOT RIGHT-- LET'S SEE...
...AH, YES...
GOOD NEWS, EVERYONE!
NEWS IS ALWAYS GOOD!
I CAN HARDLY WAIT!
HOORAY FOR BENDER!
WHAT IS IT, PROFESSOR?
I HAVE SOMETHING VERY EXCITING TO TELL ALL OF YOU!
...WE MADE IT INTO BIG APPLET'S "BEST OF NEW NEW YORK" ISSUE!
BIG APPLET
For the Discriminated New New Yorker
762ND BEST OF NEW NEW YORK ISSUE
INSIDE THIS ISSUE
BEST ALIEN ABDUCTION SERVICE
BEST GENETICALLY ENGINEERED PIZZA
HOVER CABBIE OF THE YEAR
BEST STAGE REVIVAL: TRAINSPOTTING, THE MUSICAL!
AND MORE!
HOW WONDERFUL!
SWEET PIRANHA OF GHANA!
ALL RIGHT!

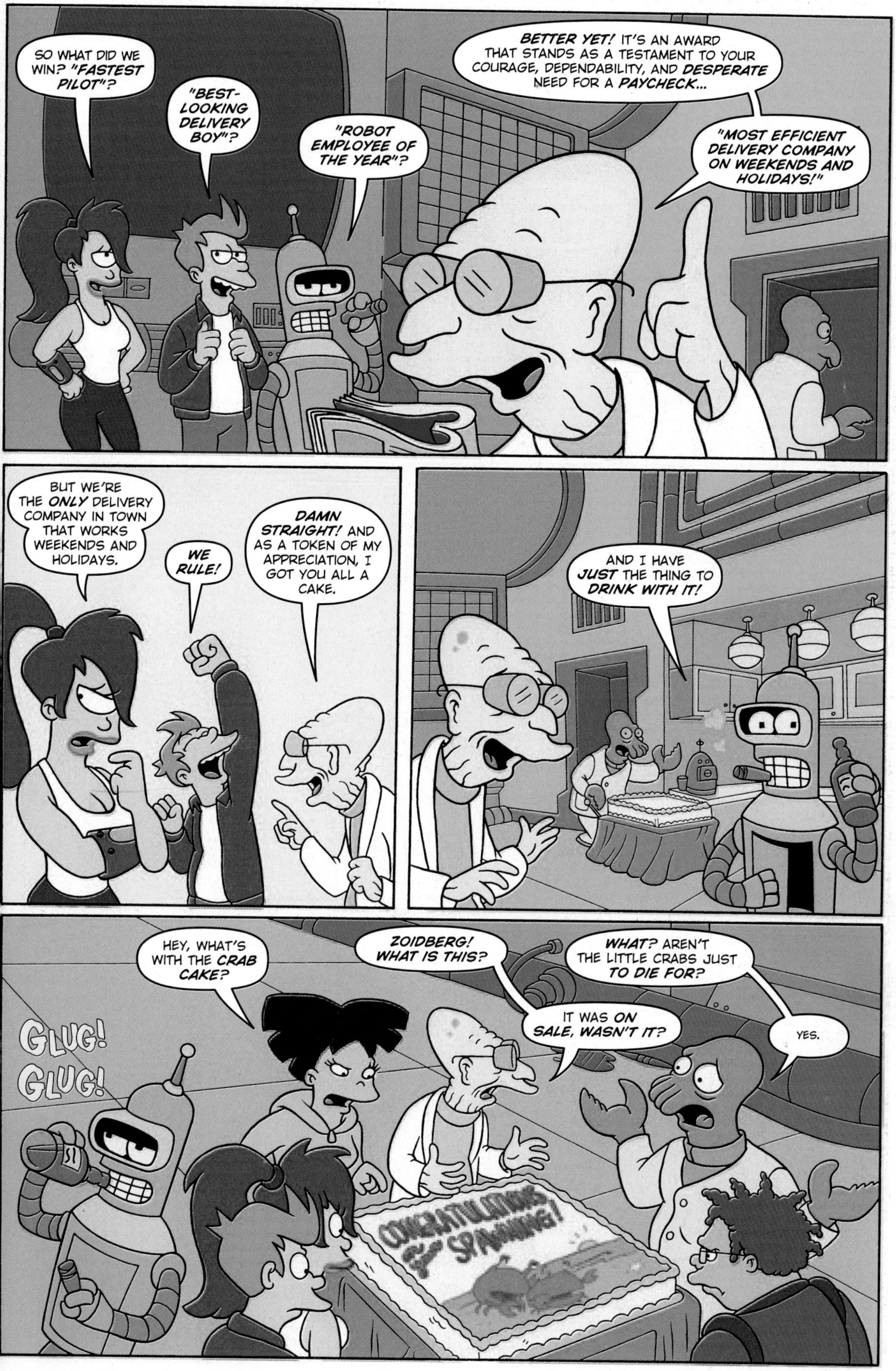
SO WHAT DID WE WIN? "FASTEST PILOT"?
"BEST-LOOKING DELIVERY BOY"?
"ROBOT EMPLOYEE OF THE YEAR"?
BETTER YET! IT'S AN AWARD THAT STANDS AS A TESTAMENT TO YOUR COURAGE, DEPENDABILITY, AND DESPERATE NEED FOR A PAYCHECK...
"MOST EFFICIENT DELIVERY COMPANY ON WEEKENDS AND HOLIDAYS!"
BUT WE'RE THE ONLY DELIVERY COMPANY IN TOWN THAT WORKS WEEKENDS AND HOLIDAYS.
WE RULE!
DAMN STRAIGHT! AND AS A TOKEN OF MY APPRECIATION, I GOT YOU ALL A CAKE.
AND I HAVE JUST THE THING TO DRINK WITH IT!
GLUG! GLUG!
HEY, WHAT'S WITH THE CRAB CAKE?
ZOIDBERG! WHAT IS THIS?
WHAT? AREN'T THE LITTLE CRABS JUST TO DIE FOR?
IT WAS ON SALE, WASN'T IT?
YES.
CONGRATULATIONS ON SPAWNING!

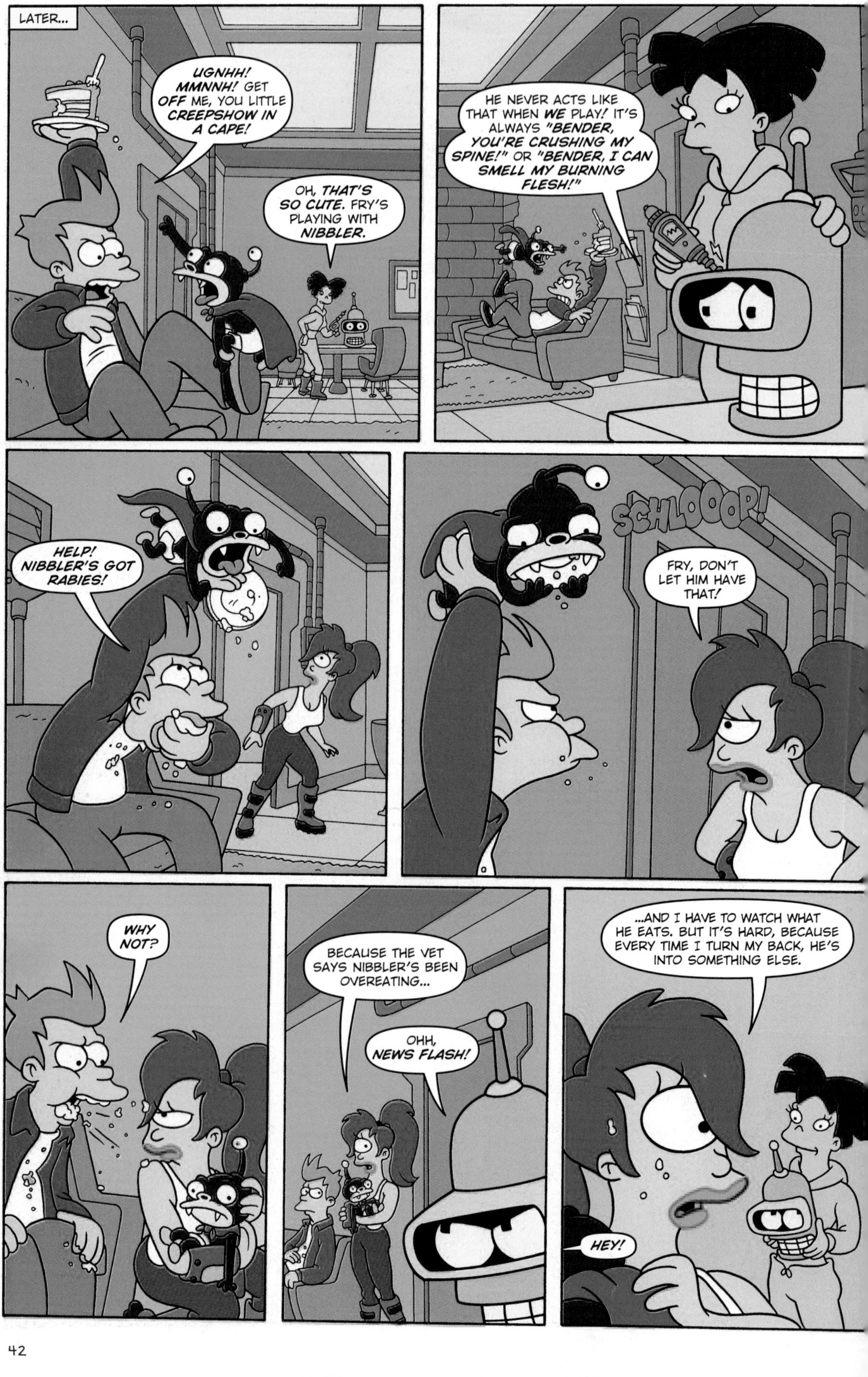
LATER...
UGNHH! MMNNH! GET OFF ME, YOU LITTLE CREEPSHOW IN A CAPE!
OH, THAT'S SO CUTE. FRY'S PLAYING WITH NIBBLER.
HE NEVER ACTS LIKE THAT WHEN WE PLAY! IT'S ALWAYS "BENDER, YOU'RE CRUSHING MY SPINE!" OR "BENDER, I CAN SMELL MY BURNING FLESH!"
HELP! NIBBLER'S GOT RABIES!
SCHLOOOP!
FRY, DON'T LET HIM HAVE THAT!
WHY NOT?
BECAUSE THE VET SAYS NIBBLER'S BEEN OVEREATING...
OHH, NEWS FLASH!
...AND I HAVE TO WATCH WHAT HE EATS. BUT IT'S HARD, BECAUSE EVERY TIME I TURN MY BACK, HE'S INTO SOMETHING ELSE.
HEY!

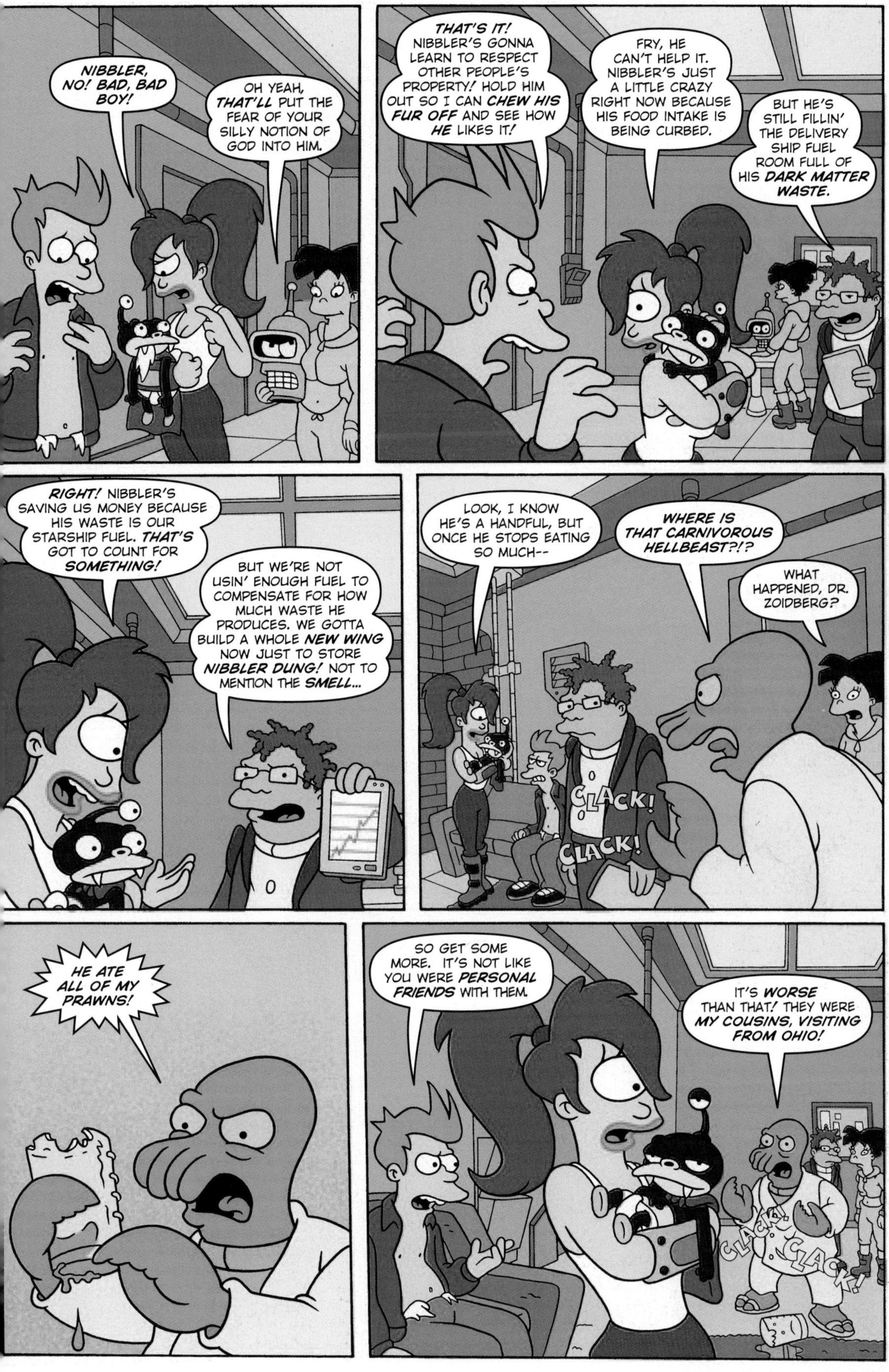

NIBBLER, NO! BAD, BAD BOY!
OH YEAH, THAT'LL PUT THE FEAR OF YOUR SILLY NOTION OF GOD INTO HIM.
THAT'S IT! NIBBLER'S GONNA LEARN TO RESPECT OTHER PEOPLE'S PROPERTY! HOLD HIM OUT SO I CAN CHEW HIS FUR OFF AND SEE HOW HE LIKES IT!
FRY, HE CAN'T HELP IT. NIBBLER'S JUST A LITTLE CRAZY RIGHT NOW BECAUSE HIS FOOD INTAKE IS BEING CURBED.
BUT HE'S STILL FILLIN' THE DELIVERY SHIP FUEL ROOM FULL OF HIS DARK MATTER WASTE.
RIGHT! NIBBLER'S SAVING US MONEY BECAUSE HIS WASTE IS OUR STARSHIP FUEL. THAT'S GOT TO COUNT FOR SOMETHING!
BUT WE'RE NOT USIN' ENOUGH FUEL TO COMPENSATE FOR HOW MUCH WASTE HE PRODUCES. WE GOTTA BUILD A WHOLE NEW WING NOW JUST TO STORE NIBBLER DUNG! NOT TO MENTION THE SMELL...
LOOK, I KNOW HE'S A HANDFUL, BUT ONCE HE STOPS EATING SO MUCH--
WHERE IS THAT CARNIVOROUS HELLBEAST?!?
WHAT HAPPENED, DR. ZOIDBERG?
CLACK!
CLACK!
HE ATE ALL OF MY PRAWNS!
SO GET SOME MORE. IT'S NOT LIKE YOU WERE PERSONAL FRIENDS WITH THEM.
IT'S WORSE THAN THAT! THEY WERE MY COUSINS, VISITING FROM OHIO!
CLACK!
CLACK!

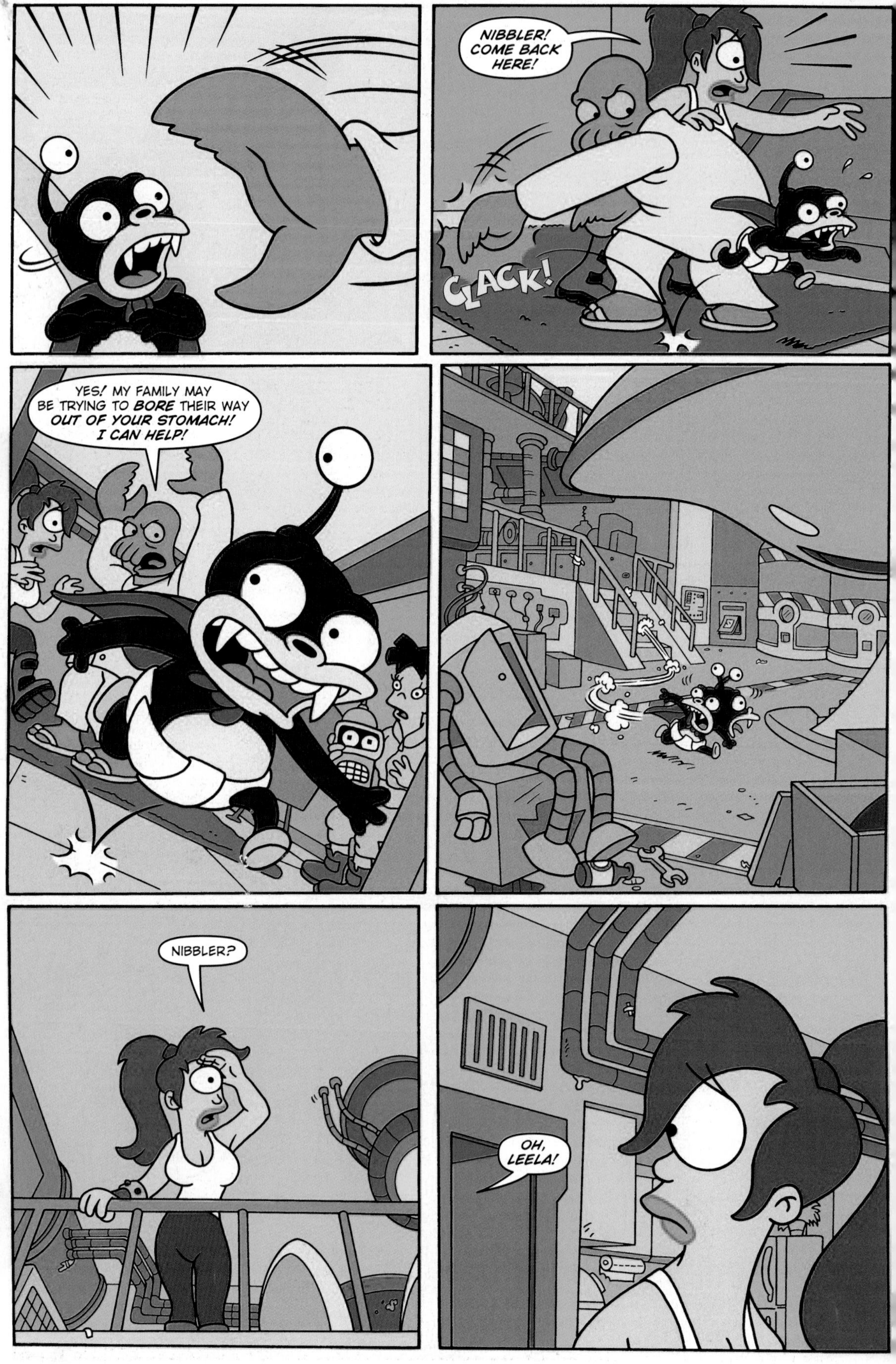
NIBBLER! COME BACK HERE!
CLACK!
YES! MY FAMILY MAY BE TRYING TO BORE THEIR WAY OUT OF YOUR STOMACH! I CAN HELP!
NIBBLER?
OH, LEELA!

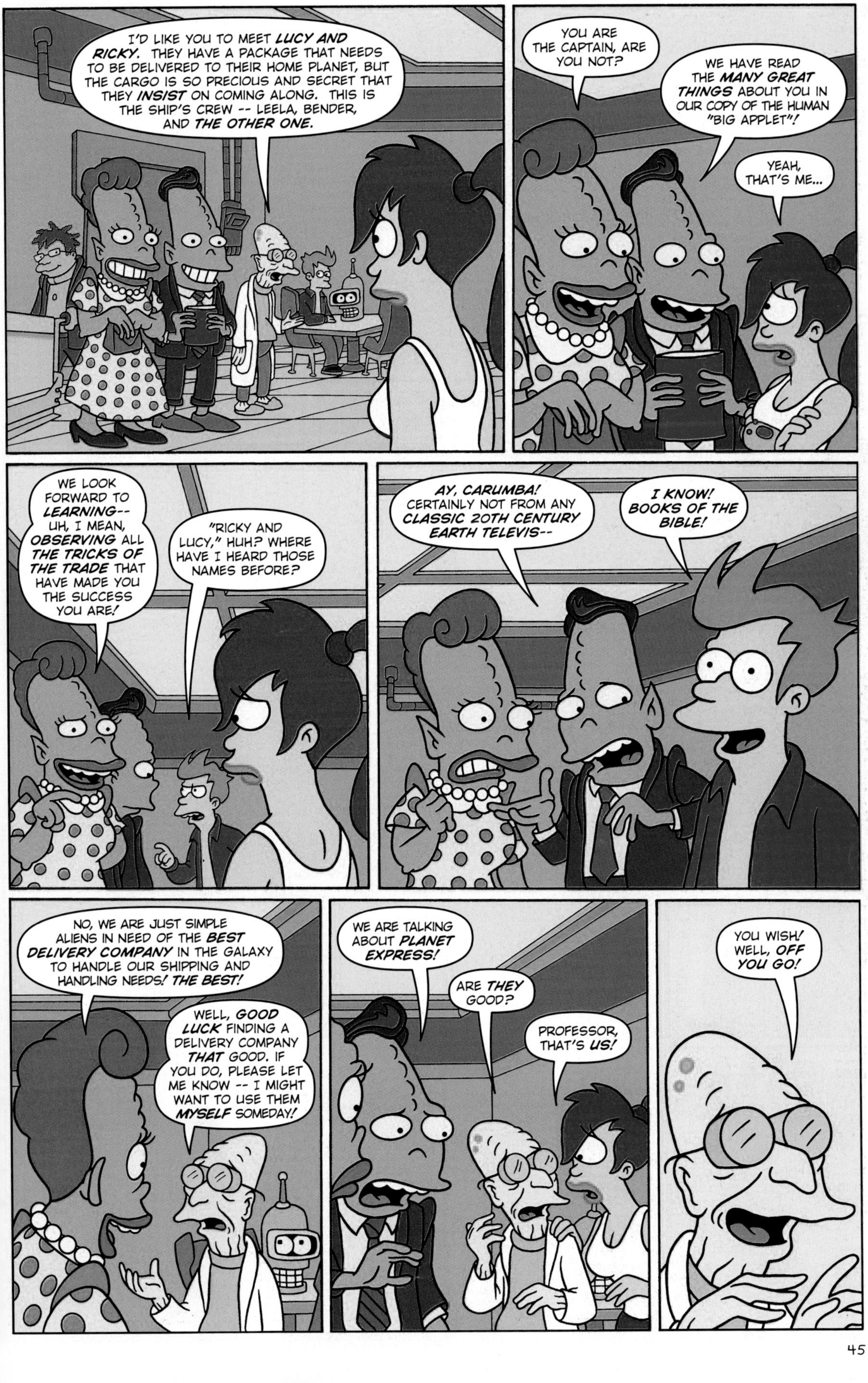
I'D LIKE YOU TO MEET LUCY AND RICKY. THEY HAVE A PACKAGE THAT NEEDS TO BE DELIVERED TO THEIR HOME PLANET, BUT THE CARGO IS SO PRECIOUS AND SECRET THAT THEY INSIST ON COMING ALONG. THIS IS THE SHIP'S CREW -- LEELA, BENDER, AND THE OTHER ONE.
YOU ARE THE CAPTAIN, ARE YOU NOT?
WE HAVE READ THE MANY GREAT THINGS ABOUT YOU IN OUR COPY OF THE HUMAN "BIG APPLET"!
YEAH, THAT'S ME...
WE LOOK FORWARD TO LEARNING-- UH, I MEAN, OBSERVING ALL THE TRICKS OF THE TRADE THAT HAVE MADE YOU THE SUCCESS YOU ARE!
"RICKY AND LUCY," HUH? WHERE HAVE I HEARD THOSE NAMES BEFORE?
AY, CARUMBA! CERTAINLY NOT FROM ANY CLASSIC 20TH CENTURY EARTH TELEVIS--
I KNOW! BOOKS OF THE BIBLE!
NO, WE ARE JUST SIMPLE ALIENS IN NEED OF THE BEST DELIVERY COMPANY IN THE GALAXY TO HANDLE OUR SHIPPING AND HANDLING NEEDS! THE BEST!
WELL, GOOD LUCK FINDING A DELIVERY COMPANY THAT GOOD. IF YOU DO, PLEASE LET ME KNOW -- I MIGHT WANT TO USE THEM MYSELF SOMEDAY!
WE ARE TALKING ABOUT PLANET EXPRESS!
ARE THEY GOOD?
PROFESSOR, THAT'S US!
YOU WISH! WELL, OFF YOU GO!

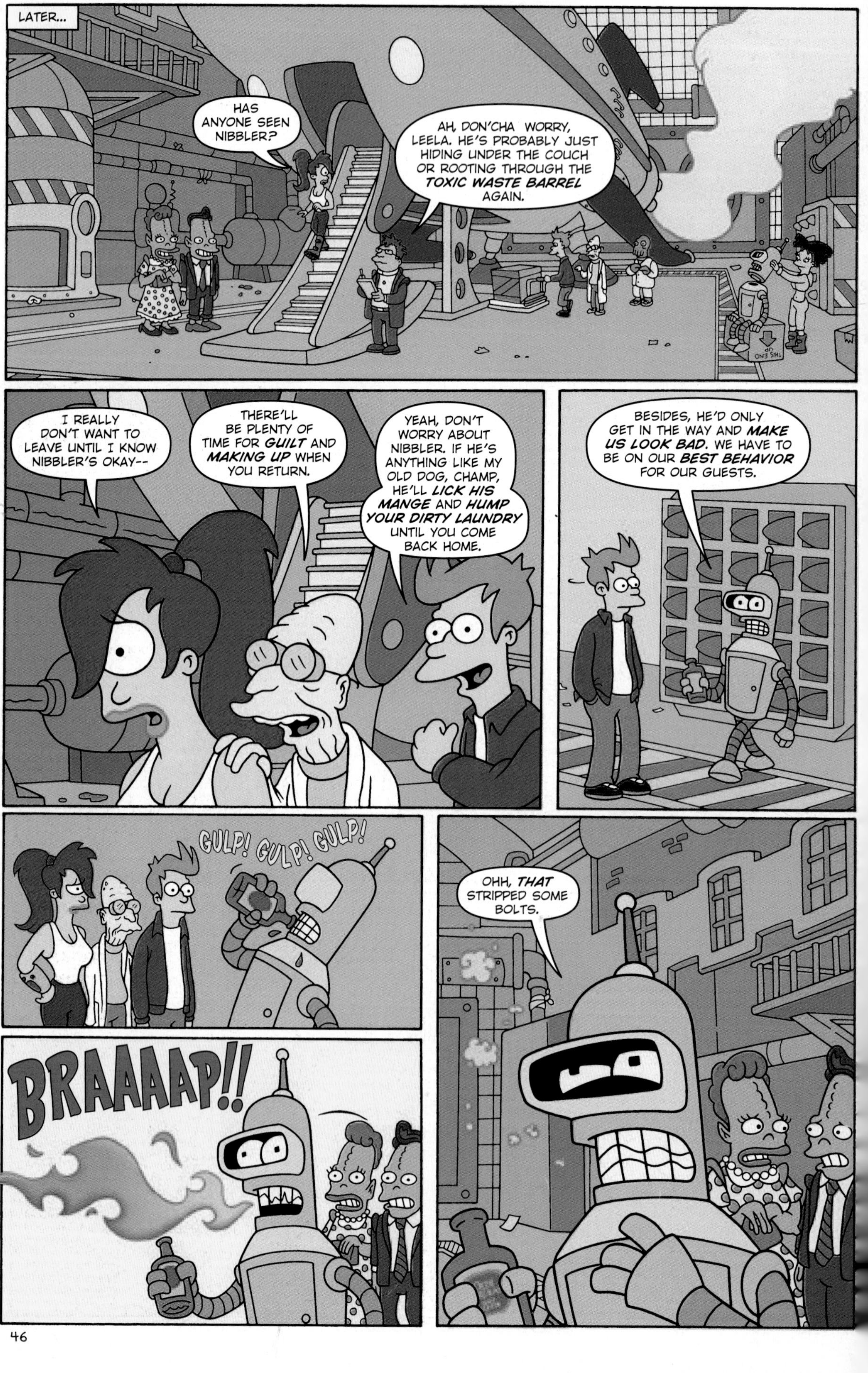
LATER...
HAS ANYONE SEEN NIBBLER?
AH, DON'CHA WORRY, LEELA. HE'S PROBABLY JUST HIDING UNDER THE COUCH OR ROOTING THROUGH THE TOXIC WASTE BARREL AGAIN.
THIS END UP
I REALLY DON'T WANT TO LEAVE UNTIL I KNOW NIBBLER'S OKAY--
THERE'LL BE PLENTY OF TIME FOR GUILT AND MAKING UP WHEN YOU RETURN.
YEAH, DON'T WORRY ABOUT NIBBLER. IF HE'S ANYTHING LIKE MY OLD DOG, CHAMP, HE'LL LICK HIS MANGE AND HUMP YOUR DIRTY LAUNDRY UNTIL YOU COME BACK HOME.
BESIDES, HE'D ONLY GET IN THE WAY AND MAKE US LOOK BAD. WE HAVE TO BE ON OUR BEST BEHAVIOR FOR OUR GUESTS.
GULP! GULP! GULP!
BRAAAAP!!
OHH, THAT STRIPPED SOME BOLTS.

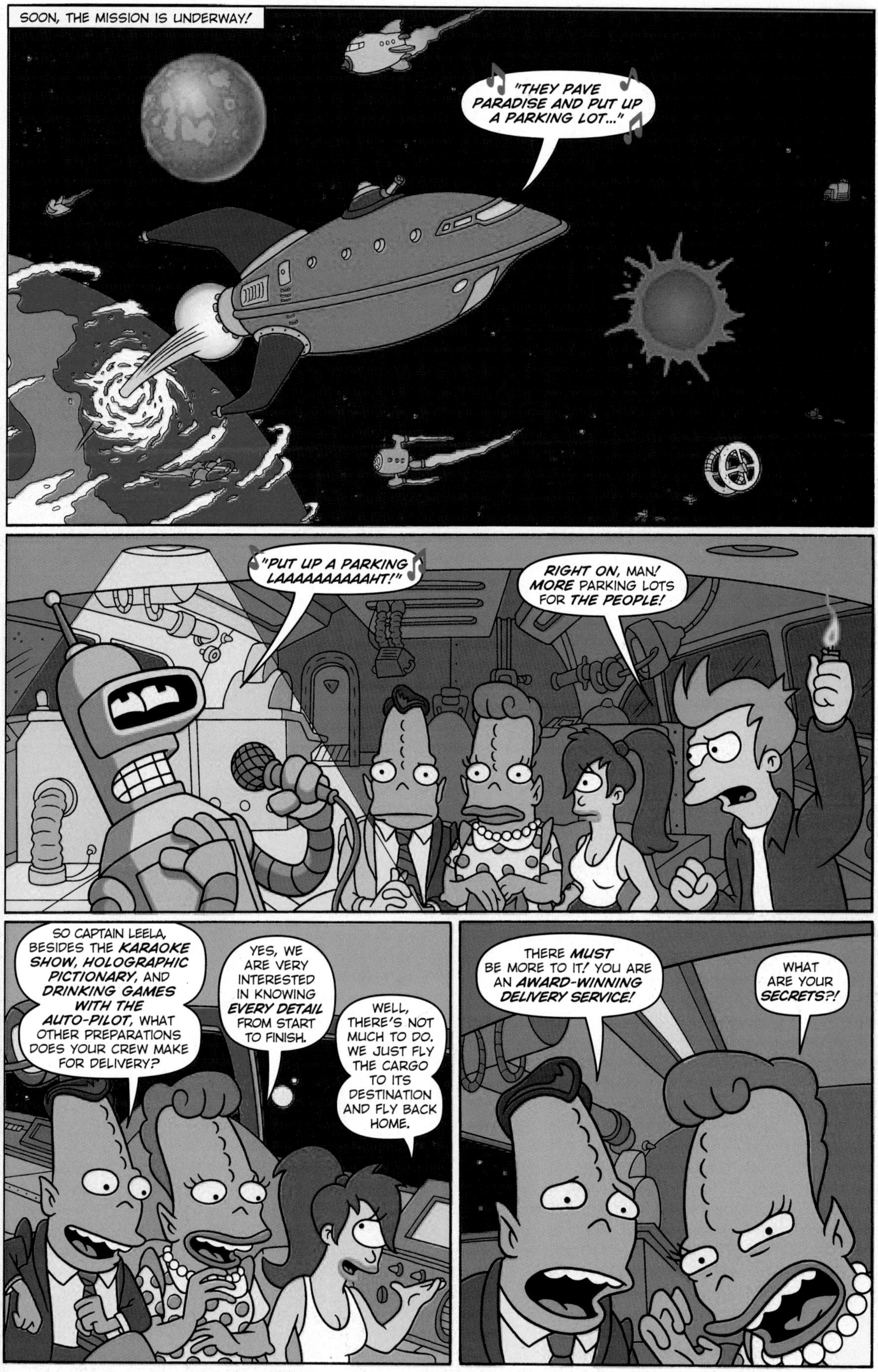
SOON, THE MISSION IS UNDERWAY!
"THEY PAVE PARADISE AND PUT UP A PARKING LOT..."
"PUT UP A PARKING LAAAAAAAAAAHT!"
RIGHT ON, MAN! MORE PARKING LOTS FOR THE PEOPLE!
SO CAPTAIN LEELA, BESIDES THE KARAOKE SHOW, HOLOGRAPHIC PICTIONARY, AND DRINKING GAMES WITH THE AUTO-PILOT, WHAT OTHER PREPARATIONS DOES YOUR CREW MAKE FOR DELIVERY?
YES, WE ARE VERY INTERESTED IN KNOWING EVERY DETAIL FROM START TO FINISH.
WELL, THERE'S NOT MUCH TO DO. WE JUST FLY THE CARGO TO ITS DESTINATION AND FLY BACK HOME.
THERE MUST BE MORE TO IT! YOU ARE AN AWARD-WINNING DELIVERY SERVICE!
WHAT ARE YOUR SECRETS?!

UH, WHAT MY FRIEND HERE MEANS TO SAY IS, THERE *MUST* BE MORE TO IT THAN SIMPLY COMING AND GOING FROM PLACE TO PLACE.

YES, *THAT IS IT!*

WELL, THERE'S REALLY NOT--

GO, GO, GO!

YES! EAT IT, DEWEY!

AND THE *AUTO PILOT* GOES *DOWN!* TIME TO PAY UP, LOSER!

AWW...

THUMP!

HEY -- THESE ARE *M&MS.* YOU WERE BETTING *SKITTLES!*

UH... *DOES NOT COMPUTE...* OR SOMETHING!

AUTO PILOT

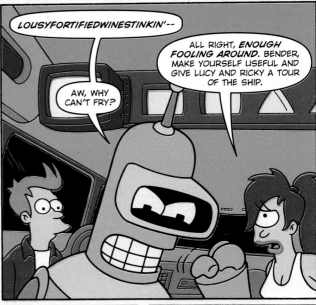

LOUSYFORTIFIEDWINESTINKIN'--

AW, WHY CAN'T FRY?

ALL RIGHT, *ENOUGH FOOLING AROUND.* BENDER, MAKE YOURSELF USEFUL AND GIVE LUCY AND RICKY A TOUR OF THE SHIP.

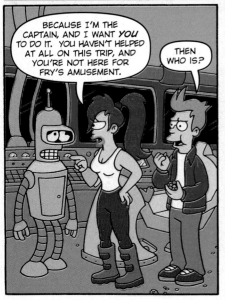

BECAUSE I'M THE CAPTAIN, AND I WANT *YOU* TO DO IT. YOU HAVEN'T HELPED AT ALL ON THIS TRIP, AND YOU'RE NOT HERE FOR FRY'S AMUSEMENT.

THEN WHO IS?

ALL RIGHT, ALL RIGHT! COME ON!

LOUSYSTINKIN UGLYONEEYED FREAKCAPTAIN JERKETTE--

SHUT YO' MOUTH!

I'M JUS' TALKIN' 'BOUT FRY!

I CAN DIG IT!

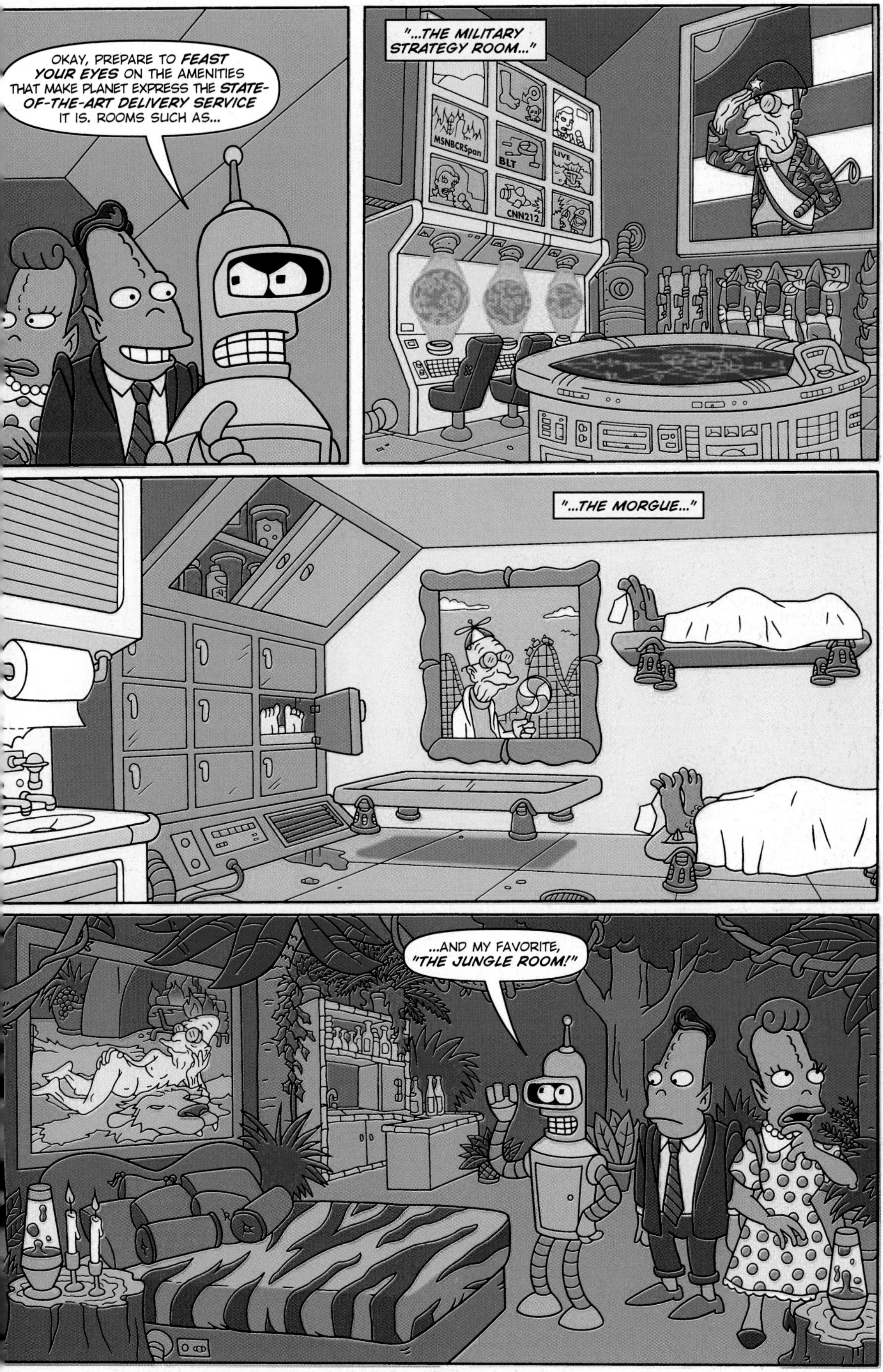

OKAY, PREPARE TO FEAST YOUR EYES ON THE AMENITIES THAT MAKE PLANET EXPRESS THE STATE-OF-THE-ART DELIVERY SERVICE IT IS. ROOMS SUCH AS...
"...THE MILITARY STRATEGY ROOM..."
MSNBCRSpan
BLT
LIVE
CNN212
"...THE MORGUE..."
...AND MY FAVORITE, "THE JUNGLE ROOM!"

SO WHAT'S YOUR POISON? *ARSENIC SHOOTERS? ETHER AND TONIC? CYANIDE DAIQUIRIS?*

UHH, WHAT DOES THIS HAVE TO DO WITH THE DELIVERY?

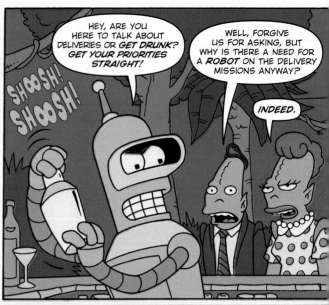

HEY, ARE YOU HERE TO TALK ABOUT DELIVERIES OR *GET DRUNK? GET YOUR PRIORITIES STRAIGHT!*

WELL, FORGIVE US FOR ASKING, BUT WHY IS THERE A NEED FOR A *ROBOT* ON THE DELIVERY MISSIONS ANYWAY?

INDEED.

SHOOSH! SHOOSH!

I'M THE SHIP'S COOK!

AND YET THE ONLY THING YOU HAVE COOKED SO FAR IS THAT *TELEPHONE-WIRE FETTUCCINI MARINATED IN MOTOR OIL.*

HEY, DON'T THANK ME. I JUST TOOK THE RECIPE FROM *ELZAR'S* "COOKING ON A BUDGET OF 8 MEGABYTES OR LESS!"

BENDER, REPORT TO FLIGHT DECK IMMEDIATELY.

WE'VE GOT TROUBLE!

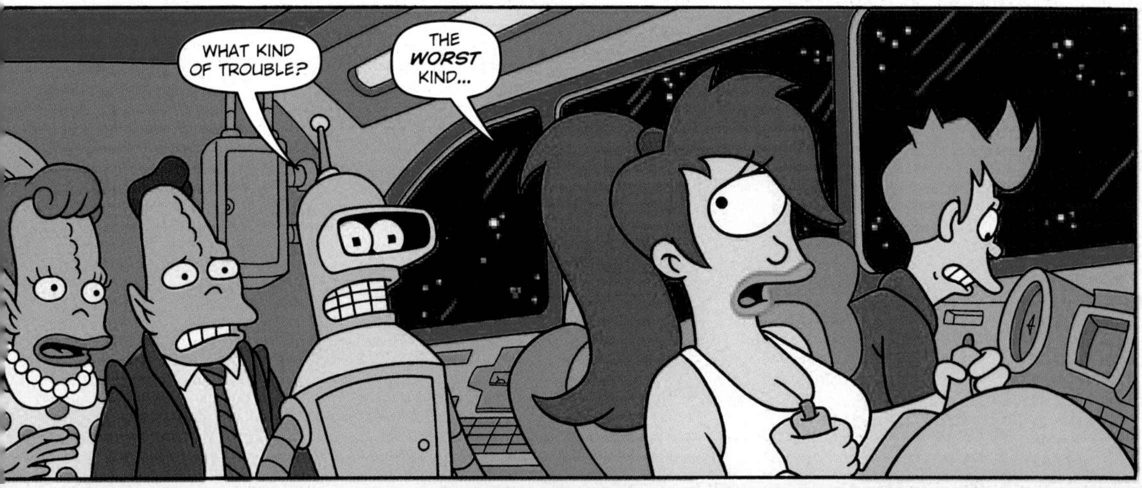
WHAT KIND OF TROUBLE?
THE WORST KIND...

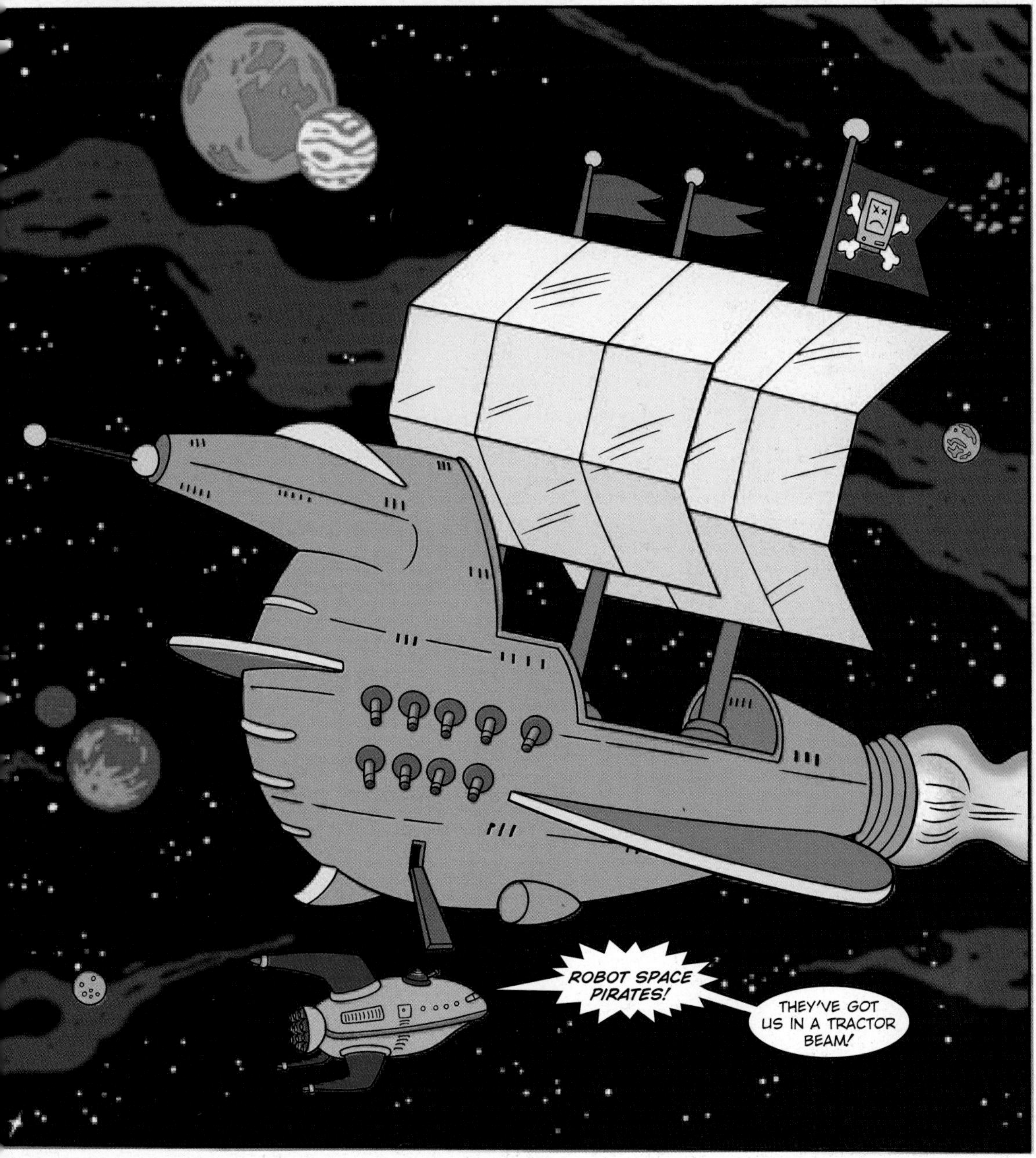
ROBOT SPACE PIRATES!
THEY'VE GOT US IN A TRACTOR BEAM!

OH NO! IT LOOKS LIKE THE SHIP OF *LONG JOHN SILICON* AND HIS CRONY *BLACKBOARD!* *TYRANTS OF THE SEA OF TRANQUILLITY!*

ARE THEY DANGEROUS?

THEY ARE IF YOU HAVE *VALUABLE CARGO.*

EEP! THAT'S *ME!*

LUCY AND RICKY, IF WE'RE GOING TO SURVIVE, WE *HAVE TO KNOW* WHAT'S IN THE CRATE.

UHH, I AM AFRAID THAT IS IMPOSSIBLE, CAPTAIN LEELA.

BUT IT COULD *COST OUR LIVES* IF WE DON'T TELL THEM!

CAN WE NOT JUST GIVE THEM *THE ROBOT?* HE HAS PROVEN HIMSELF QUITE *UNNECESSARY* AS IT IS.

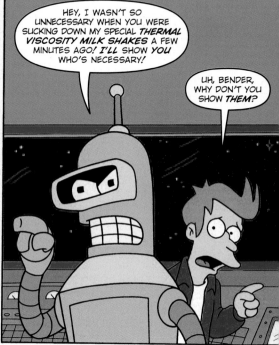

HEY, I WASN'T SO UNNECESSARY WHEN YOU WERE SUCKING DOWN MY SPECIAL *THERMAL VISCOSITY MILK SHAKES* A FEW MINUTES AGO! *I'LL* SHOW *YOU* WHO'S NECESSARY!

UH, BENDER, WHY DON'T YOU SHOW *THEM?*

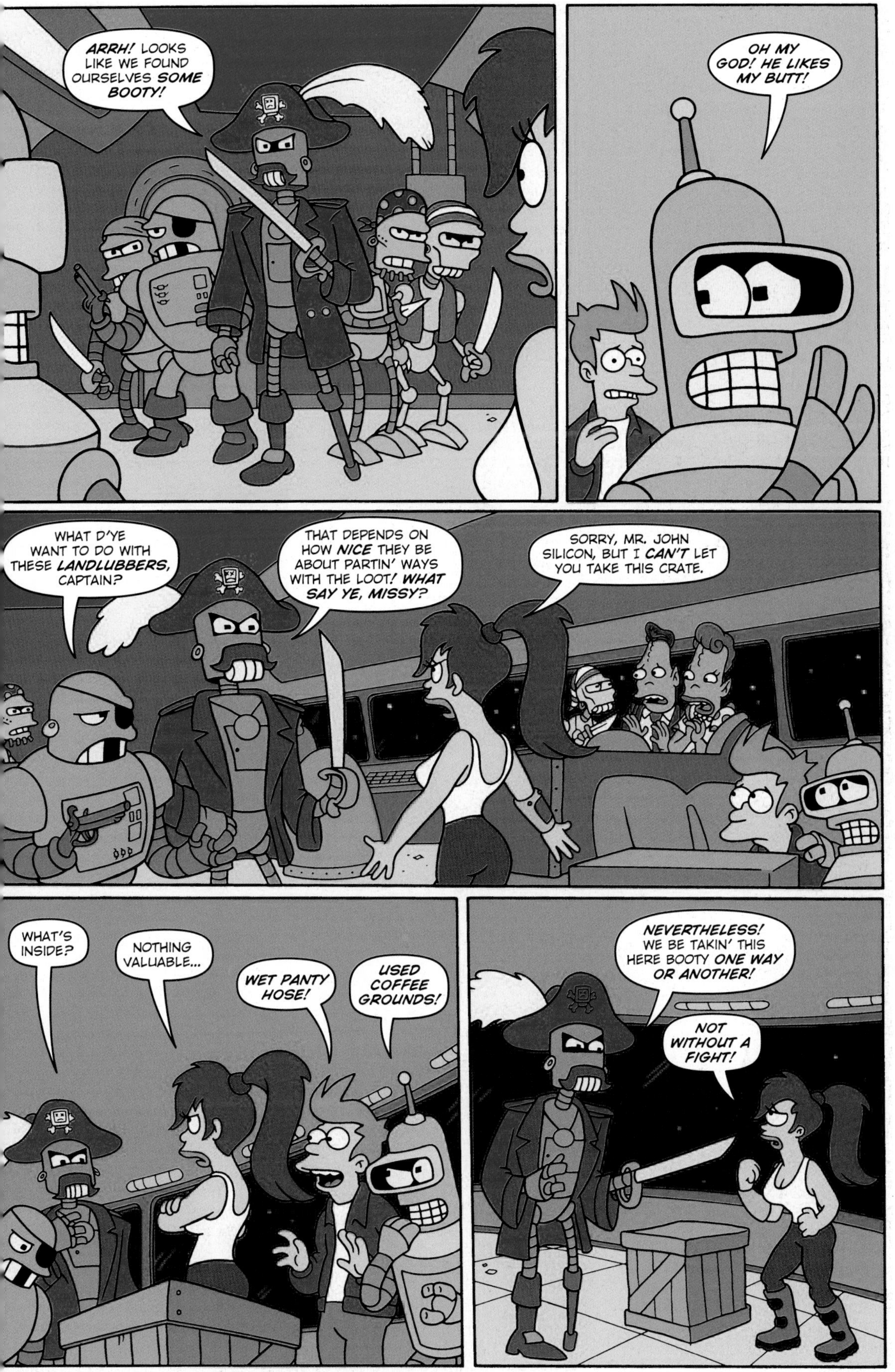
ARRH! LOOKS LIKE WE FOUND OURSELVES SOME BOOTY!
OH MY GOD! HE LIKES MY BUTT!
WHAT D'YE WANT TO DO WITH THESE LANDLUBBERS, CAPTAIN?
THAT DEPENDS ON HOW NICE THEY BE ABOUT PARTIN' WAYS WITH THE LOOT! WHAT SAY YE, MISSY?
SORRY, MR. JOHN SILICON, BUT I CAN'T LET YOU TAKE THIS CRATE.
WHAT'S INSIDE?
NOTHING VALUABLE...
WET PANTY HOSE!
USED COFFEE GROUNDS!
NEVERTHELESS! WE BE TAKIN' THIS HERE BOOTY ONE WAY OR ANOTHER!
NOT WITHOUT A FIGHT!

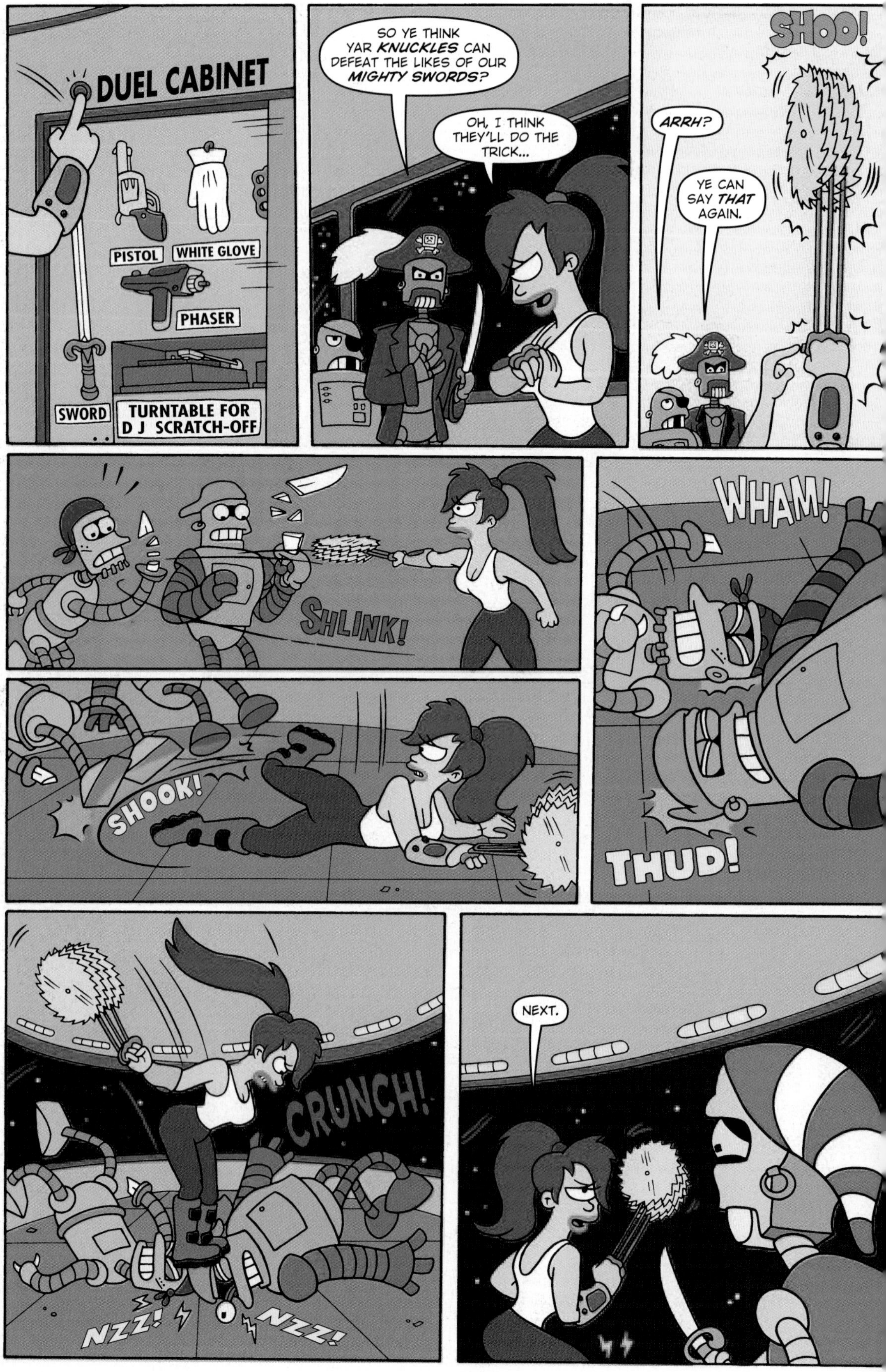
DUEL CABINET
PISTOL
WHITE GLOVE
PHASER
SWORD
TURNTABLE FOR D J SCRATCH-OFF
SO YE THINK YAR KNUCKLES CAN DEFEAT THE LIKES OF OUR MIGHTY SWORDS?
OH, I THINK THEY'LL DO THE TRICK...
SHOO!
ARRH?
YE CAN SAY THAT AGAIN.
SHLINK!
WHAM!
SHOOK!
THUD!
CRUNCH!
NZZ!
NZZ!
NEXT.

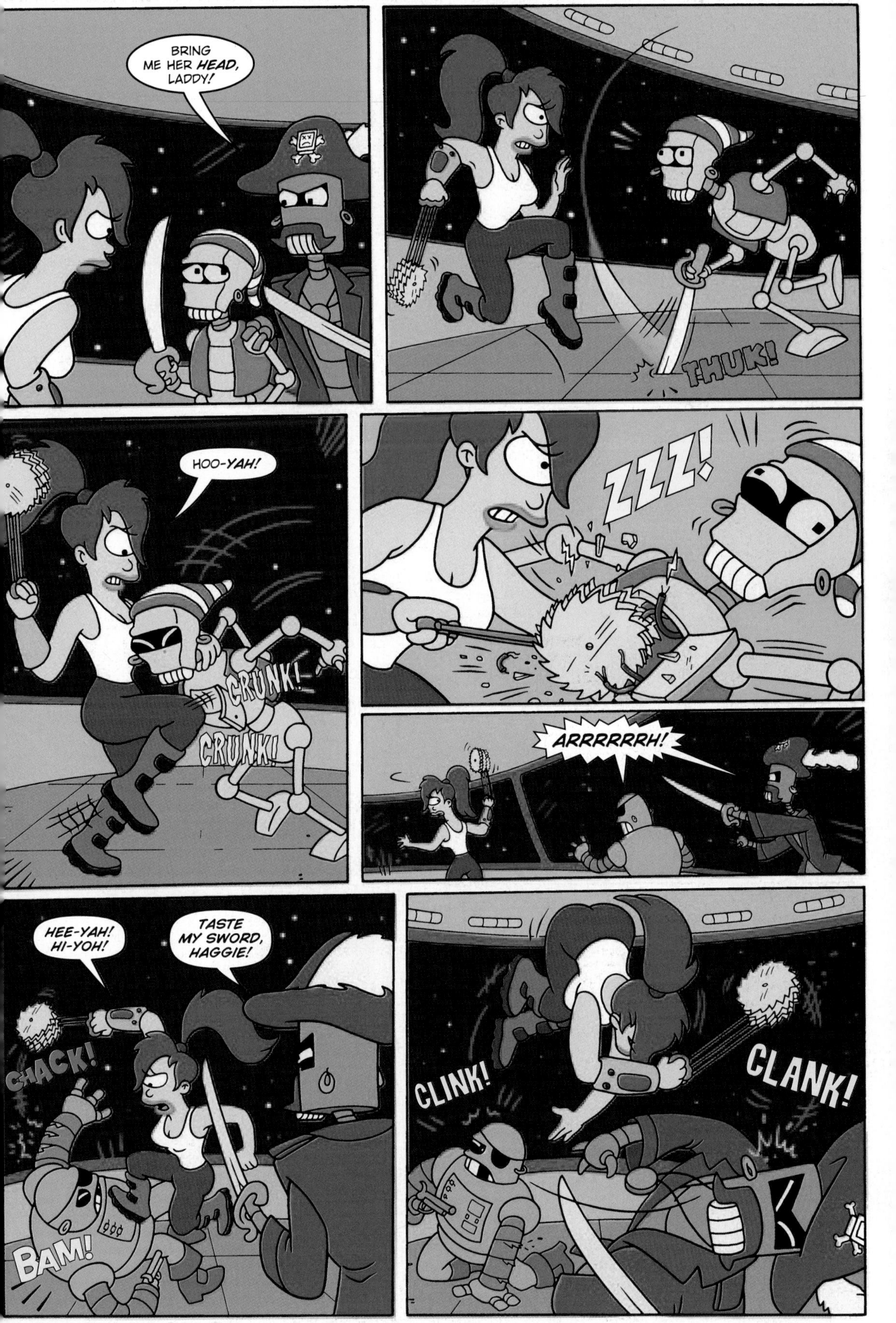
BRING ME HER HEAD, LADDY!
THUK!
HOO-YAH!
CRUNK!
CRUNK!
ZZZ!
ARRRRRRH!
HEE-YAH! HI-YOH!
TASTE MY SWORD, HAGGIE!
CHACK!
BAM!
CLINK!
CLANK!

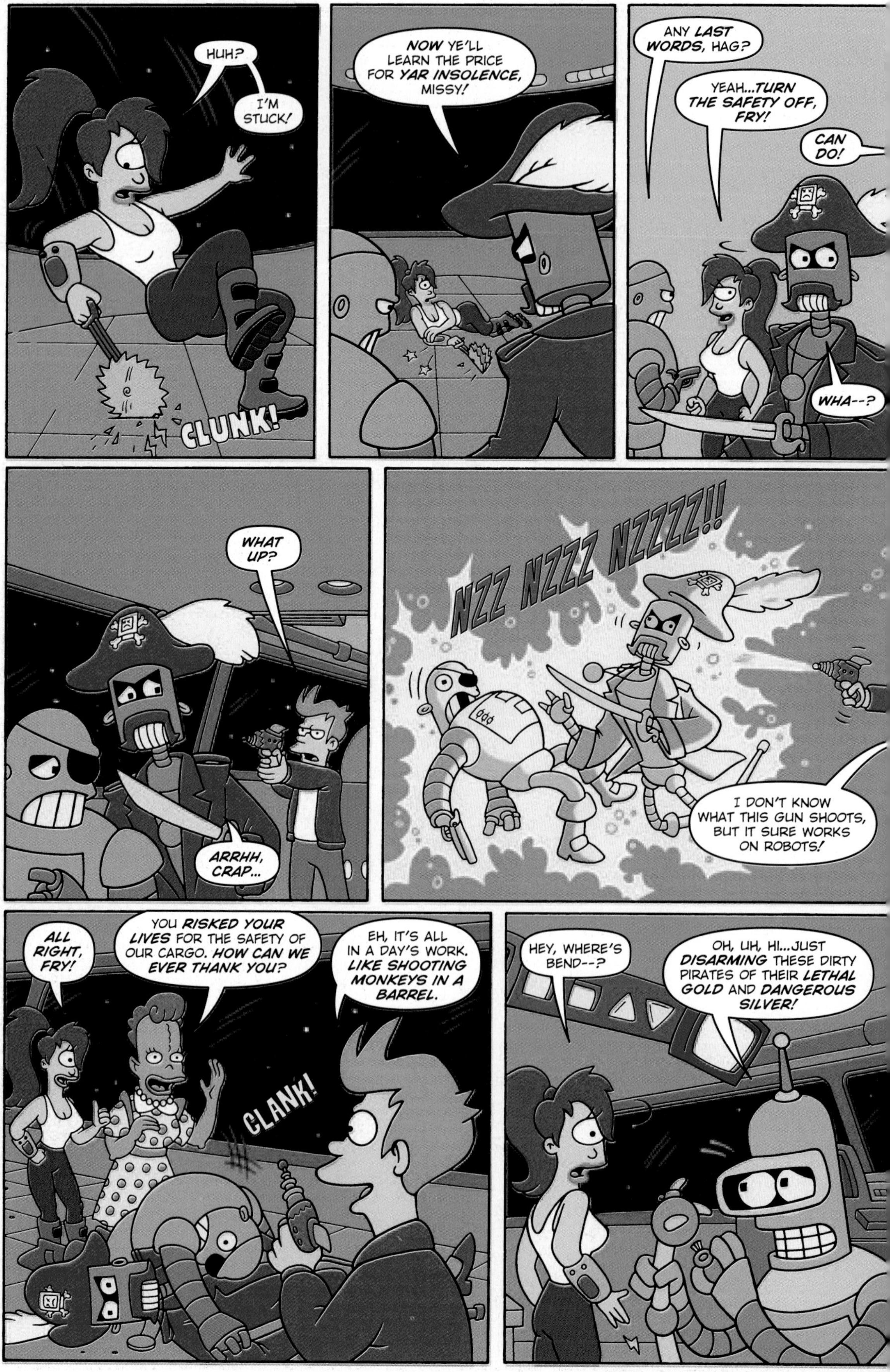
HUH?
I'M STUCK!
CLUNK!
NOW YE'LL LEARN THE PRICE FOR YAR INSOLENCE, MISSY!
ANY LAST WORDS, HAG?
YEAH...TURN THE SAFETY OFF, FRY!
CAN DO!
WHA--?
WHAT UP?
ARRHH, CRAP...
NZZ NZZZ NZZZZ!!
I DON'T KNOW WHAT THIS GUN SHOOTS, BUT IT SURE WORKS ON ROBOTS!
ALL RIGHT, FRY!
YOU RISKED YOUR LIVES FOR THE SAFETY OF OUR CARGO. HOW CAN WE EVER THANK YOU?
EH, IT'S ALL IN A DAY'S WORK. LIKE SHOOTING MONKEYS IN A BARREL.
CLANK!
HEY, WHERE'S BEND--?
OH, UH, HI...JUST DISARMING THESE DIRTY PIRATES OF THEIR LETHAL GOLD AND DANGEROUS SILVER!

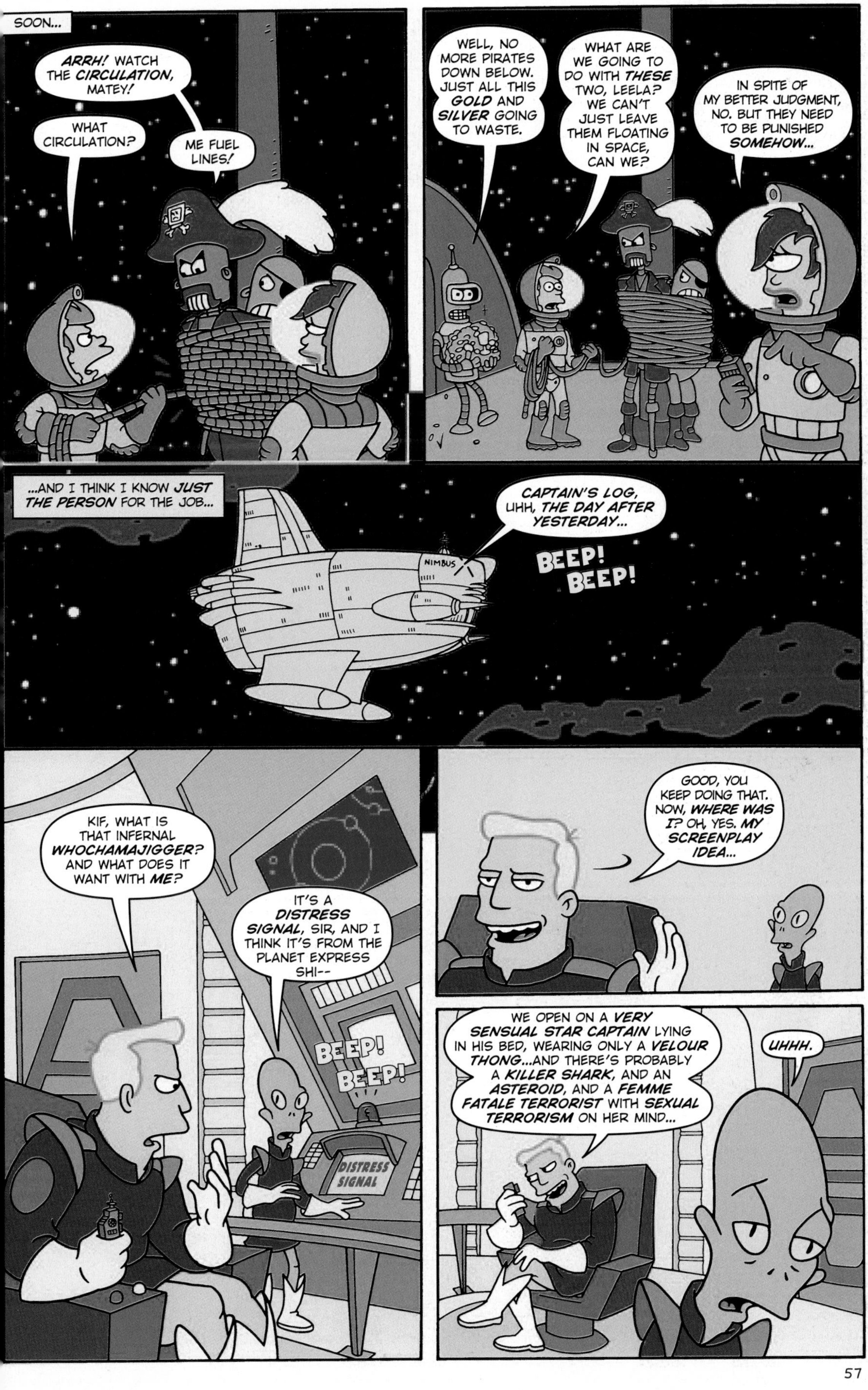
SOON...
ARRH! WATCH THE CIRCULATION, MATEY!
WHAT CIRCULATION?
ME FUEL LINES!
WELL, NO MORE PIRATES DOWN BELOW. JUST ALL THIS GOLD AND SILVER GOING TO WASTE.
WHAT ARE WE GOING TO DO WITH THESE TWO, LEELA? WE CAN'T JUST LEAVE THEM FLOATING IN SPACE, CAN WE?
IN SPITE OF MY BETTER JUDGMENT, NO. BUT THEY NEED TO BE PUNISHED SOMEHOW...
...AND I THINK I KNOW JUST THE PERSON FOR THE JOB...
NIMBUS
CAPTAIN'S LOG, UHH, THE DAY AFTER YESTERDAY...
BEEP! BEEP!
KIF, WHAT IS THAT INFERNAL WHOCHAMAJIGGER? AND WHAT DOES IT WANT WITH ME?
IT'S A DISTRESS SIGNAL, SIR, AND I THINK IT'S FROM THE PLANET EXPRESS SHI--
BEEP! BEEP!
DISTRESS SIGNAL
GOOD, YOU KEEP DOING THAT. NOW, WHERE WAS I? OH, YES. MY SCREENPLAY IDEA...
WE OPEN ON A VERY SENSUAL STAR CAPTAIN LYING IN HIS BED, WEARING ONLY A VELOUR THONG...AND THERE'S PROBABLY A KILLER SHARK, AND AN ASTEROID, AND A FEMME FATALE TERRORIST WITH SEXUAL TERRORISM ON HER MIND...
UHHH.

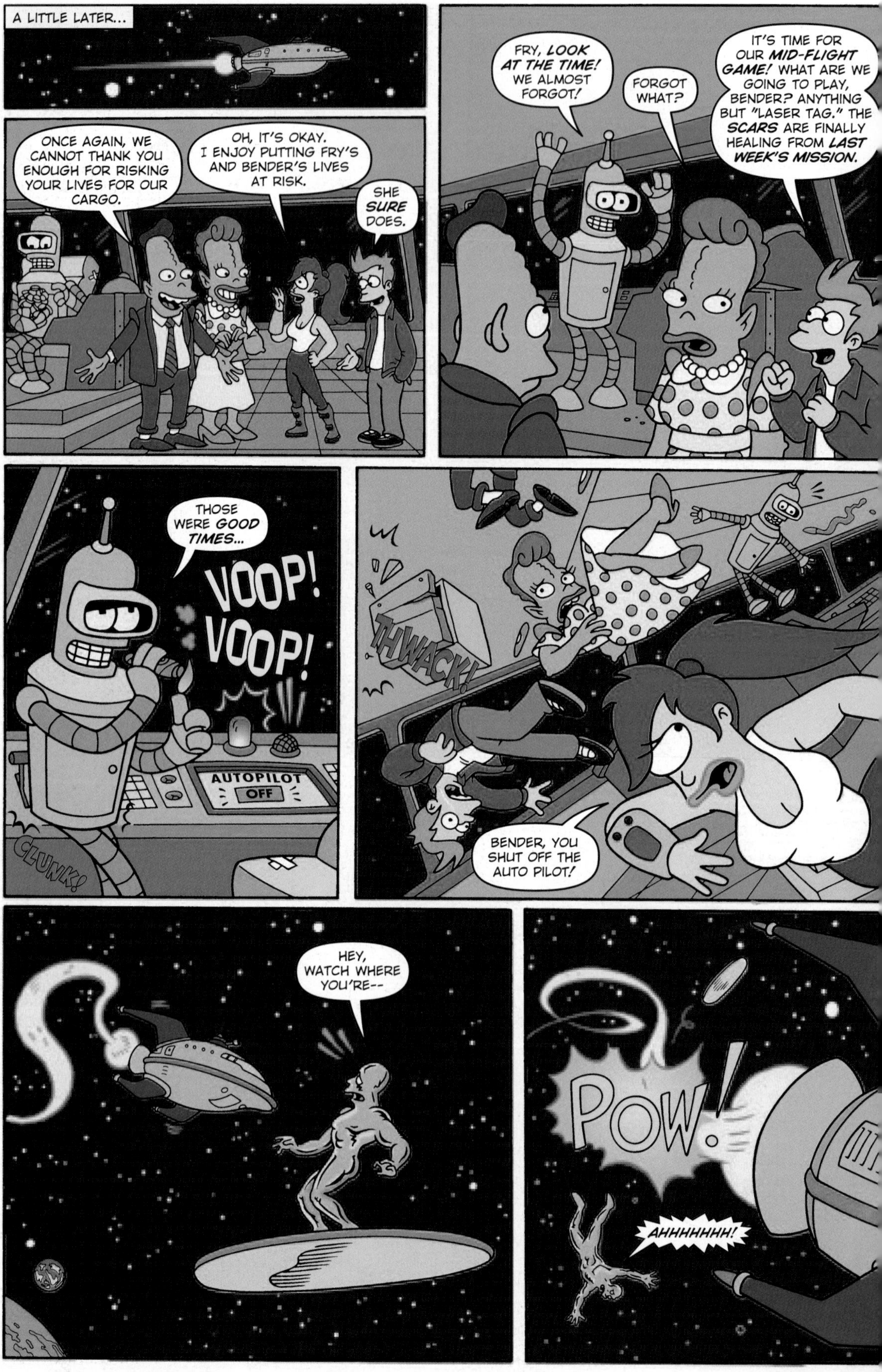
A LITTLE LATER...
ONCE AGAIN, WE CANNOT THANK YOU ENOUGH FOR RISKING YOUR LIVES FOR OUR CARGO.
OH, IT'S OKAY. I ENJOY PUTTING FRY'S AND BENDER'S LIVES AT RISK.
SHE SURE DOES.
FRY, LOOK AT THE TIME! WE ALMOST FORGOT!
FORGOT WHAT?
IT'S TIME FOR OUR MID-FLIGHT GAME! WHAT ARE WE GOING TO PLAY, BENDER? ANYTHING BUT "LASER TAG." THE SCARS ARE FINALLY HEALING FROM LAST WEEK'S MISSION.
THOSE WERE GOOD TIMES...
VOOP! VOOP!
AUTOPILOT
OFF
CLUNK!
THWACK!
BENDER, YOU SHUT OFF THE AUTO PILOT!
HEY, WATCH WHERE YOU'RE--
POW!
AHHHHHHH!

UH-OH!

ZZEW!

ZZEW!

ZZEW!

THAT WAS CLOSE!

WHAT THE--?

OWWW!

ARE YOU GUYS OKAY?

WE'RE FINE, THANKS.

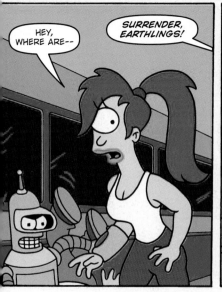

HEY, WHERE ARE--

SURRENDER, EARTHLINGS!

THERE WERE GUNS IN THAT CRATE? I COULDA SWORE THEY WERE PUPPIES!

YOU OWE ME TEN BUCKS...

SILENCE!!

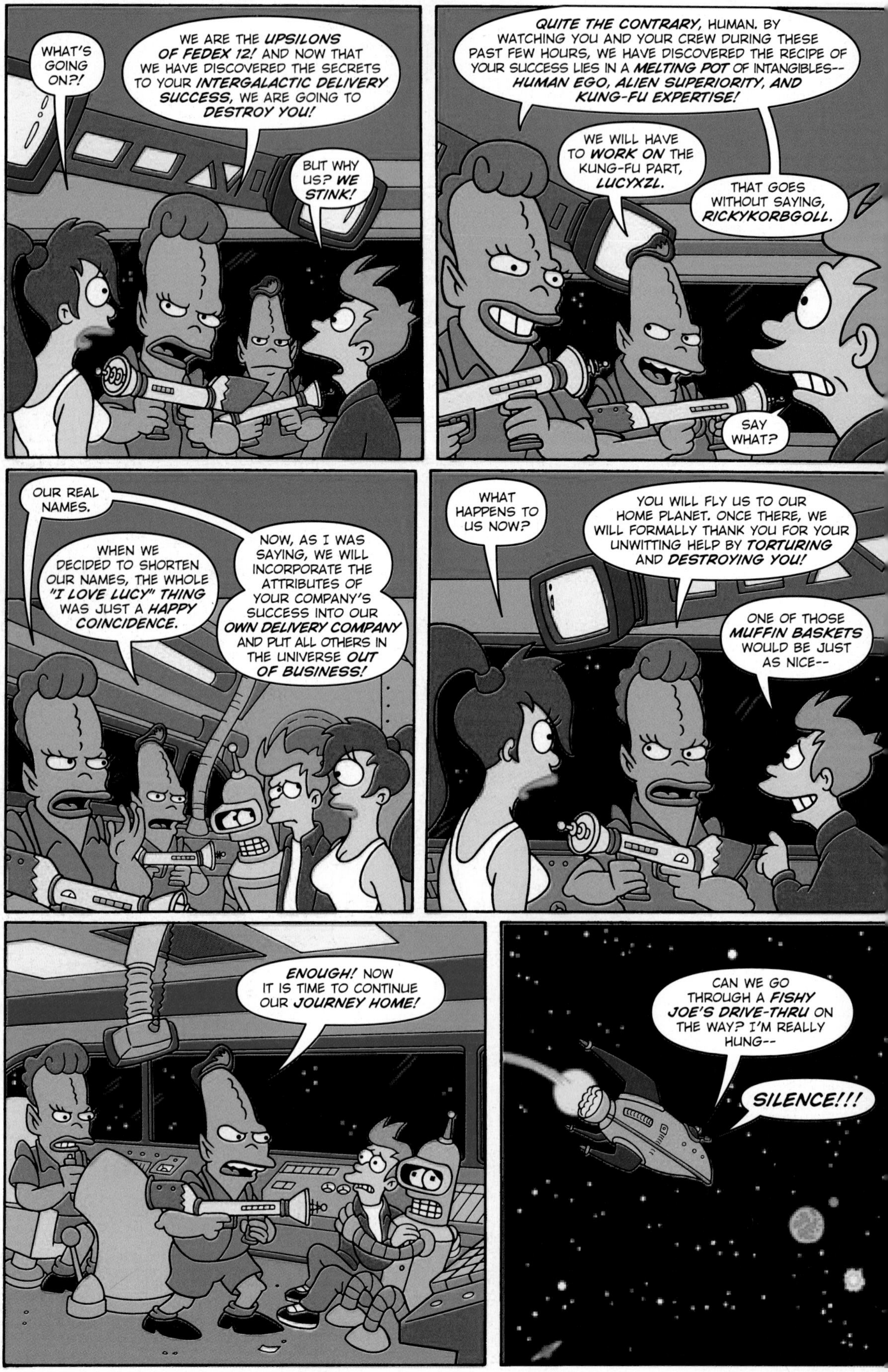

WHAT'S GOING ON?!
WE ARE THE UPSILONS OF FEDEX 12! AND NOW THAT WE HAVE DISCOVERED THE SECRETS TO YOUR INTERGALACTIC DELIVERY SUCCESS, WE ARE GOING TO DESTROY YOU!
BUT WHY US? WE STINK!
QUITE THE CONTRARY, HUMAN. BY WATCHING YOU AND YOUR CREW DURING THESE PAST FEW HOURS, WE HAVE DISCOVERED THE RECIPE OF YOUR SUCCESS LIES IN A MELTING POT OF INTANGIBLES-- HUMAN EGO, ALIEN SUPERIORITY, AND KUNG-FU EXPERTISE!
WE WILL HAVE TO WORK ON THE KUNG-FU PART, LUCYXZL.
THAT GOES WITHOUT SAYING, RICKYKORBGOLL.
SAY WHAT?
OUR REAL NAMES.
WHEN WE DECIDED TO SHORTEN OUR NAMES, THE WHOLE "I LOVE LUCY" THING WAS JUST A HAPPY COINCIDENCE.
NOW, AS I WAS SAYING, WE WILL INCORPORATE THE ATTRIBUTES OF YOUR COMPANY'S SUCCESS INTO OUR OWN DELIVERY COMPANY AND PUT ALL OTHERS IN THE UNIVERSE OUT OF BUSINESS!
WHAT HAPPENS TO US NOW?
YOU WILL FLY US TO OUR HOME PLANET. ONCE THERE, WE WILL FORMALLY THANK YOU FOR YOUR UNWITTING HELP BY TORTURING AND DESTROYING YOU!
ONE OF THOSE MUFFIN BASKETS WOULD BE JUST AS NICE--
ENOUGH! NOW IT IS TIME TO CONTINUE OUR JOURNEY HOME!
CAN WE GO THROUGH A FISHY JOE'S DRIVE-THRU ON THE WAY? I'M REALLY HUNG--
SILENCE!!!

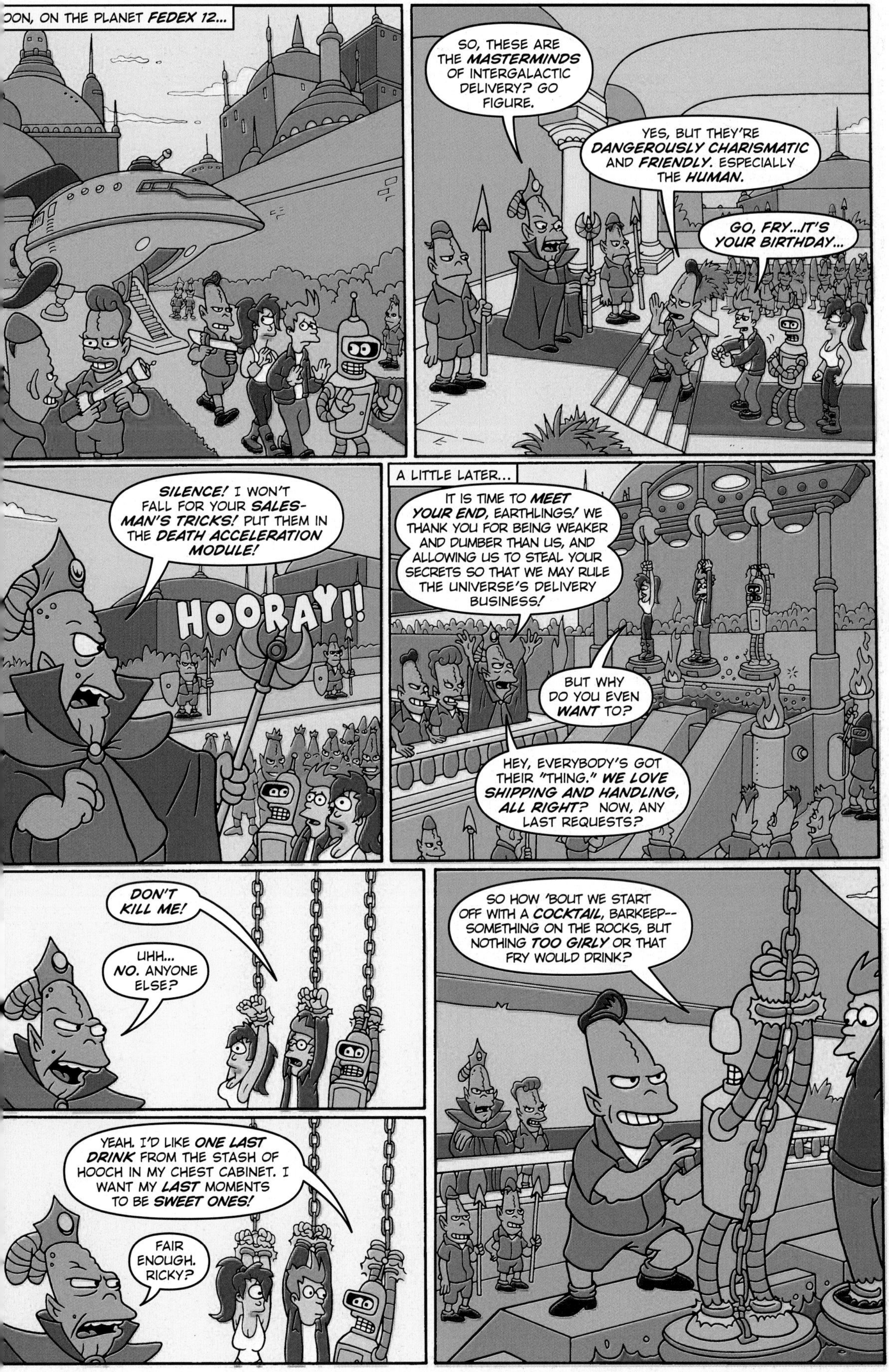

OON, ON THE PLANET FEDEX 12...
SO, THESE ARE THE MASTERMINDS OF INTERGALACTIC DELIVERY? GO FIGURE.
YES, BUT THEY'RE DANGEROUSLY CHARISMATIC AND FRIENDLY. ESPECIALLY THE HUMAN.
GO, FRY...IT'S YOUR BIRTHDAY...
SILENCE! I WON'T FALL FOR YOUR SALES-MAN'S TRICKS! PUT THEM IN THE DEATH ACCELERATION MODULE!
HOORAY!!
A LITTLE LATER...
IT IS TIME TO MEET YOUR END, EARTHLINGS! WE THANK YOU FOR BEING WEAKER AND DUMBER THAN US, AND ALLOWING US TO STEAL YOUR SECRETS SO THAT WE MAY RULE THE UNIVERSE'S DELIVERY BUSINESS!
BUT WHY DO YOU EVEN WANT TO?
HEY, EVERYBODY'S GOT THEIR "THING." WE LOVE SHIPPING AND HANDLING, ALL RIGHT? NOW, ANY LAST REQUESTS?
DON'T KILL ME!
UHH... NO. ANYONE ELSE?
YEAH. I'D LIKE ONE LAST DRINK FROM THE STASH OF HOOCH IN MY CHEST CABINET. I WANT MY LAST MOMENTS TO BE SWEET ONES!
FAIR ENOUGH. RICKY?
SO HOW 'BOUT WE START OFF WITH A COCKTAIL, BARKEEP-- SOMETHING ON THE ROCKS, BUT NOTHING TOO GIRLY OR THAT FRY WOULD DRINK?

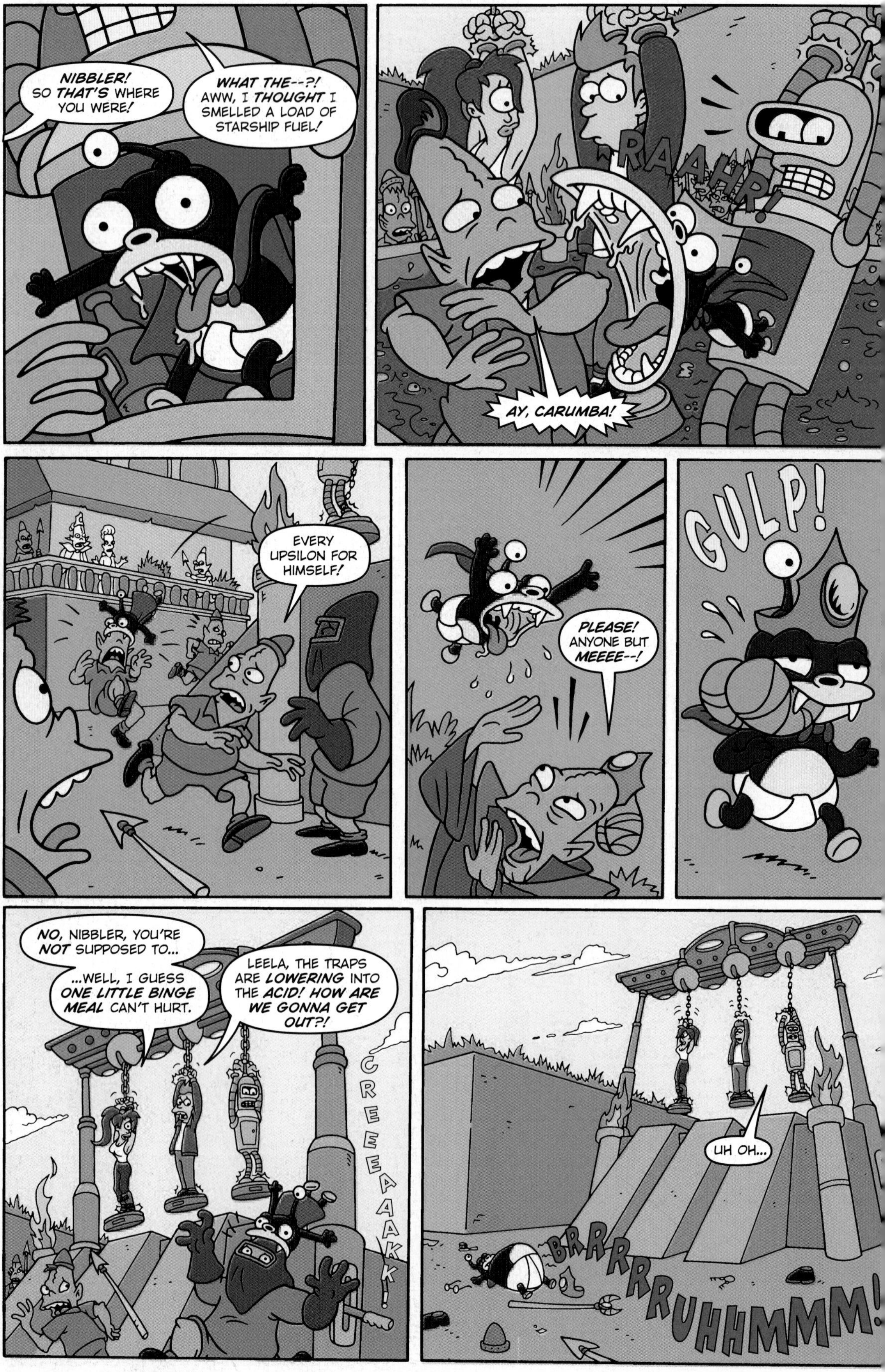
NIBBLER! SO THAT'S WHERE YOU WERE!
WHAT THE--?! AWW, I THOUGHT I SMELLED A LOAD OF STARSHIP FUEL!
RAAHR!
AY, CARUMBA!
EVERY UPSILON FOR HIMSELF!
PLEASE! ANYONE BUT MEEEE--!
GULP!
NO, NIBBLER, YOU'RE NOT SUPPOSED TO...
...WELL, I GUESS ONE LITTLE BINGE MEAL CAN'T HURT.
LEELA, THE TRAPS ARE LOWERING INTO THE ACID! HOW ARE WE GONNA GET OUT?!
CREEEAAAK!
UH OH...
BRRRRRUHHMMM!

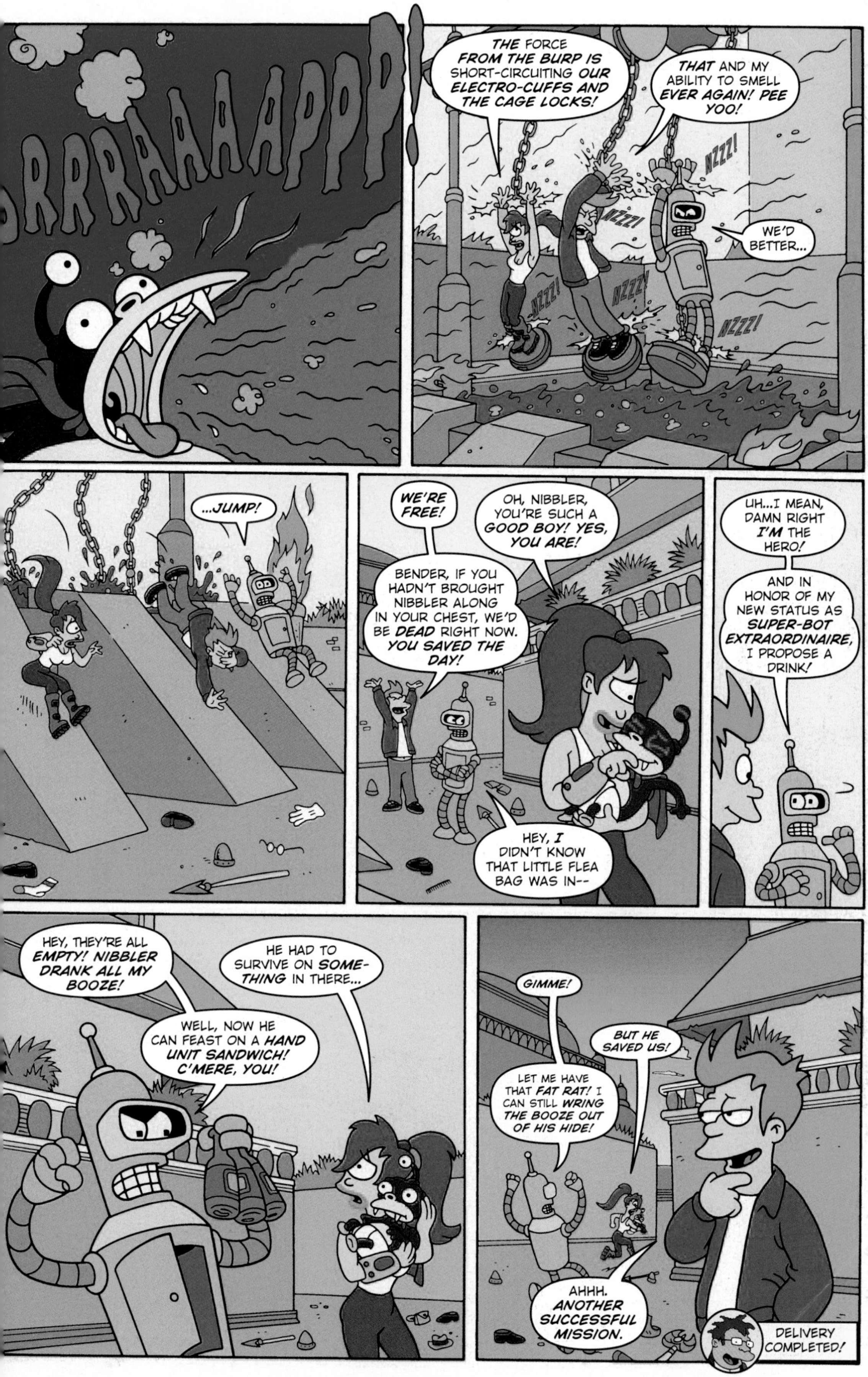
BRRRAAAAAPPP!
THE FORCE FROM THE BURP IS SHORT-CIRCUITING OUR ELECTRO-CUFFS AND THE CAGE LOCKS!
THAT AND MY ABILITY TO SMELL EVER AGAIN! PEE YOO!
NZZZ!
NZZZ!
NZZZ!
NZZZ!
NZZZ!
WE'D BETTER...
...JUMP!
WE'RE FREE!
BENDER, IF YOU HADN'T BROUGHT NIBBLER ALONG IN YOUR CHEST, WE'D BE DEAD RIGHT NOW. YOU SAVED THE DAY!
OH, NIBBLER, YOU'RE SUCH A GOOD BOY! YES, YOU ARE!
HEY, I DIDN'T KNOW THAT LITTLE FLEA BAG WAS IN--
UH...I MEAN, DAMN RIGHT I'M THE HERO!
AND IN HONOR OF MY NEW STATUS AS SUPER-BOT EXTRAORDINAIRE, I PROPOSE A DRINK!
HEY, THEY'RE ALL EMPTY! NIBBLER DRANK ALL MY BOOZE!
HE HAD TO SURVIVE ON SOME-THING IN THERE...
WELL, NOW HE CAN FEAST ON A HAND UNIT SANDWICH! C'MERE, YOU!
GIMME!
BUT HE SAVED US!
LET ME HAVE THAT FAT RAT! I CAN STILL WRING THE BOOZE OUT OF HIS HIDE!
AHHH. ANOTHER SUCCESSFUL MISSION.
DELIVERY COMPLETED!

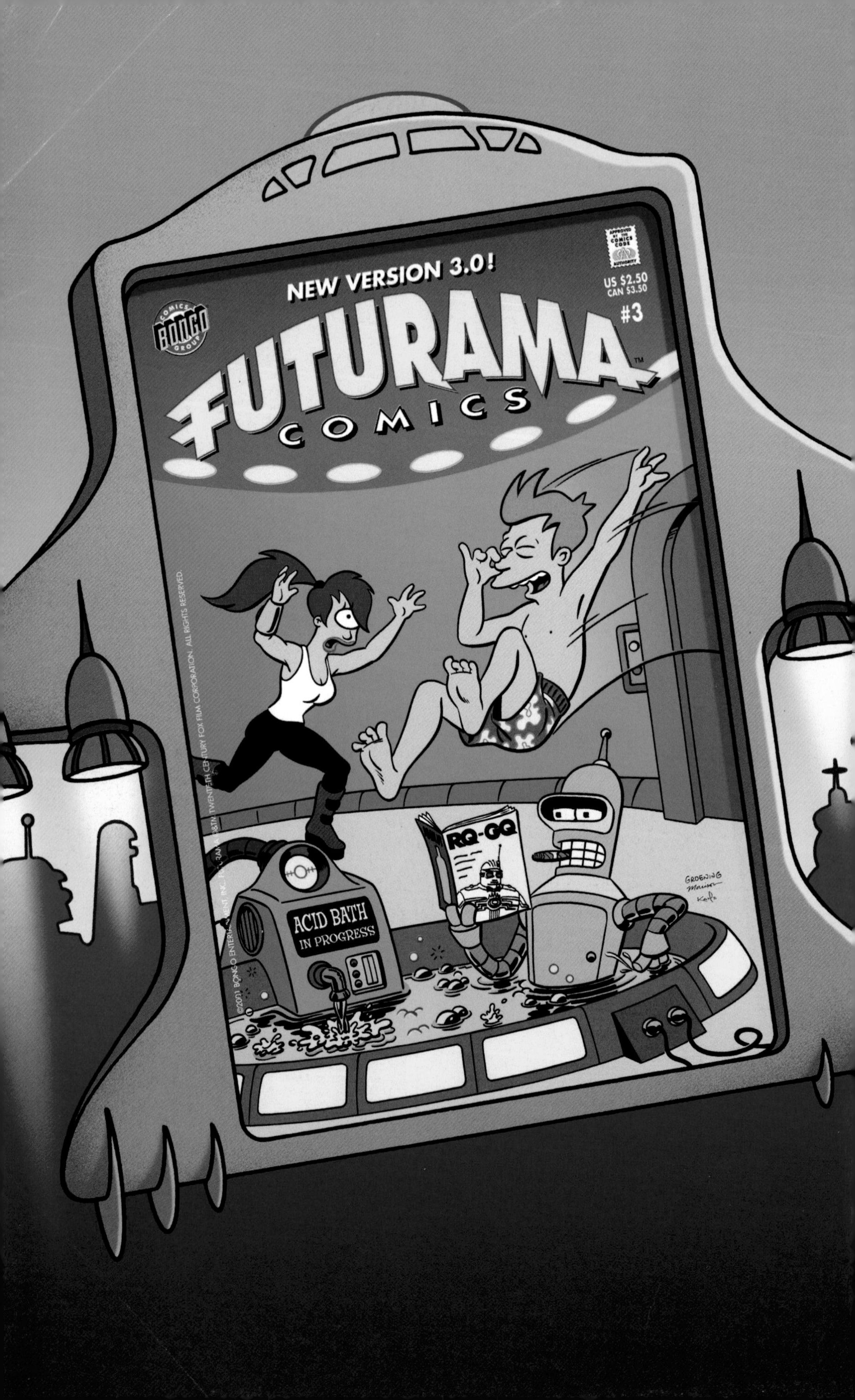

NEW VERSION 3.0!
APPROVED BY THE COMICS CODE AUTHORITY
US $2.50
CAN $3.50
#3
COMICS BONGO GROUP
FUTURAMA™
COMICS
RQ-GQ
ACID BATH
IN PROGRESS
GROENING
FOX FILM CORPORATION. ALL RIGHTS RESERVED.

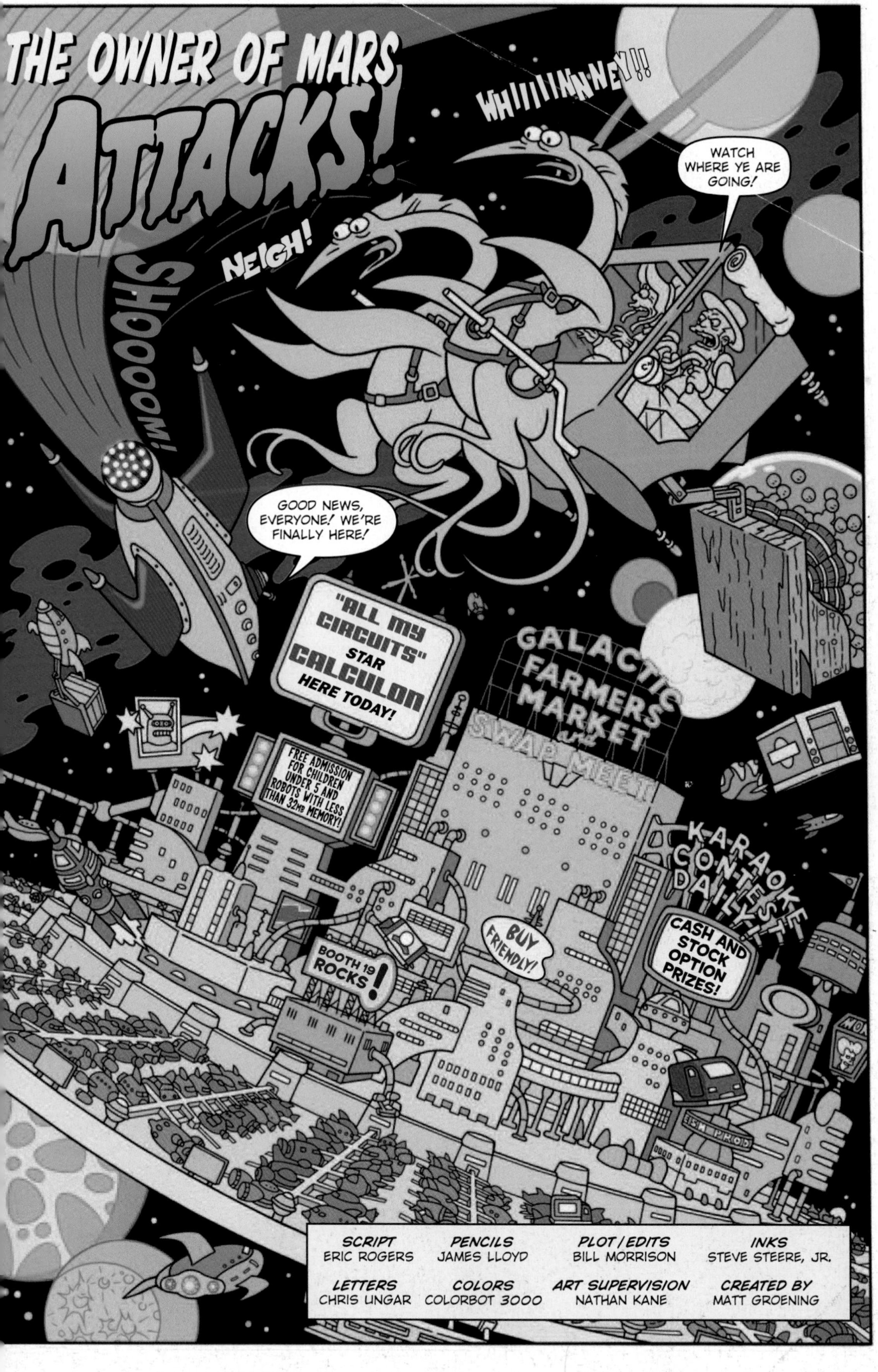
THE OWNER OF MARS
ATTACKS!
WHIIIIINNNEY!!
WATCH WHERE YE ARE GOING!
NEIGH!
SHOOOOOM!
GOOD NEWS, EVERYONE! WE'RE FINALLY HERE!
"ALL MY CIRCUITS" STAR CALCULON HERE TODAY!
FREE ADMISSION FOR CHILDREN UNDER 5 AND ROBOTS WITH LESS THAN 32MB MEMORY!
GALACTIC FARMERS MARKET and SWAP MEET
KARAOKE CONTEST DAILY!
CASH AND STOCK OPTION PRIZES!
BUY FRIENDLY!
BOOTH 19 ROCKS!
SCRIPT ERIC ROGERS
PENCILS JAMES LLOYD
PLOT / EDITS BILL MORRISON
INKS STEVE STEERE, JR.
LETTERS CHRIS UNGAR
COLORS COLORBOT 3000
ART SUPERVISION NATHAN KANE
CREATED BY MATT GROENING

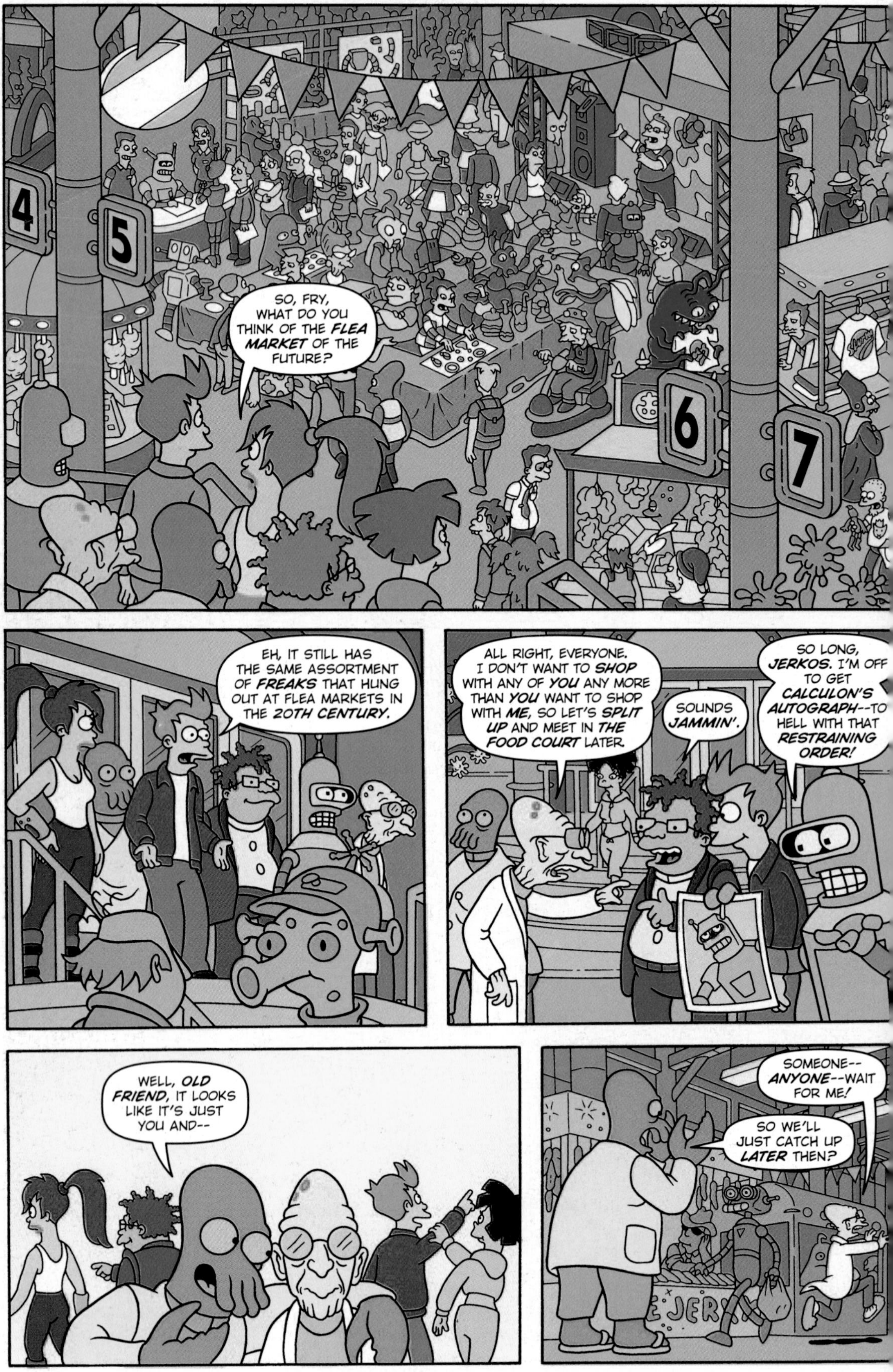
SO, FRY, WHAT DO YOU THINK OF THE FLEA MARKET OF THE FUTURE?
EH, IT STILL HAS THE SAME ASSORTMENT OF FREAKS THAT HUNG OUT AT FLEA MARKETS IN THE 20TH CENTURY.
ALL RIGHT, EVERYONE. I DON'T WANT TO SHOP WITH ANY OF YOU ANY MORE THAN YOU WANT TO SHOP WITH ME, SO LET'S SPLIT UP AND MEET IN THE FOOD COURT LATER.
SOUNDS JAMMIN'.
SO LONG, JERKOS. I'M OFF TO GET CALCULON'S AUTOGRAPH--TO HELL WITH THAT RESTRAINING ORDER!
WELL, OLD FRIEND, IT LOOKS LIKE IT'S JUST YOU AND--
SOMEONE--ANYONE--WAIT FOR ME!
SO WE'LL JUST CATCH UP LATER THEN?

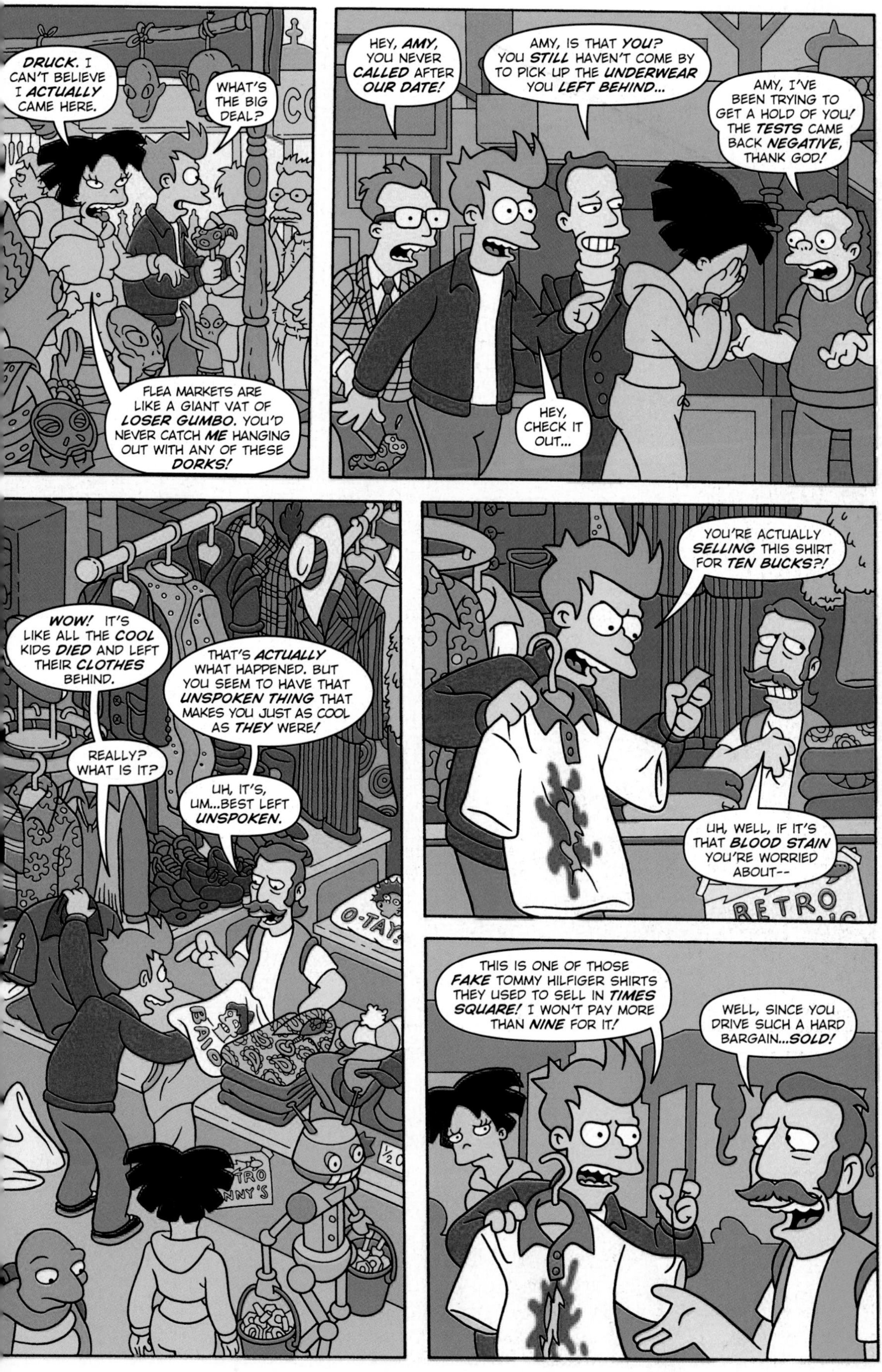
DRUCK. I CAN'T BELIEVE I ACTUALLY CAME HERE.
WHAT'S THE BIG DEAL?
FLEA MARKETS ARE LIKE A GIANT VAT OF LOSER GUMBO. YOU'D NEVER CATCH ME HANGING OUT WITH ANY OF THESE DORKS!
HEY, AMY, YOU NEVER CALLED AFTER OUR DATE!
AMY, IS THAT YOU? YOU STILL HAVEN'T COME BY TO PICK UP THE UNDERWEAR YOU LEFT BEHIND...
AMY, I'VE BEEN TRYING TO GET A HOLD OF YOU! THE TESTS CAME BACK NEGATIVE, THANK GOD!
HEY, CHECK IT OUT...
WOW! IT'S LIKE ALL THE COOL KIDS DIED AND LEFT THEIR CLOTHES BEHIND.
THAT'S ACTUALLY WHAT HAPPENED. BUT YOU SEEM TO HAVE THAT UNSPOKEN THING THAT MAKES YOU JUST AS COOL AS THEY WERE!
REALLY? WHAT IS IT?
UH, IT'S, UM...BEST LEFT UNSPOKEN.
O-TAY!
BAIO
YOU'RE ACTUALLY SELLING THIS SHIRT FOR TEN BUCKS?!
UH, WELL, IF IT'S THAT BLOOD STAIN YOU'RE WORRIED ABOUT--
RETRO
THIS IS ONE OF THOSE FAKE TOMMY HILFIGER SHIRTS THEY USED TO SELL IN TIMES SQUARE! I WON'T PAY MORE THAN NINE FOR IT!
WELL, SINCE YOU DRIVE SUCH A HARD BARGAIN...SOLD!

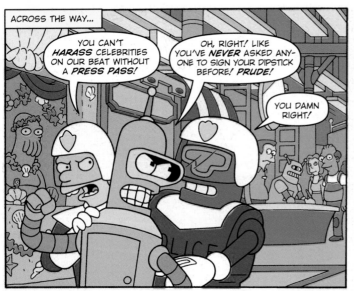

ACROSS THE WAY...

YOU CAN'T *HARASS* CELEBRITIES ON OUR BEAT WITHOUT A *PRESS PASS!*

OH, RIGHT! LIKE YOU'VE *NEVER* ASKED ANY-ONE TO SIGN YOUR DIPSTICK BEFORE! *PRUDE!*

YOU DAMN RIGHT!

RANDY'S COINS, COLLECTIBLES & CRAP

NOGOODLAWSPROTECTING THEINNOCENT--

I SEE YOU'RE A CALCULON FAN. MAYBE I CAN INTEREST YOU IN *THIS...*

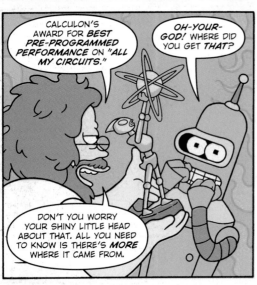

CALCULON'S AWARD FOR *BEST PRE-PROGRAMMED PERFORMANCE* ON *"ALL MY CIRCUITS."*

OH-YOUR-GOD! WHERE DID YOU GET *THAT?*

DON'T YOU WORRY YOUR SHINY LITTLE HEAD ABOUT THAT. ALL YOU NEED TO KNOW IS THERE'S *MORE* WHERE IT CAME FROM.

LOOK AT ALL THIS *BEAUTIFUL, EXQUISITE CRAP!* PEOPLE ACTUALLY *BUY* THIS *JUNK?!*

HUMAN ORGANS

HUMAN ORGANS

WELL, NOT *THAT*, BUT EVERYTHING ELSE! LET ME TELL YOU ABOUT PEOPLE--IF THERE'S *ONE THING* THEY LOVE, IT'S *EVERYTHING!*

The Family Guy

ALL 723 EPISODES!

CRAZY, SEXY, COOL

"PEOPLE...LOVE... EVERYTHING..."

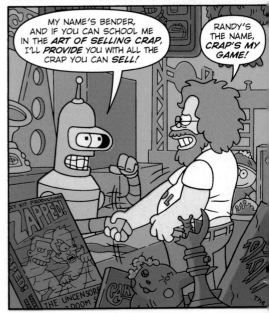

MY NAME'S BENDER, AND IF YOU CAN SCHOOL ME IN THE *ART OF SELLING CRAP*, I'LL *PROVIDE* YOU WITH ALL THE CRAP YOU CAN *SELL!*

RANDY'S THE NAME, *CRAP'S MY GAME!*

68

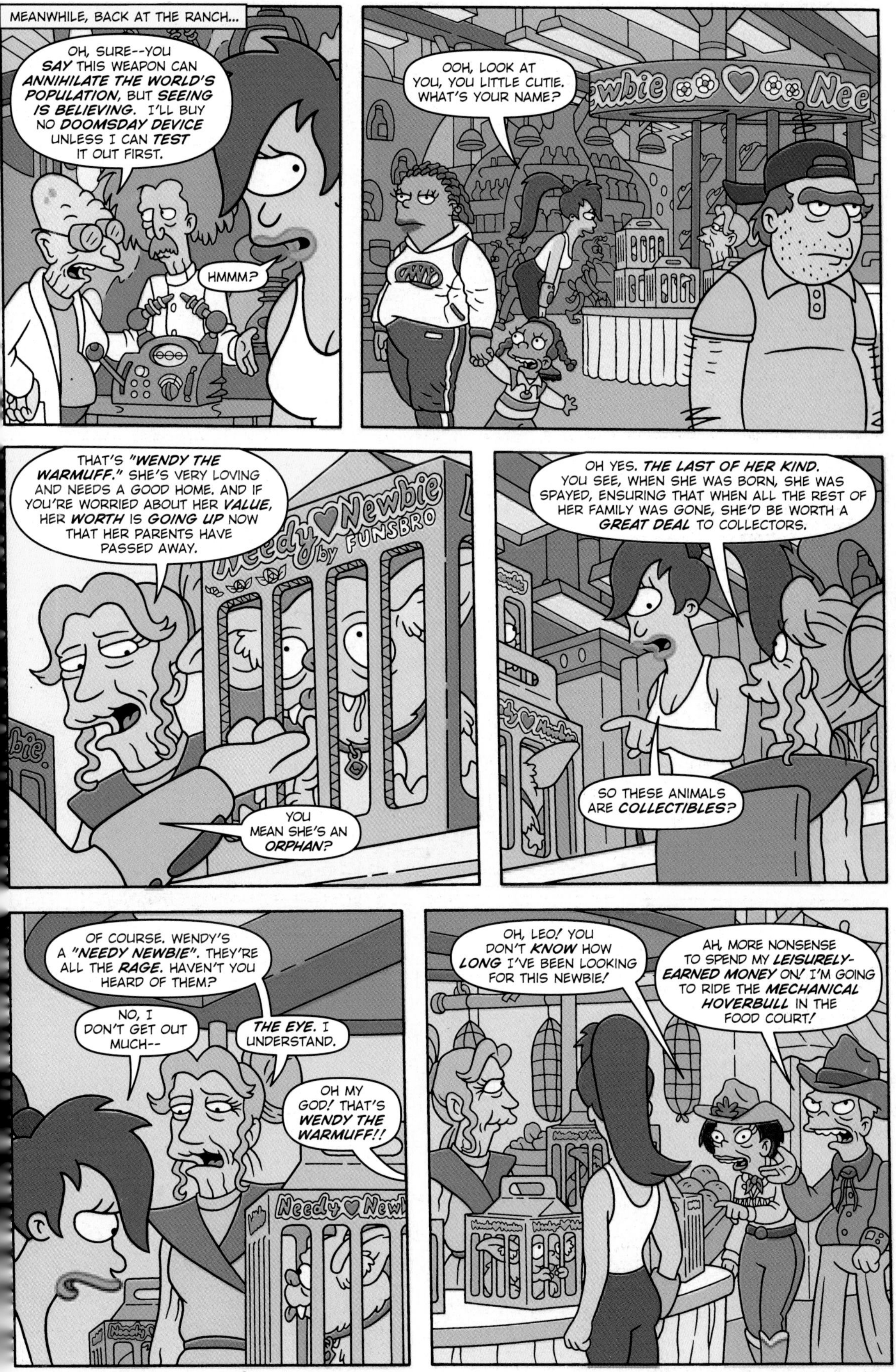
MEANWHILE, BACK AT THE RANCH...
OH, SURE--YOU SAY THIS WEAPON CAN ANNIHILATE THE WORLD'S POPULATION, BUT SEEING IS BELIEVING. I'LL BUY NO DOOMSDAY DEVICE UNLESS I CAN TEST IT OUT FIRST.
HMMM?
OOH, LOOK AT YOU, YOU LITTLE CUTIE. WHAT'S YOUR NAME?
THAT'S "WENDY THE WARMUFF." SHE'S VERY LOVING AND NEEDS A GOOD HOME. AND IF YOU'RE WORRIED ABOUT HER VALUE, HER WORTH IS GOING UP NOW THAT HER PARENTS HAVE PASSED AWAY.
Needy Newbie by FUNSBRO
YOU MEAN SHE'S AN ORPHAN?
OH YES. THE LAST OF HER KIND. YOU SEE, WHEN SHE WAS BORN, SHE WAS SPAYED, ENSURING THAT WHEN ALL THE REST OF HER FAMILY WAS GONE, SHE'D BE WORTH A GREAT DEAL TO COLLECTORS.
SO THESE ANIMALS ARE COLLECTIBLES?
OF COURSE. WENDY'S A "NEEDY NEWBIE". THEY'RE ALL THE RAGE. HAVEN'T YOU HEARD OF THEM?
NO, I DON'T GET OUT MUCH--
THE EYE. I UNDERSTAND.
OH MY GOD! THAT'S WENDY THE WARMUFF!!
OH, LEO! YOU DON'T KNOW HOW LONG I'VE BEEN LOOKING FOR THIS NEWBIE!
AH, MORE NONSENSE TO SPEND MY LEISURELY-EARNED MONEY ON! I'M GOING TO RIDE THE MECHANICAL HOVERBULL IN THE FOOD COURT!

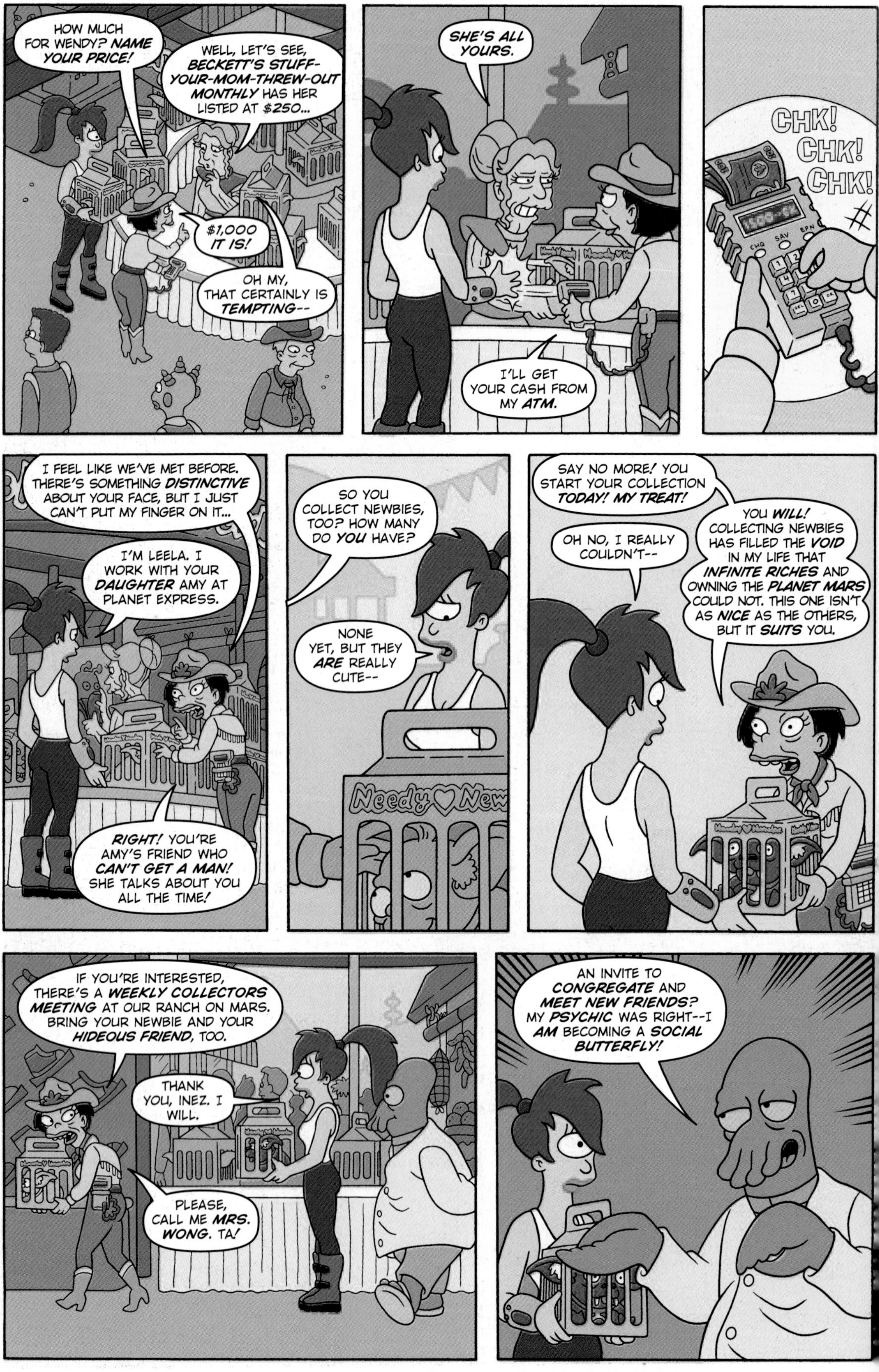
HOW MUCH FOR WENDY? NAME YOUR PRICE!
WELL, LET'S SEE, BECKETT'S STUFF-YOUR-MOM-THREW-OUT MONTHLY HAS HER LISTED AT $250...
$1,000 IT IS!
OH MY, THAT CERTAINLY IS TEMPTING--
SHE'S ALL YOURS.
I'LL GET YOUR CASH FROM MY ATM.
CHK!
CHK!
CHK!
I FEEL LIKE WE'VE MET BEFORE. THERE'S SOMETHING DISTINCTIVE ABOUT YOUR FACE, BUT I JUST CAN'T PUT MY FINGER ON IT...
I'M LEELA. I WORK WITH YOUR DAUGHTER AMY AT PLANET EXPRESS.
RIGHT! YOU'RE AMY'S FRIEND WHO CAN'T GET A MAN! SHE TALKS ABOUT YOU ALL THE TIME!
SO YOU COLLECT NEWBIES, TOO? HOW MANY DO YOU HAVE?
NONE YET, BUT THEY ARE REALLY CUTE--
SAY NO MORE! YOU START YOUR COLLECTION TODAY! MY TREAT!
OH NO, I REALLY COULDN'T--
YOU WILL! COLLECTING NEWBIES HAS FILLED THE VOID IN MY LIFE THAT INFINITE RICHES AND OWNING THE PLANET MARS COULD NOT. THIS ONE ISN'T AS NICE AS THE OTHERS, BUT IT SUITS YOU.
IF YOU'RE INTERESTED, THERE'S A WEEKLY COLLECTORS MEETING AT OUR RANCH ON MARS. BRING YOUR NEWBIE AND YOUR HIDEOUS FRIEND, TOO.
THANK YOU, INEZ. I WILL.
PLEASE, CALL ME MRS. WONG. TA!
AN INVITE TO CONGREGATE AND MEET NEW FRIENDS? MY PSYCHIC WAS RIGHT--I AM BECOMING A SOCIAL BUTTERFLY!

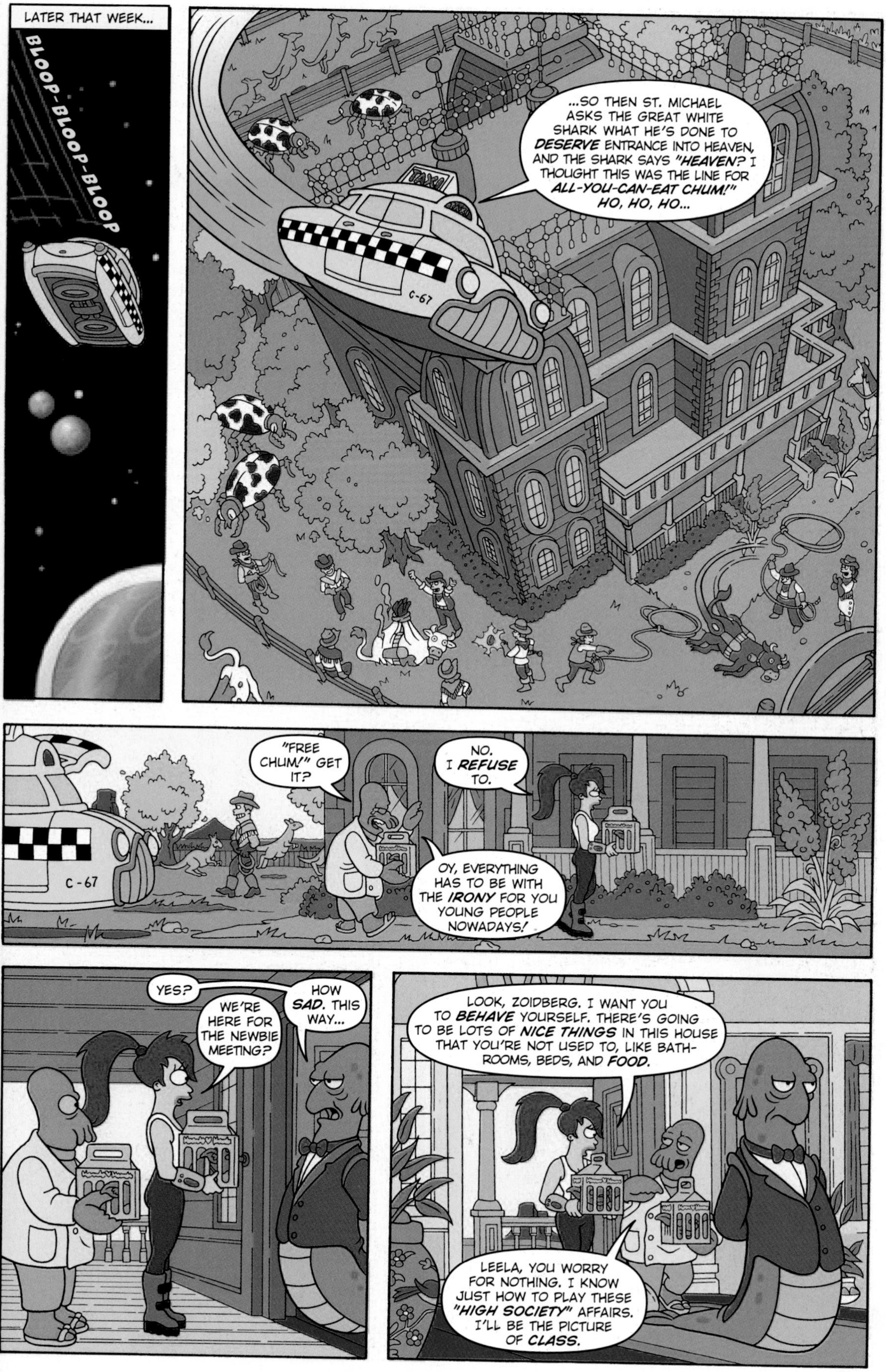
LATER THAT WEEK...
BLOOP-BLOOP-BLOOP-BLOOP
TAXI
C-67
...SO THEN ST. MICHAEL ASKS THE GREAT WHITE SHARK WHAT HE'S DONE TO DESERVE ENTRANCE INTO HEAVEN, AND THE SHARK SAYS "HEAVEN? I THOUGHT THIS WAS THE LINE FOR ALL-YOU-CAN-EAT CHUM!" HO, HO, HO...
C-67
"FREE CHUM!" GET IT?
NO. I REFUSE TO.
OY, EVERYTHING HAS TO BE WITH THE IRONY FOR YOU YOUNG PEOPLE NOWADAYS!
YES?
WE'RE HERE FOR THE NEWBIE MEETING?
HOW SAD. THIS WAY...
LOOK, ZOIDBERG. I WANT YOU TO BEHAVE YOURSELF. THERE'S GOING TO BE LOTS OF NICE THINGS IN THIS HOUSE THAT YOU'RE NOT USED TO, LIKE BATHROOMS, BEDS, AND FOOD.
LEELA, YOU WORRY FOR NOTHING. I KNOW JUST HOW TO PLAY THESE "HIGH SOCIETY" AFFAIRS. I'LL BE THE PICTURE OF CLASS.

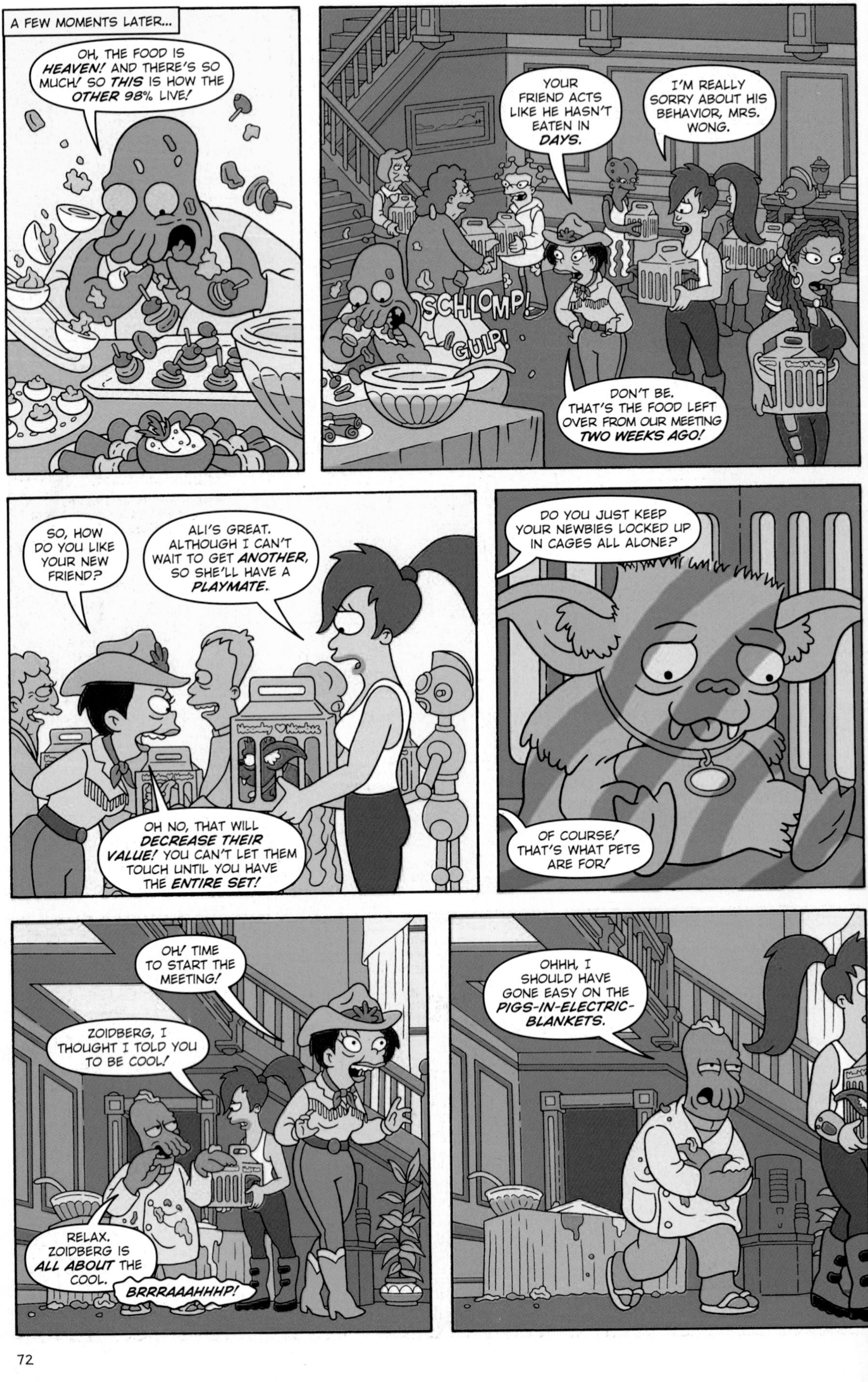
A FEW MOMENTS LATER...
OH, THE FOOD IS HEAVEN! AND THERE'S SO MUCH! SO THIS IS HOW THE OTHER 98% LIVE!
YOUR FRIEND ACTS LIKE HE HASN'T EATEN IN DAYS.
I'M REALLY SORRY ABOUT HIS BEHAVIOR, MRS. WONG.
SCHLOMP!
GULP!
DON'T BE. THAT'S THE FOOD LEFT OVER FROM OUR MEETING TWO WEEKS AGO!
SO, HOW DO YOU LIKE YOUR NEW FRIEND?
ALI'S GREAT. ALTHOUGH I CAN'T WAIT TO GET ANOTHER, SO SHE'LL HAVE A PLAYMATE.
OH NO, THAT WILL DECREASE THEIR VALUE! YOU CAN'T LET THEM TOUCH UNTIL YOU HAVE THE ENTIRE SET!
DO YOU JUST KEEP YOUR NEWBIES LOCKED UP IN CAGES ALL ALONE?
OF COURSE! THAT'S WHAT PETS ARE FOR!
OH! TIME TO START THE MEETING!
ZOIDBERG, I THOUGHT I TOLD YOU TO BE COOL!
RELAX. ZOIDBERG IS ALL ABOUT THE COOL.
BRRRAAAHHHP!
OHHH, I SHOULD HAVE GONE EASY ON THE PIGS-IN-ELECTRIC-BLANKETS.

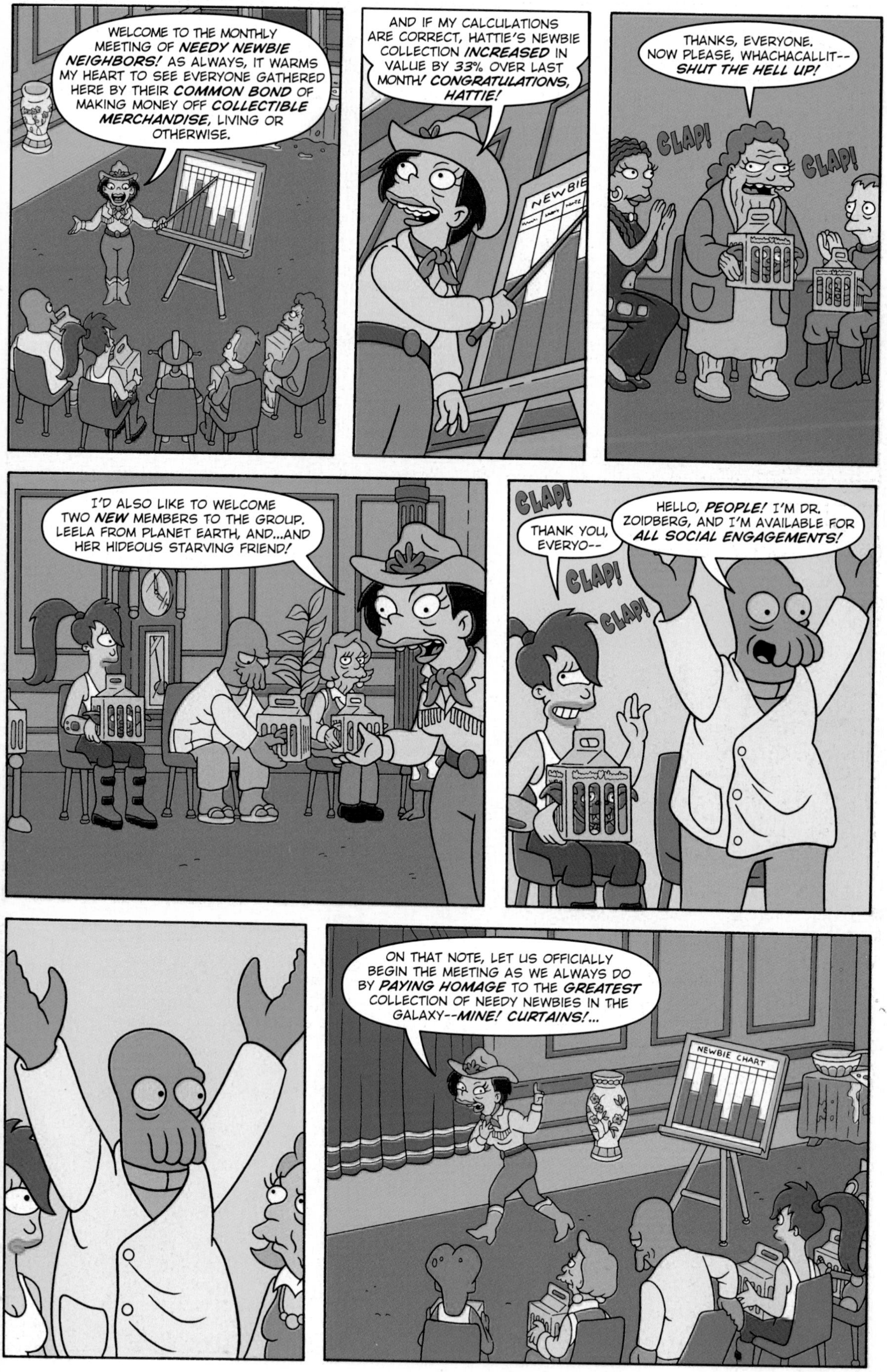
WELCOME TO THE MONTHLY MEETING OF NEEDY NEWBIE NEIGHBORS! AS ALWAYS, IT WARMS MY HEART TO SEE EVERYONE GATHERED HERE BY THEIR COMMON BOND OF MAKING MONEY OFF COLLECTIBLE MERCHANDISE, LIVING OR OTHERWISE.
AND IF MY CALCULATIONS ARE CORRECT, HATTIE'S NEWBIE COLLECTION INCREASED IN VALUE BY 33% OVER LAST MONTH! CONGRATULATIONS, HATTIE!
NEWBIE
THANKS, EVERYONE. NOW PLEASE, WHACHACALLIT-- SHUT THE HELL UP!
CLAP!
CLAP!
I'D ALSO LIKE TO WELCOME TWO NEW MEMBERS TO THE GROUP. LEELA FROM PLANET EARTH, AND...AND HER HIDEOUS STARVING FRIEND!
CLAP!
THANK YOU, EVERYO--
HELLO, PEOPLE! I'M DR. ZOIDBERG, AND I'M AVAILABLE FOR ALL SOCIAL ENGAGEMENTS!
CLAP!
CLAP!
ON THAT NOTE, LET US OFFICIALLY BEGIN THE MEETING AS WE ALWAYS DO BY PAYING HOMAGE TO THE GREATEST COLLECTION OF NEEDY NEWBIES IN THE GALAXY--MINE! CURTAINS!...
NEWBIE CHART

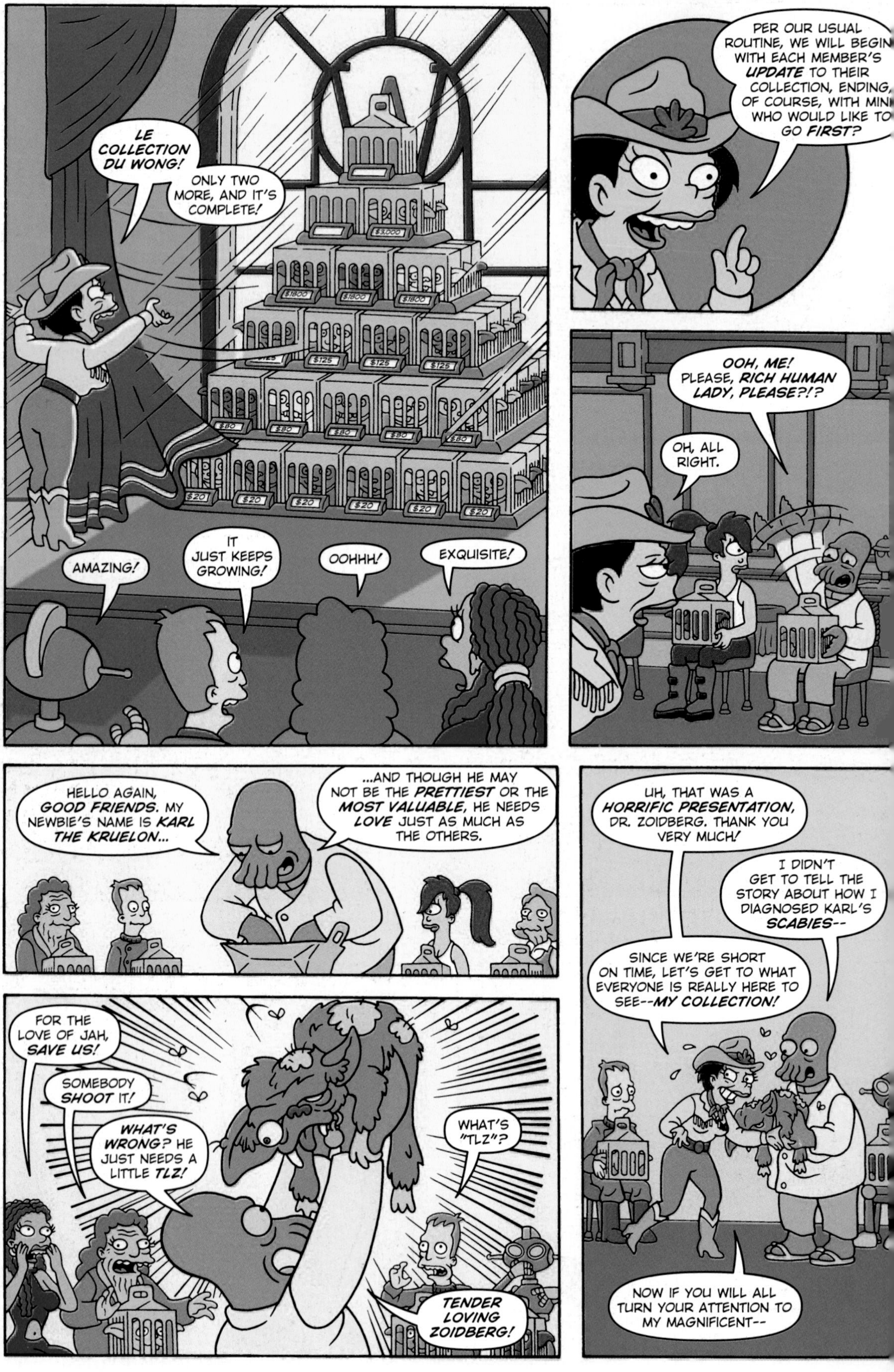
LE COLLECTION DU WONG!
ONLY TWO MORE, AND IT'S COMPLETE!
AMAZING!
IT JUST KEEPS GROWING!
OOHHH!
EXQUISITE!
PER OUR USUAL ROUTINE, WE WILL BEGIN WITH EACH MEMBER'S UPDATE TO THEIR COLLECTION, ENDING, OF COURSE, WITH MIN WHO WOULD LIKE TO GO FIRST?
OOH, ME! PLEASE, RICH HUMAN LADY, PLEASE?!?
OH, ALL RIGHT.
HELLO AGAIN, GOOD FRIENDS. MY NEWBIE'S NAME IS KARL THE KRUELON...
...AND THOUGH HE MAY NOT BE THE PRETTIEST OR THE MOST VALUABLE, HE NEEDS LOVE JUST AS MUCH AS THE OTHERS.
FOR THE LOVE OF JAH, SAVE US!
SOMEBODY SHOOT IT!
WHAT'S WRONG? HE JUST NEEDS A LITTLE TLZ!
WHAT'S "TLZ"?
TENDER LOVING ZOIDBERG!
UH, THAT WAS A HORRIFIC PRESENTATION, DR. ZOIDBERG. THANK YOU VERY MUCH!
I DIDN'T GET TO TELL THE STORY ABOUT HOW I DIAGNOSED KARL'S SCABIES--
SINCE WE'RE SHORT ON TIME, LET'S GET TO WHAT EVERYONE IS REALLY HERE TO SEE--MY COLLECTION!
NOW IF YOU WILL ALL TURN YOUR ATTENTION TO MY MAGNIFICENT--

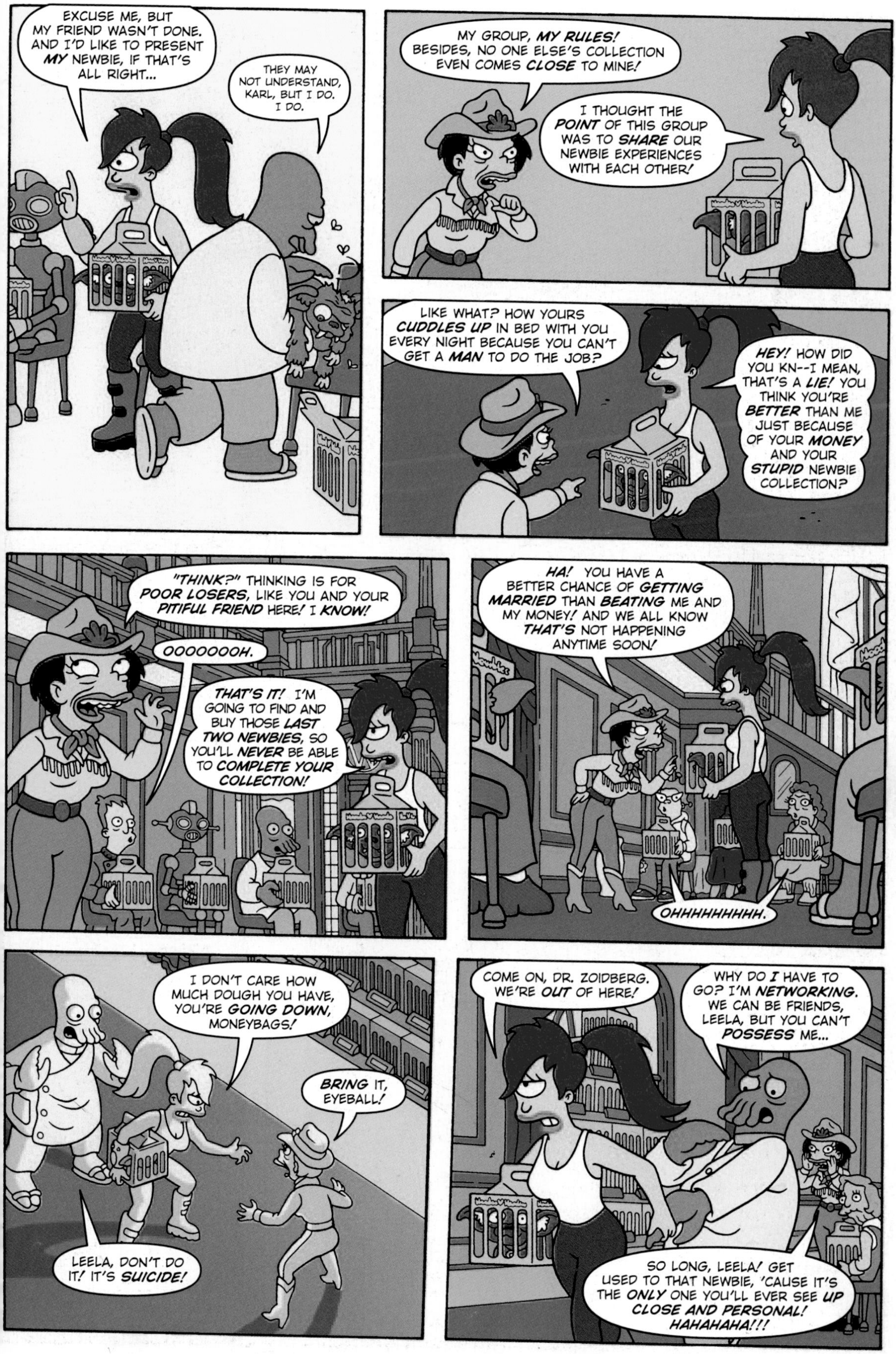

EXCUSE ME, BUT MY FRIEND WASN'T DONE. AND I'D LIKE TO PRESENT MY NEWBIE, IF THAT'S ALL RIGHT...
THEY MAY NOT UNDERSTAND, KARL, BUT I DO. I DO.
MY GROUP, MY RULES! BESIDES, NO ONE ELSE'S COLLECTION EVEN COMES CLOSE TO MINE!
I THOUGHT THE POINT OF THIS GROUP WAS TO SHARE OUR NEWBIE EXPERIENCES WITH EACH OTHER!
LIKE WHAT? HOW YOURS CUDDLES UP IN BED WITH YOU EVERY NIGHT BECAUSE YOU CAN'T GET A MAN TO DO THE JOB?
HEY! HOW DID YOU KN--I MEAN, THAT'S A LIE! YOU THINK YOU'RE BETTER THAN ME JUST BECAUSE OF YOUR MONEY AND YOUR STUPID NEWBIE COLLECTION?
"THINK?" THINKING IS FOR POOR LOSERS, LIKE YOU AND YOUR PITIFUL FRIEND HERE! I KNOW!
OOOOOOOH.
THAT'S IT! I'M GOING TO FIND AND BUY THOSE LAST TWO NEWBIES, SO YOU'LL NEVER BE ABLE TO COMPLETE YOUR COLLECTION!
HA! YOU HAVE A BETTER CHANCE OF GETTING MARRIED THAN BEATING ME AND MY MONEY! AND WE ALL KNOW THAT'S NOT HAPPENING ANYTIME SOON!
OHHHHHHHHH.
I DON'T CARE HOW MUCH DOUGH YOU HAVE, YOU'RE GOING DOWN, MONEYBAGS!
BRING IT, EYEBALL!
LEELA, DON'T DO IT! IT'S SUICIDE!
COME ON, DR. ZOIDBERG. WE'RE OUT OF HERE!
WHY DO I HAVE TO GO? I'M NETWORKING. WE CAN BE FRIENDS, LEELA, BUT YOU CAN'T POSSESS ME...
SO LONG, LEELA! GET USED TO THAT NEWBIE, 'CAUSE IT'S THE ONLY ONE YOU'LL EVER SEE UP CLOSE AND PERSONAL! HAHAHAHA!!!

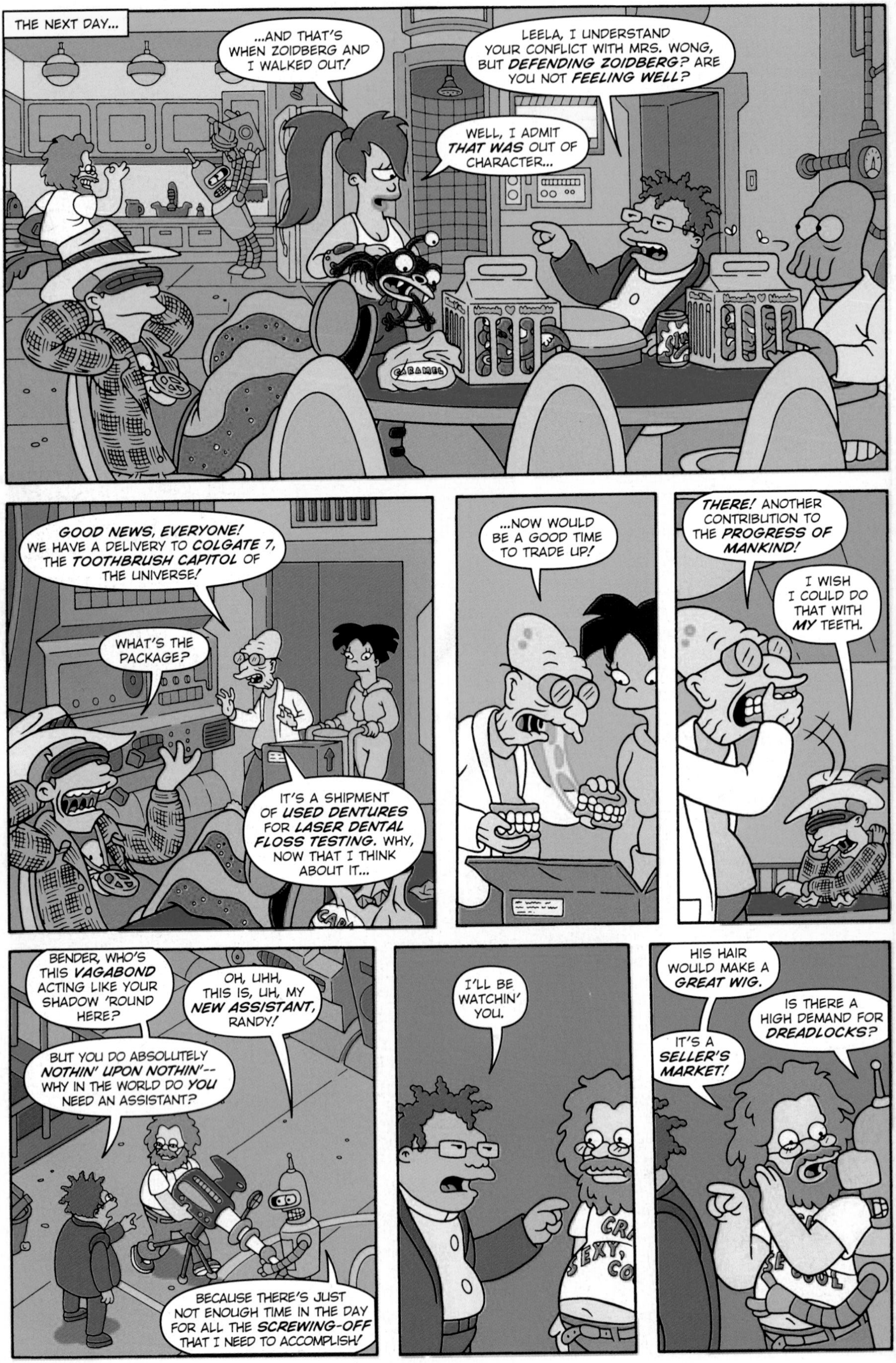
THE NEXT DAY...
...AND THAT'S WHEN ZOIDBERG AND I WALKED OUT!
LEELA, I UNDERSTAND YOUR CONFLICT WITH MRS. WONG, BUT DEFENDING ZOIDBERG? ARE YOU NOT FEELING WELL?
WELL, I ADMIT THAT WAS OUT OF CHARACTER...
CARAMEL
GOOD NEWS, EVERYONE! WE HAVE A DELIVERY TO COLGATE 7, THE TOOTHBRUSH CAPITOL OF THE UNIVERSE!
WHAT'S THE PACKAGE?
IT'S A SHIPMENT OF USED DENTURES FOR LASER DENTAL FLOSS TESTING. WHY, NOW THAT I THINK ABOUT IT...
...NOW WOULD BE A GOOD TIME TO TRADE UP!
THERE! ANOTHER CONTRIBUTION TO THE PROGRESS OF MANKIND!
I WISH I COULD DO THAT WITH MY TEETH.
BENDER, WHO'S THIS VAGABOND ACTING LIKE YOUR SHADOW 'ROUND HERE?
OH, UHH, THIS IS, UH, MY NEW ASSISTANT, RANDY!
BUT YOU DO ABSOLUTELY NOTHIN' UPON NOTHIN'-- WHY IN THE WORLD DO YOU NEED AN ASSISTANT?
BECAUSE THERE'S JUST NOT ENOUGH TIME IN THE DAY FOR ALL THE SCREWING-OFF THAT I NEED TO ACCOMPLISH!
I'LL BE WATCHIN' YOU.
HIS HAIR WOULD MAKE A GREAT WIG.
IS THERE A HIGH DEMAND FOR DREADLOCKS?
IT'S A SELLER'S MARKET!

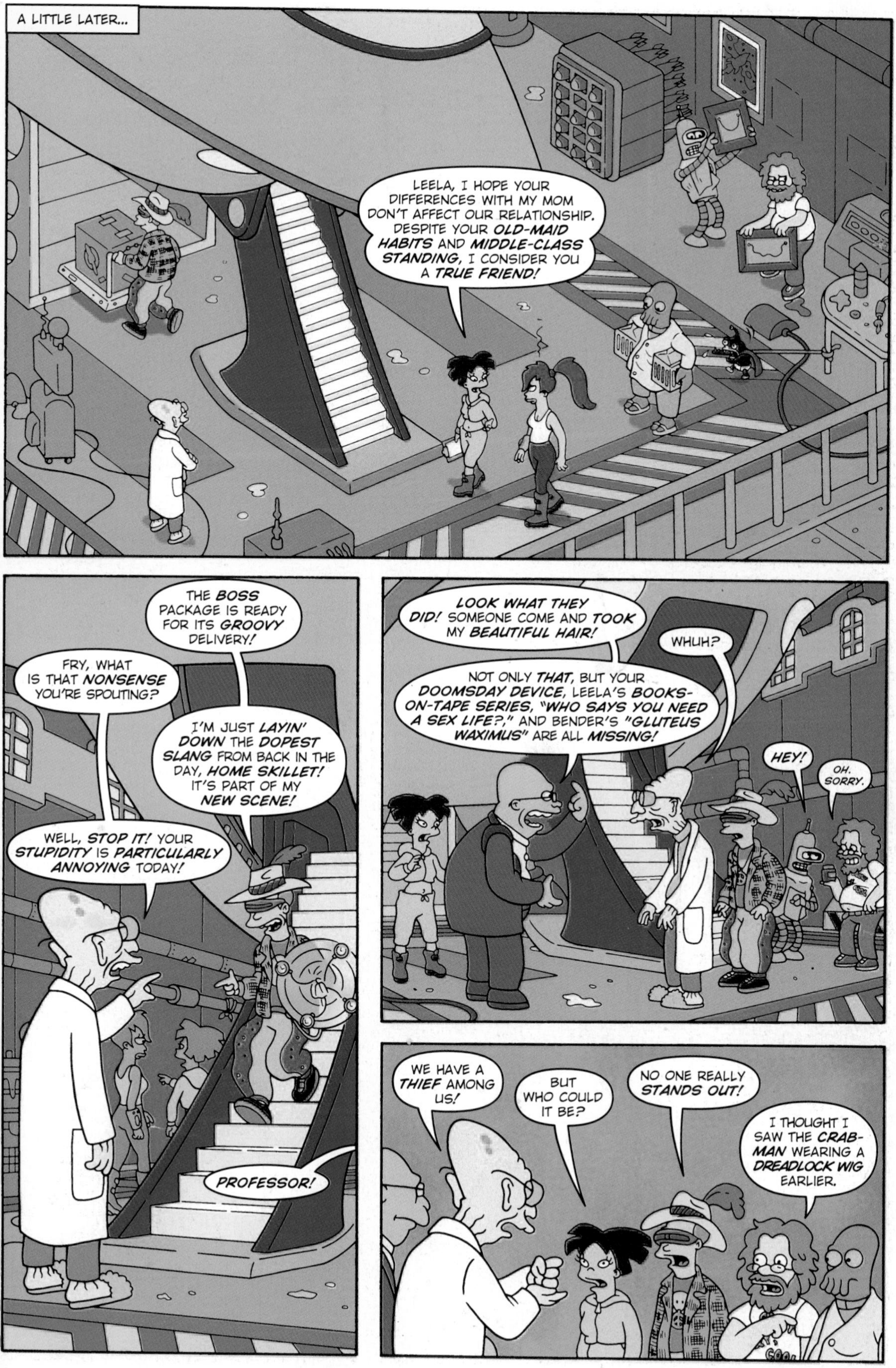
A LITTLE LATER...
LEELA, I HOPE YOUR DIFFERENCES WITH MY MOM DON'T AFFECT OUR RELATIONSHIP. DESPITE YOUR OLD-MAID HABITS AND MIDDLE-CLASS STANDING, I CONSIDER YOU A TRUE FRIEND!
FRY, WHAT IS THAT NONSENSE YOU'RE SPOUTING?
THE BOSS PACKAGE IS READY FOR ITS GROOVY DELIVERY!
I'M JUST LAYIN' DOWN THE DOPEST SLANG FROM BACK IN THE DAY, HOME SKILLET! IT'S PART OF MY NEW SCENE!
WELL, STOP IT! YOUR STUPIDITY IS PARTICULARLY ANNOYING TODAY!
PROFESSOR!
LOOK WHAT THEY DID! SOMEONE COME AND TOOK MY BEAUTIFUL HAIR!
WHUH?
NOT ONLY THAT, BUT YOUR DOOMSDAY DEVICE, LEELA'S BOOKS-ON-TAPE SERIES, "WHO SAYS YOU NEED A SEX LIFE?," AND BENDER'S "GLUTEUS WAXIMUS" ARE ALL MISSING!
HEY!
OH. SORRY.
WE HAVE A THIEF AMONG US!
BUT WHO COULD IT BE?
NO ONE REALLY STANDS OUT!
I THOUGHT I SAW THE CRAB-MAN WEARING A DREADLOCK WIG EARLIER.

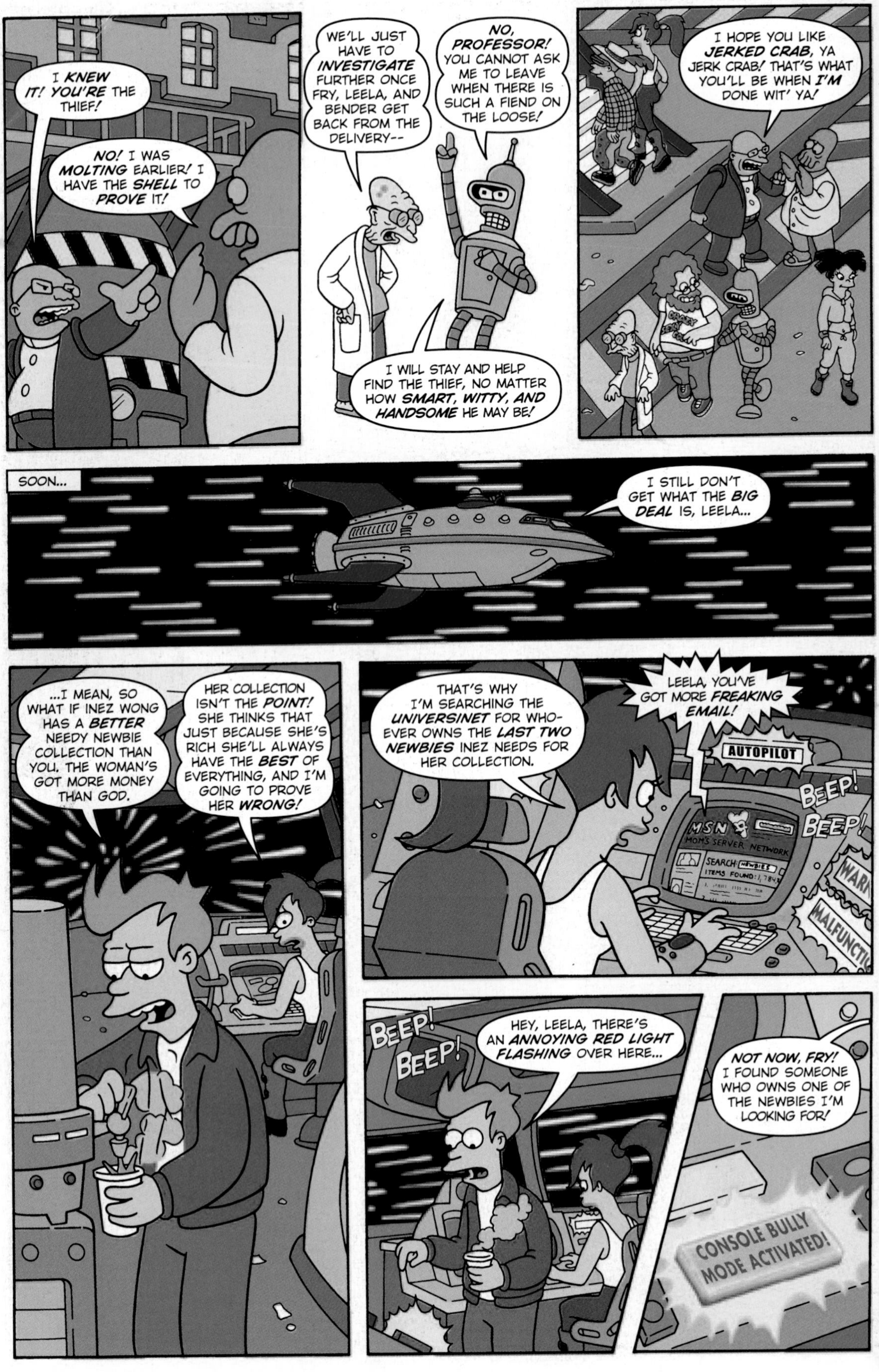

I KNEW IT! YOU'RE THE THIEF!
NO! I WAS MOLTING EARLIER! I HAVE THE SHELL TO PROVE IT!
WE'LL JUST HAVE TO INVESTIGATE FURTHER ONCE FRY, LEELA, AND BENDER GET BACK FROM THE DELIVERY--
NO, PROFESSOR! YOU CANNOT ASK ME TO LEAVE WHEN THERE IS SUCH A FIEND ON THE LOOSE!
I WILL STAY AND HELP FIND THE THIEF, NO MATTER HOW SMART, WITTY, AND HANDSOME HE MAY BE!
I HOPE YOU LIKE JERKED CRAB, YA JERK CRAB! THAT'S WHAT YOU'LL BE WHEN I'M DONE WIT' YA!
SOON...
I STILL DON'T GET WHAT THE BIG DEAL IS, LEELA...
...I MEAN, SO WHAT IF INEZ WONG HAS A BETTER NEEDY NEWBIE COLLECTION THAN YOU. THE WOMAN'S GOT MORE MONEY THAN GOD.
HER COLLECTION ISN'T THE POINT! SHE THINKS THAT JUST BECAUSE SHE'S RICH SHE'LL ALWAYS HAVE THE BEST OF EVERYTHING, AND I'M GOING TO PROVE HER WRONG!
THAT'S WHY I'M SEARCHING THE UNIVERSINET FOR WHO-EVER OWNS THE LAST TWO NEWBIES INEZ NEEDS FOR HER COLLECTION.
LEELA, YOU'VE GOT MORE FREAKING EMAIL!
AUTOPILOT
MSN
MOM'S SERVER NETWORK
SEARCH: NEWBIES
BEEP!
BEEP!
BEEP!
BEEP!
HEY, LEELA, THERE'S AN ANNOYING RED LIGHT FLASHING OVER HERE...
NOT NOW, FRY! I FOUND SOMEONE WHO OWNS ONE OF THE NEWBIES I'M LOOKING FOR!
CONSOLE BULLY MODE ACTIVATED!

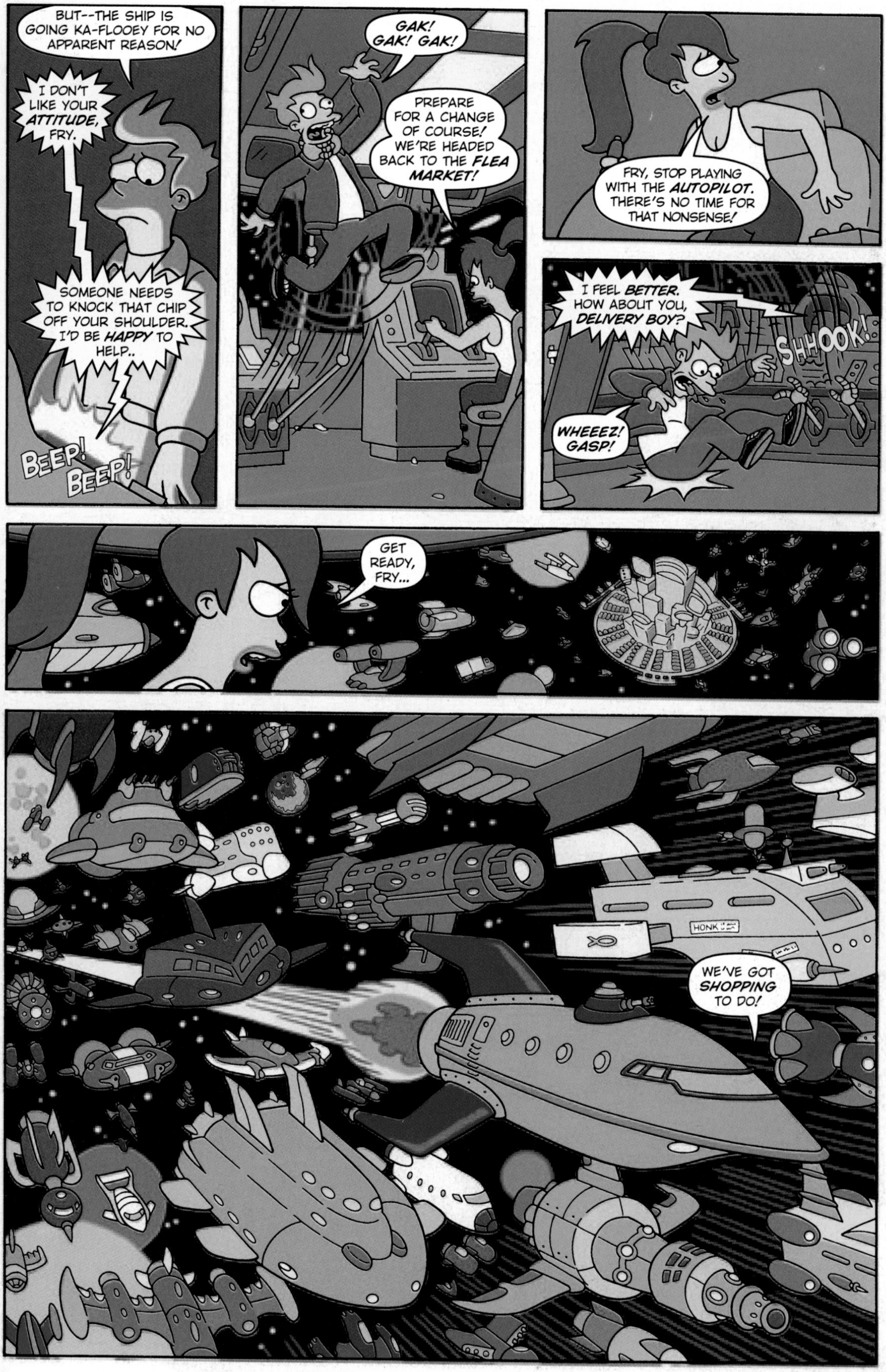
BUT--THE SHIP IS GOING KA-FLOOEY FOR NO APPARENT REASON!
I DON'T LIKE YOUR ATTITUDE, FRY.
SOMEONE NEEDS TO KNOCK THAT CHIP OFF YOUR SHOULDER. I'D BE HAPPY TO HELP..
BEEP! BEEP!
GAK! GAK! GAK!
PREPARE FOR A CHANGE OF COURSE! WE'RE HEADED BACK TO THE FLEA MARKET!
FRY, STOP PLAYING WITH THE AUTOPILOT. THERE'S NO TIME FOR THAT NONSENSE!
I FEEL BETTER. HOW ABOUT YOU, DELIVERY BOY?
SHHOOK!
WHEEEZ! GASP!
GET READY, FRY...
HONK
WE'VE GOT SHOPPING TO DO!

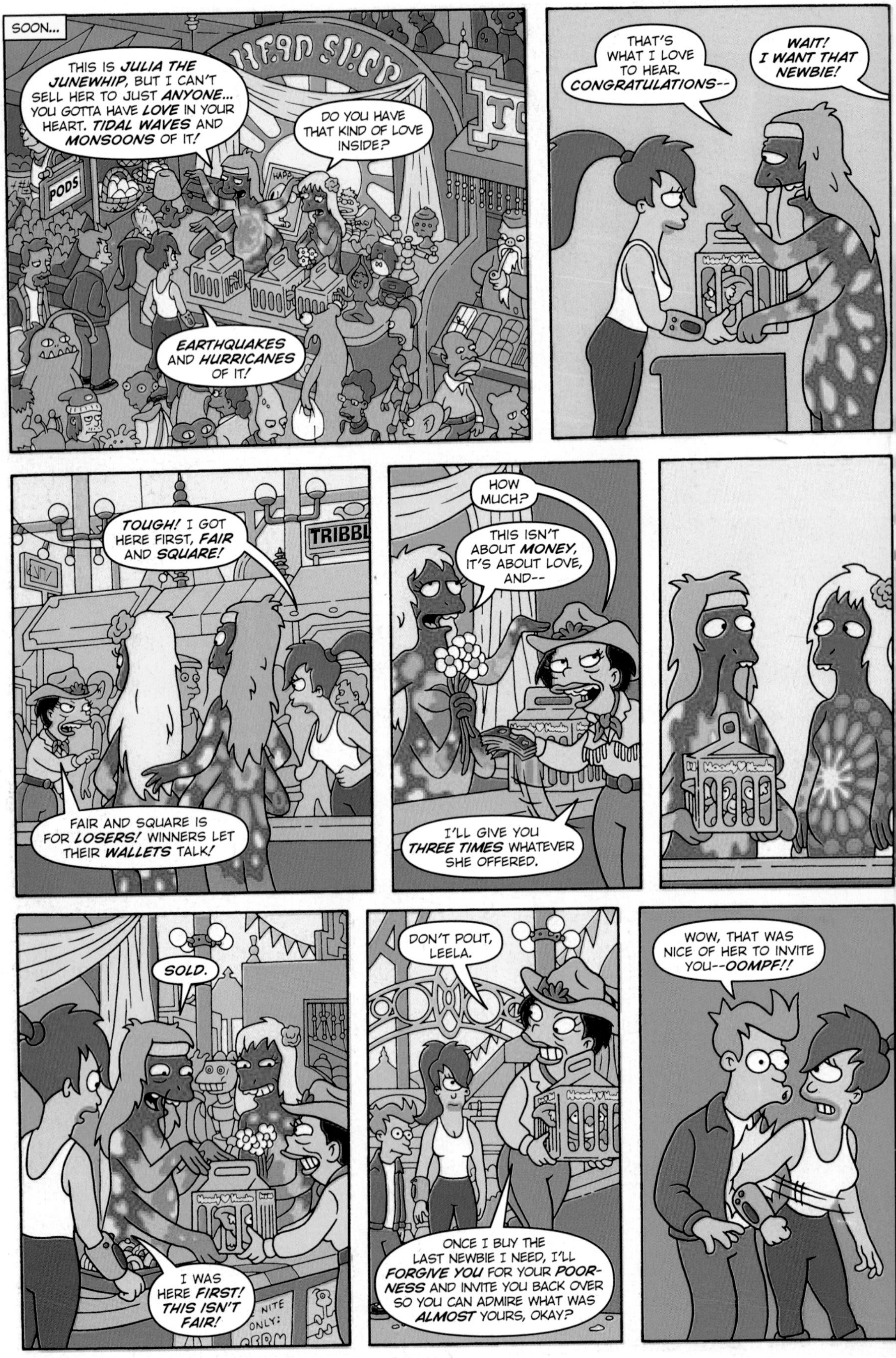
SOON...
THIS IS JULIA THE JUNEWHIP, BUT I CAN'T SELL HER TO JUST ANYONE... YOU GOTTA HAVE LOVE IN YOUR HEART. TIDAL WAVES AND MONSOONS OF IT!
DO YOU HAVE THAT KIND OF LOVE INSIDE?
PODS
EARTHQUAKES AND HURRICANES OF IT!
THAT'S WHAT I LOVE TO HEAR. CONGRATULATIONS--
WAIT! I WANT THAT NEWBIE!
TOUGH! I GOT HERE FIRST, FAIR AND SQUARE!
TRIBBL
FAIR AND SQUARE IS FOR LOSERS! WINNERS LET THEIR WALLETS TALK!
HOW MUCH?
THIS ISN'T ABOUT MONEY, IT'S ABOUT LOVE, AND--
I'LL GIVE YOU THREE TIMES WHATEVER SHE OFFERED.
SOLD.
I WAS HERE FIRST! THIS ISN'T FAIR!
NITE ONLY:
DON'T POUT, LEELA.
ONCE I BUY THE LAST NEWBIE I NEED, I'LL FORGIVE YOU FOR YOUR POORNESS AND INVITE YOU BACK OVER SO YOU CAN ADMIRE WHAT WAS ALMOST YOURS, OKAY?
WOW, THAT WAS NICE OF HER TO INVITE YOU--OOMPF!!

A FEW MINUTES LATER...

...AND IT WAS AT THAT MOMENT THAT I KNEW THERE WOULD NEVER BE A GREATER ROCK-N-ROLL BAND THAN *KAJAGOOGOO*. YOU WANT ME TO SING ONE OF THEIR SONGS FOR YOU?

NOT NOW.

AW, COME ON, LEELA. THERE'S GOTTA BE *SOMETHING* THAT CAN CHEER YOU UP...

LOOK!

WHOA, *CHECK OUT THE HIP THREADS!* WHO'S THE IDIOT THAT LET *THIS* STUFF SLIP AWAY?

WHY THAT BELONGED TO A REAL JACKASS HUMAN I USED TO--

OFFICIAL MEDICAL SUPPLIES

--FRY! FRY--FRY-- *FRIGHTENING FACE* YOU HAVE THERE!

HEY, YOU LOOK FAMILIAR. ARE YOU A BENDER UNIT?

A BENDER?! SURELY YOU JEST! I WOULDN'T BE *CAUGHT DEAD* ACTING LIKE ONE OF THOSE *LOVABLE AND SEXY FELLOWS!*

HEY, FRY...

WHO DIED and made you ELVISBOT?

THESE LOOK LIKE SOME OF THE PARTS THAT ARE MISSING FROM THE SHIP. THAT MUST BE WHY THE *AUTOPILOT MALFUNCTIONED!*

AND HERE I THOUGHT HE WAS JUST JEALOUS OF *MY INFINITE NATURAL GASES!*

WORD #7 ALBUM WHY HUMANS SUCK: A PHILISOPHICAL ESSAY

EXCUSE ME, SIR. I'D LIKE TO PURCHASE THESE PARTS.

SURE. ANYTHING FOR A *STAR...*

HEE HEE HEE HEE...

:SIGH:

ZAPPED! ZAPPED! ZAPPED! THE UNCENS... BEDR...

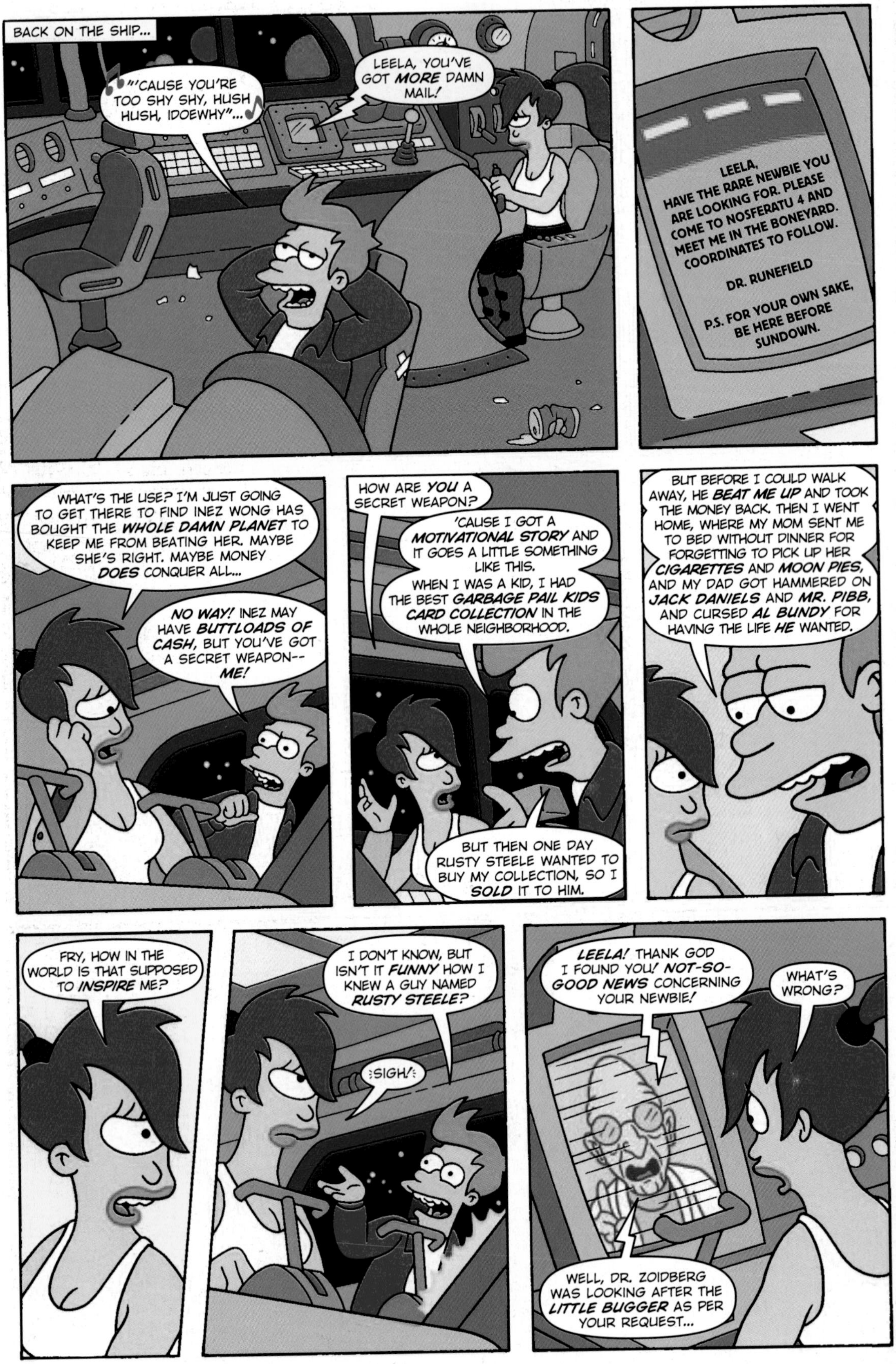
BACK ON THE SHIP...
"'CAUSE YOU'RE TOO SHY SHY, HUSH HUSH, IDOEWHY"...
LEELA, YOU'VE GOT MORE DAMN MAIL!
LEELA,
HAVE THE RARE NEWBIE YOU ARE LOOKING FOR. PLEASE COME TO NOSFERATU 4 AND MEET ME IN THE BONEYARD. COORDINATES TO FOLLOW.
DR. RUNEFIELD
P.S. FOR YOUR OWN SAKE, BE HERE BEFORE SUNDOWN.
WHAT'S THE USE? I'M JUST GOING TO GET THERE TO FIND INEZ WONG HAS BOUGHT THE WHOLE DAMN PLANET TO KEEP ME FROM BEATING HER. MAYBE SHE'S RIGHT. MAYBE MONEY DOES CONQUER ALL...
NO WAY! INEZ MAY HAVE BUTTLOADS OF CASH, BUT YOU'VE GOT A SECRET WEAPON-- ME!
HOW ARE YOU A SECRET WEAPON?
'CAUSE I GOT A MOTIVATIONAL STORY AND IT GOES A LITTLE SOMETHING LIKE THIS.
WHEN I WAS A KID, I HAD THE BEST GARBAGE PAIL KIDS CARD COLLECTION IN THE WHOLE NEIGHBORHOOD.
BUT THEN ONE DAY RUSTY STEELE WANTED TO BUY MY COLLECTION, SO I SOLD IT TO HIM.
BUT BEFORE I COULD WALK AWAY, HE BEAT ME UP AND TOOK THE MONEY BACK. THEN I WENT HOME, WHERE MY MOM SENT ME TO BED WITHOUT DINNER FOR FORGETTING TO PICK UP HER CIGARETTES AND MOON PIES, AND MY DAD GOT HAMMERED ON JACK DANIELS AND MR. PIBB, AND CURSED AL BUNDY FOR HAVING THE LIFE HE WANTED.
FRY, HOW IN THE WORLD IS THAT SUPPOSED TO INSPIRE ME?
I DON'T KNOW, BUT ISN'T IT FUNNY HOW I KNEW A GUY NAMED RUSTY STEELE?
SIGH!
LEELA! THANK GOD I FOUND YOU! NOT-SO-GOOD NEWS CONCERNING YOUR NEWBIE!
WHAT'S WRONG?
WELL, DR. ZOIDBERG WAS LOOKING AFTER THE LITTLE BUGGER AS PER YOUR REQUEST...

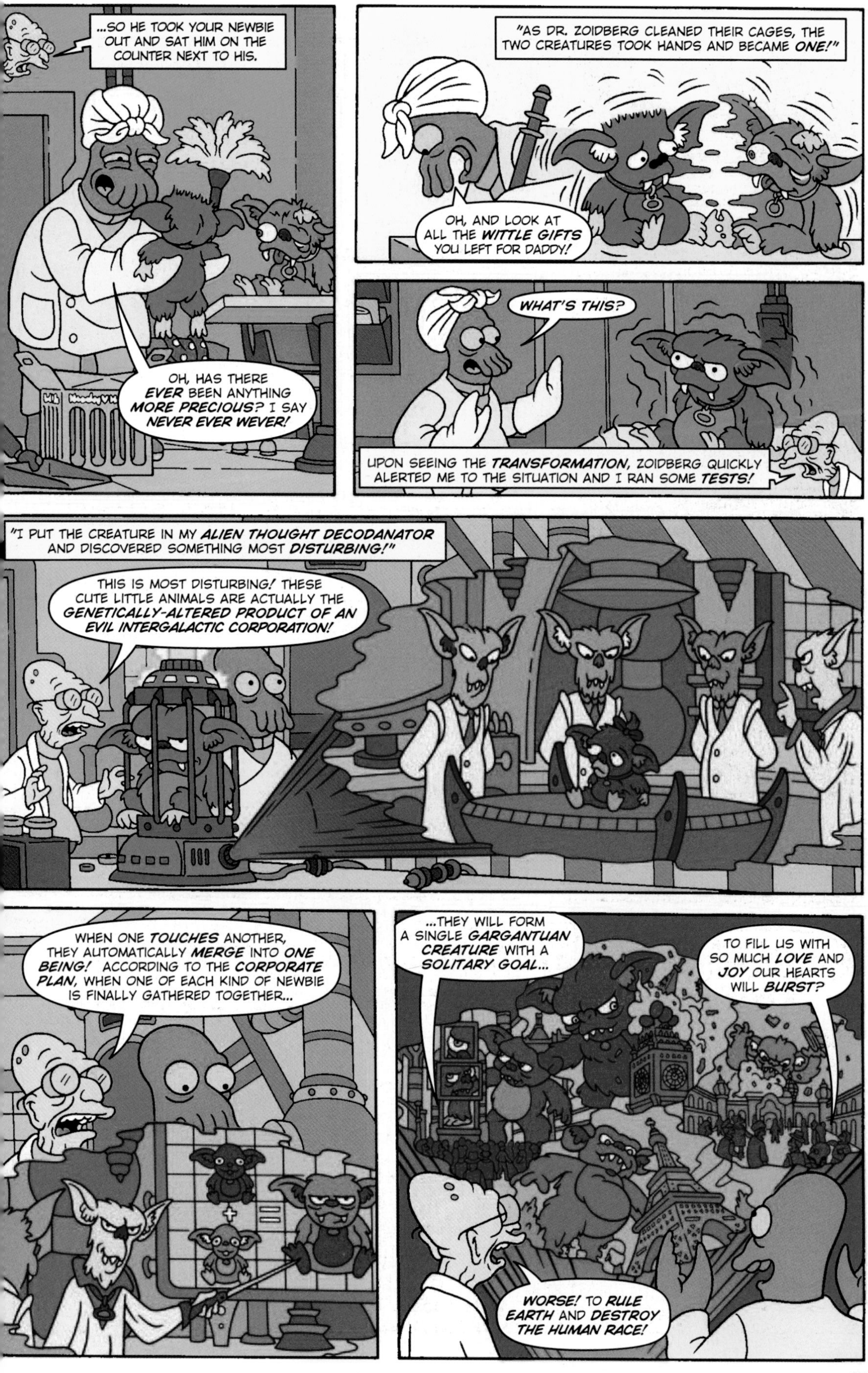
...SO HE TOOK YOUR NEWBIE OUT AND SAT HIM ON THE COUNTER NEXT TO HIS.
OH, HAS THERE EVER BEEN ANYTHING MORE PRECIOUS? I SAY NEVER EVER WEVER!
"AS DR. ZOIDBERG CLEANED THEIR CAGES, THE TWO CREATURES TOOK HANDS AND BECAME ONE!"
OH, AND LOOK AT ALL THE WITTLE GIFTS YOU LEFT FOR DADDY!
WHAT'S THIS?
UPON SEEING THE TRANSFORMATION, ZOIDBERG QUICKLY ALERTED ME TO THE SITUATION AND I RAN SOME TESTS!
"I PUT THE CREATURE IN MY ALIEN THOUGHT DECODANATOR AND DISCOVERED SOMETHING MOST DISTURBING!"
THIS IS MOST DISTURBING! THESE CUTE LITTLE ANIMALS ARE ACTUALLY THE GENETICALLY-ALTERED PRODUCT OF AN EVIL INTERGALACTIC CORPORATION!
WHEN ONE TOUCHES ANOTHER, THEY AUTOMATICALLY MERGE INTO ONE BEING! ACCORDING TO THE CORPORATE PLAN, WHEN ONE OF EACH KIND OF NEWBIE IS FINALLY GATHERED TOGETHER...
...THEY WILL FORM A SINGLE GARGANTUAN CREATURE WITH A SOLITARY GOAL...
TO FILL US WITH SO MUCH LOVE AND JOY OUR HEARTS WILL BURST?
WORSE! TO RULE EARTH AND DESTROY THE HUMAN RACE!

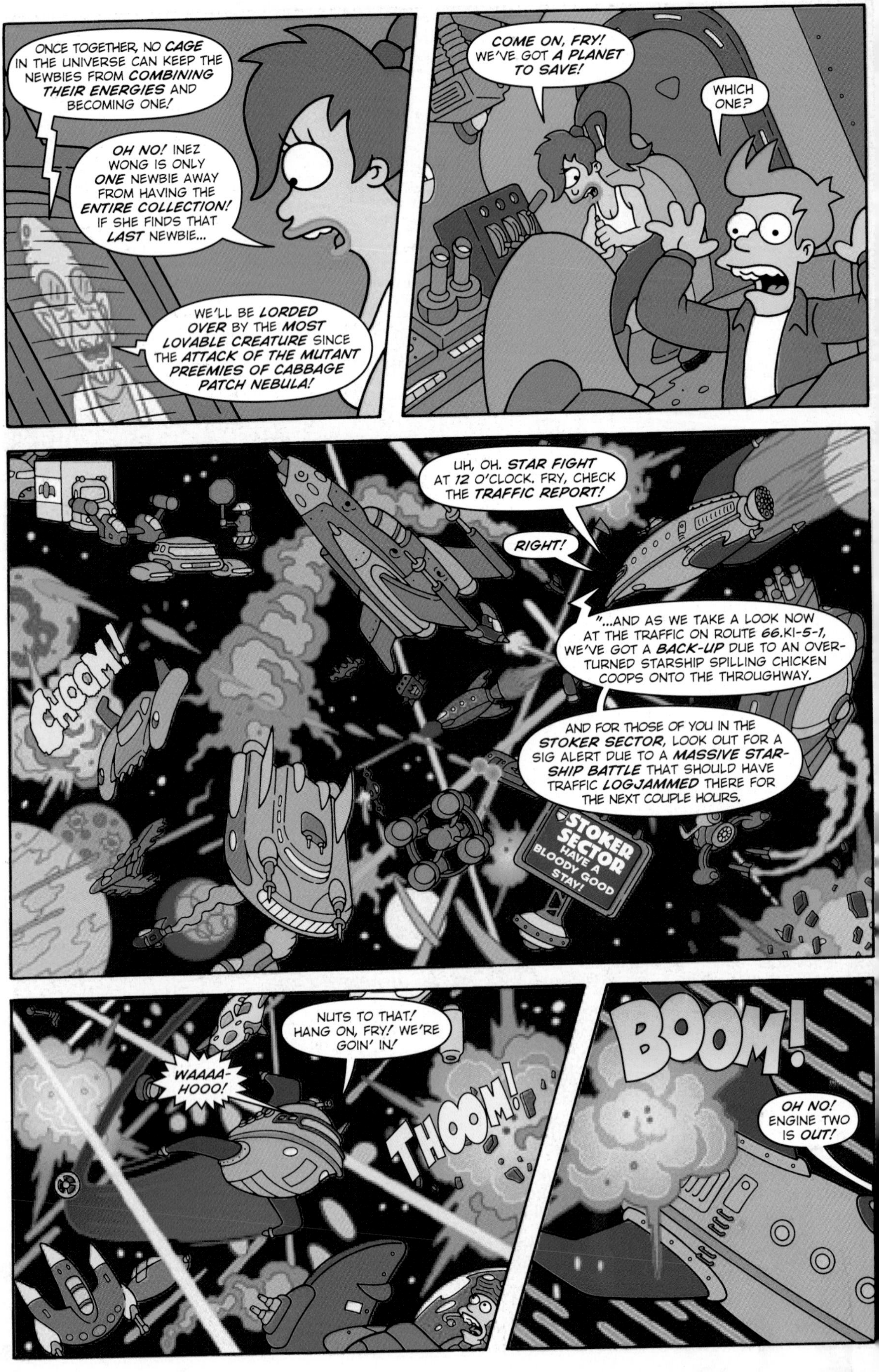
ONCE TOGETHER, NO CAGE IN THE UNIVERSE CAN KEEP THE NEWBIES FROM COMBINING THEIR ENERGIES AND BECOMING ONE!
OH NO! INEZ WONG IS ONLY ONE NEWBIE AWAY FROM HAVING THE ENTIRE COLLECTION! IF SHE FINDS THAT LAST NEWBIE...
WE'LL BE LORDED OVER BY THE MOST LOVABLE CREATURE SINCE THE ATTACK OF THE MUTANT PREEMIES OF CABBAGE PATCH NEBULA!
COME ON, FRY! WE'VE GOT A PLANET TO SAVE!
WHICH ONE?
UH, OH. STAR FIGHT AT 12 O'CLOCK. FRY, CHECK THE TRAFFIC REPORT!
RIGHT!
"...AND AS WE TAKE A LOOK NOW AT THE TRAFFIC ON ROUTE 66.KI-5-1, WE'VE GOT A BACK-UP DUE TO AN OVER-TURNED STARSHIP SPILLING CHICKEN COOPS ONTO THE THROUGHWAY.
AND FOR THOSE OF YOU IN THE STOKER SECTOR, LOOK OUT FOR A SIG ALERT DUE TO A MASSIVE STAR-SHIP BATTLE THAT SHOULD HAVE TRAFFIC LOGJAMMED THERE FOR THE NEXT COUPLE HOURS.
CHOOM!
STOKER SECTOR HAVE A BLOODY GOOD STAY!
NUTS TO THAT! HANG ON, FRY! WE'RE GOIN' IN!
WAAAA-HOOO!
THOOM!
BOOM!
OH NO! ENGINE TWO IS OUT!

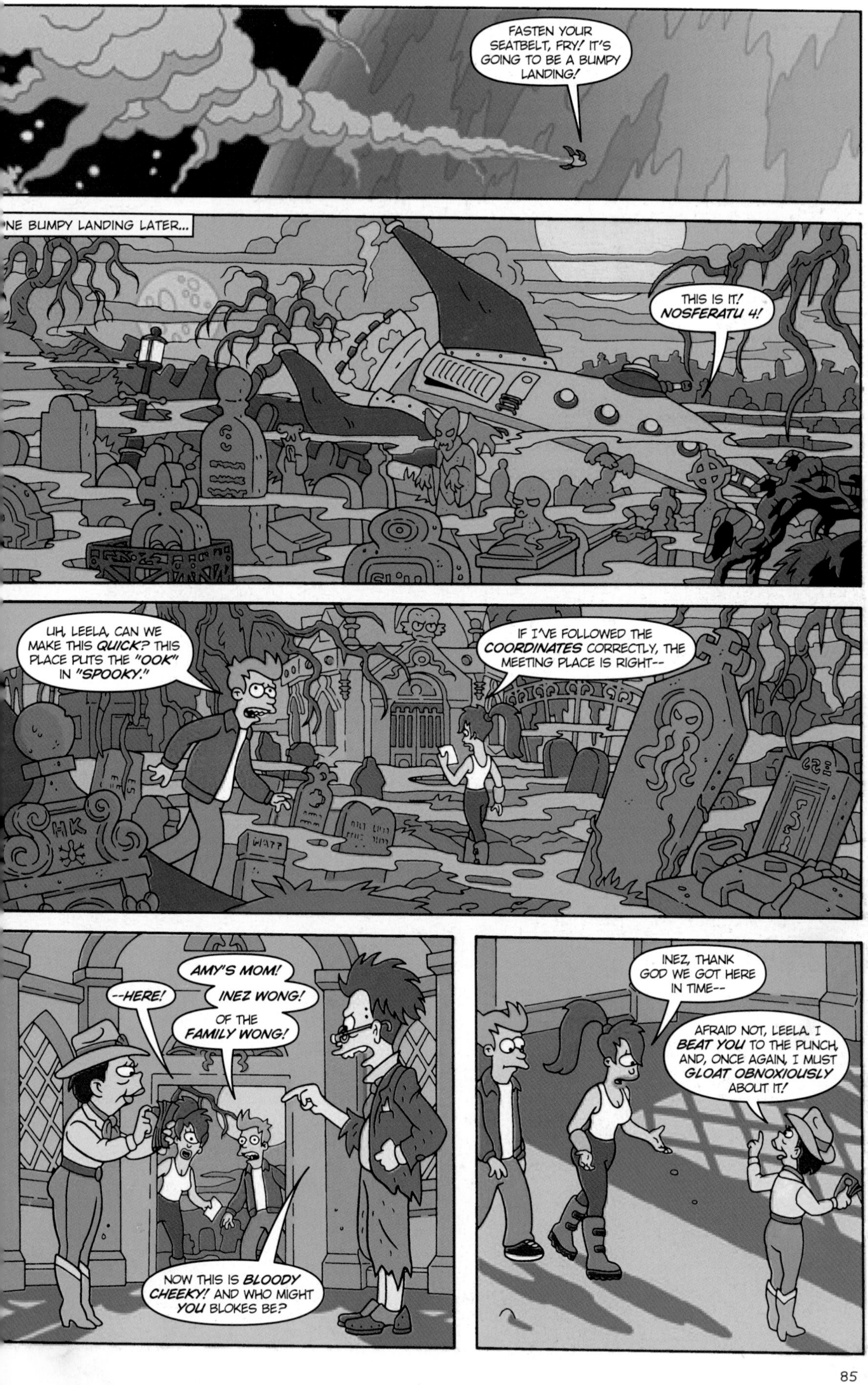
FASTEN YOUR SEATBELT, FRY! IT'S GOING TO BE A BUMPY LANDING!
NE BUMPY LANDING LATER...
THIS IS IT! NOSFERATU 4!
UH, LEELA, CAN WE MAKE THIS QUICK? THIS PLACE PUTS THE "OOK" IN "SPOOKY."
IF I'VE FOLLOWED THE COORDINATES CORRECTLY, THE MEETING PLACE IS RIGHT--
--HERE!
AMY'S MOM!
INEZ WONG!
OF THE FAMILY WONG!
NOW THIS IS BLOODY CHEEKY! AND WHO MIGHT YOU BLOKES BE?
INEZ, THANK GOD WE GOT HERE IN TIME--
AFRAID NOT, LEELA. I BEAT YOU TO THE PUNCH, AND, ONCE AGAIN, I MUST GLOAT OBNOXIOUSLY ABOUT IT!

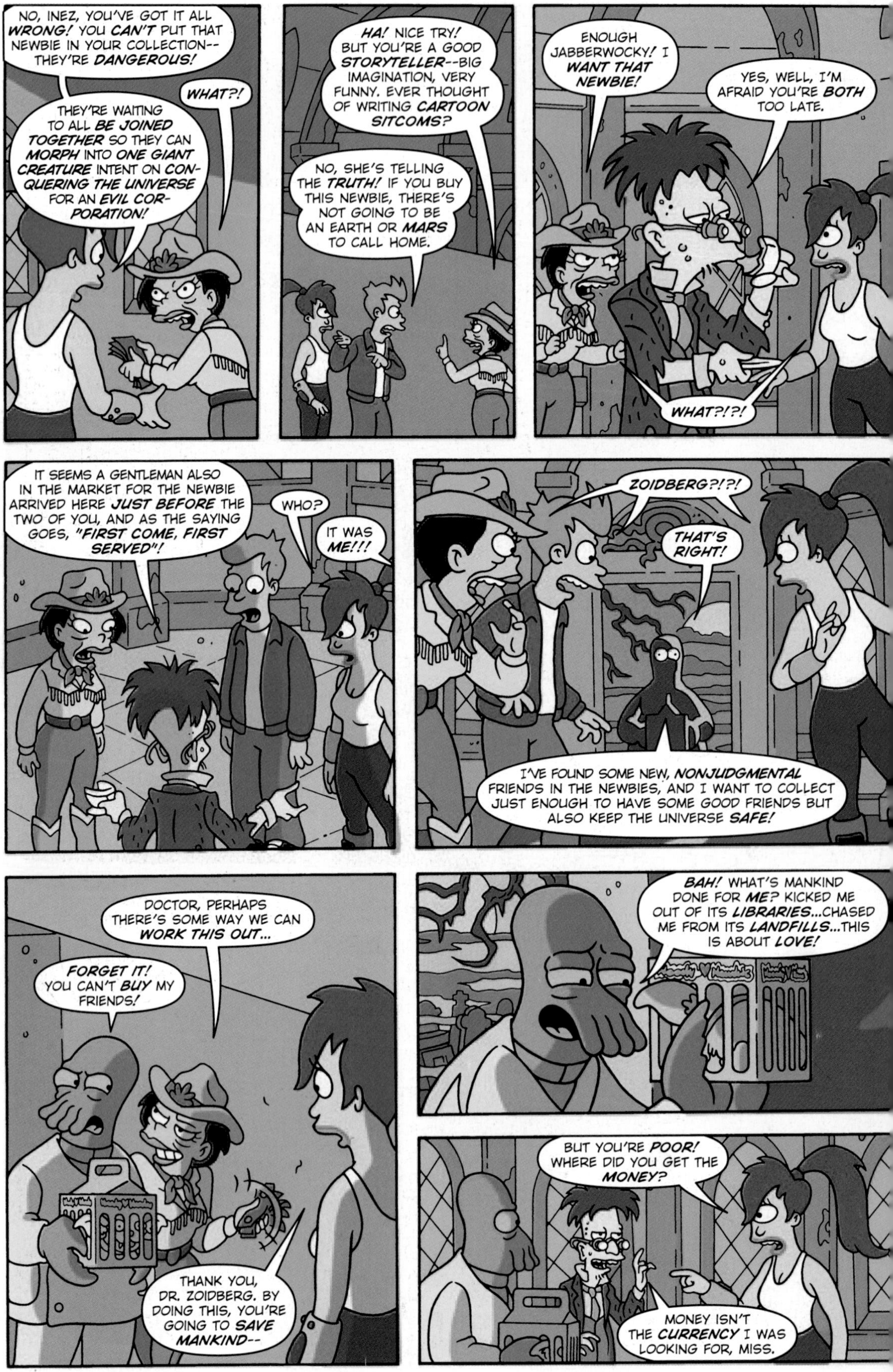
NO, INEZ, YOU'VE GOT IT ALL WRONG! YOU CAN'T PUT THAT NEWBIE IN YOUR COLLECTION--THEY'RE DANGEROUS!
WHAT?!
THEY'RE WAITING TO ALL BE JOINED TOGETHER SO THEY CAN MORPH INTO ONE GIANT CREATURE INTENT ON CONQUERING THE UNIVERSE FOR AN EVIL CORPORATION!
HA! NICE TRY! BUT YOU'RE A GOOD STORYTELLER--BIG IMAGINATION, VERY FUNNY. EVER THOUGHT OF WRITING CARTOON SITCOMS?
NO, SHE'S TELLING THE TRUTH! IF YOU BUY THIS NEWBIE, THERE'S NOT GOING TO BE AN EARTH OR MARS TO CALL HOME.
ENOUGH JABBERWOCKY! I WANT THAT NEWBIE!
YES, WELL, I'M AFRAID YOU'RE BOTH TOO LATE.
WHAT?!?!
IT SEEMS A GENTLEMAN ALSO IN THE MARKET FOR THE NEWBIE ARRIVED HERE JUST BEFORE THE TWO OF YOU, AND AS THE SAYING GOES, "FIRST COME, FIRST SERVED"!
WHO?
IT WAS ME!!!
ZOIDBERG?!?!
THAT'S RIGHT!
I'VE FOUND SOME NEW, NONJUDGMENTAL FRIENDS IN THE NEWBIES, AND I WANT TO COLLECT JUST ENOUGH TO HAVE SOME GOOD FRIENDS BUT ALSO KEEP THE UNIVERSE SAFE!
DOCTOR, PERHAPS THERE'S SOME WAY WE CAN WORK THIS OUT...
FORGET IT! YOU CAN'T BUY MY FRIENDS!
THANK YOU, DR. ZOIDBERG. BY DOING THIS, YOU'RE GOING TO SAVE MANKIND--
BAH! WHAT'S MANKIND DONE FOR ME? KICKED ME OUT OF ITS LIBRARIES...CHASED ME FROM ITS LANDFILLS...THIS IS ABOUT LOVE!
BUT YOU'RE POOR! WHERE DID YOU GET THE MONEY?
MONEY ISN'T THE CURRENCY I WAS LOOKING FOR, MISS.

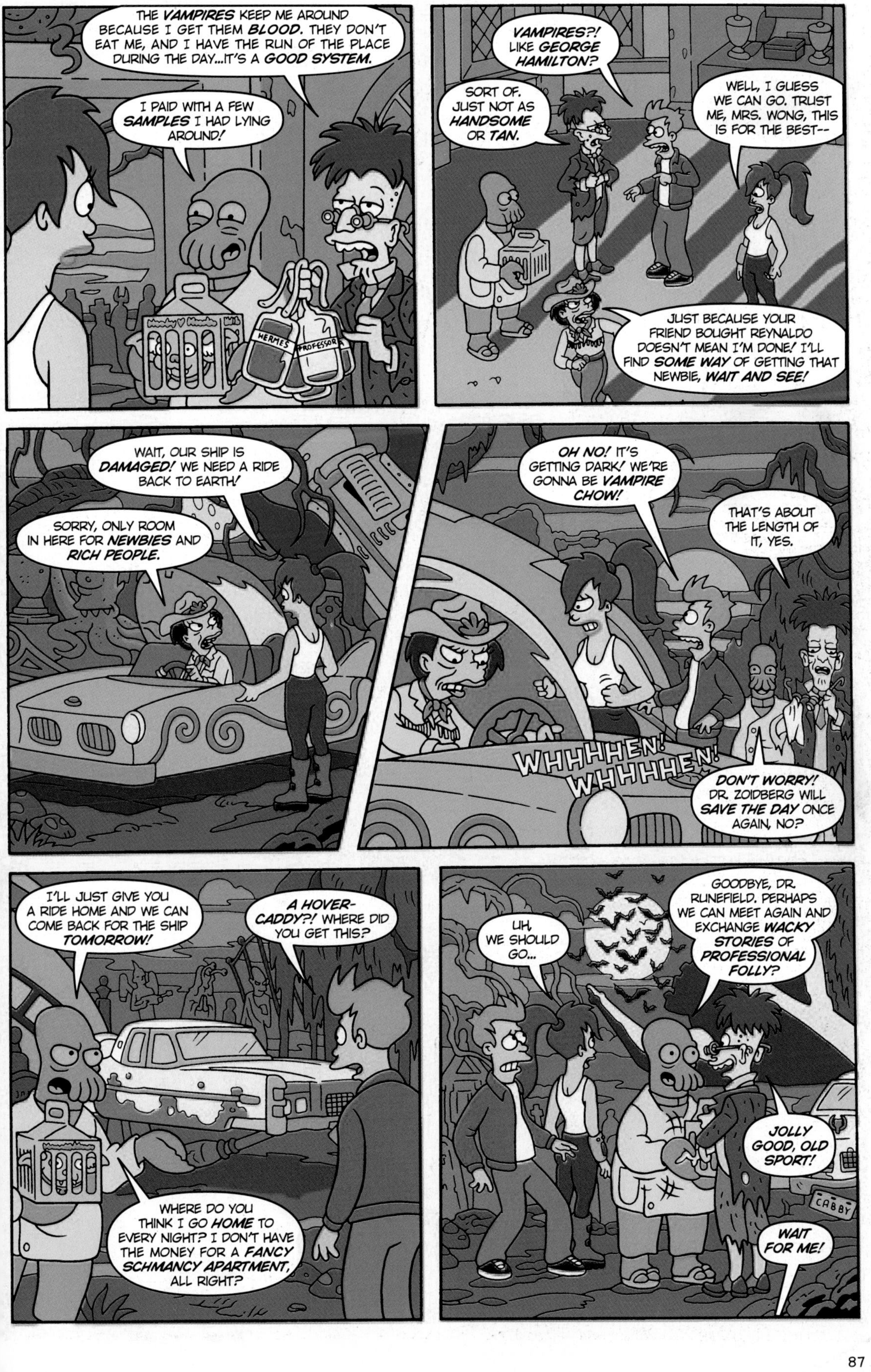
THE VAMPIRES KEEP ME AROUND BECAUSE I GET THEM BLOOD. THEY DON'T EAT ME, AND I HAVE THE RUN OF THE PLACE DURING THE DAY...IT'S A GOOD SYSTEM.
I PAID WITH A FEW SAMPLES I HAD LYING AROUND!
HERMES
PROFESSOR
VAMPIRES?! LIKE GEORGE HAMILTON?
SORT OF. JUST NOT AS HANDSOME OR TAN.
WELL, I GUESS WE CAN GO. TRUST ME, MRS. WONG, THIS IS FOR THE BEST--
JUST BECAUSE YOUR FRIEND BOUGHT REYNALDO DOESN'T MEAN I'M DONE! I'LL FIND SOME WAY OF GETTING THAT NEWBIE, WAIT AND SEE!
WAIT, OUR SHIP IS DAMAGED! WE NEED A RIDE BACK TO EARTH!
SORRY, ONLY ROOM IN HERE FOR NEWBIES AND RICH PEOPLE.
OH NO! IT'S GETTING DARK! WE'RE GONNA BE VAMPIRE CHOW!
THAT'S ABOUT THE LENGTH OF IT, YES.
WHHHHEN! WHHHHEN!
DON'T WORRY! DR. ZOIDBERG WILL SAVE THE DAY ONCE AGAIN, NO?
I'LL JUST GIVE YOU A RIDE HOME AND WE CAN COME BACK FOR THE SHIP TOMORROW!
A HOVER-CADDY?! WHERE DID YOU GET THIS?
WHERE DO YOU THINK I GO HOME TO EVERY NIGHT? I DON'T HAVE THE MONEY FOR A FANCY SCHMANCY APARTMENT, ALL RIGHT?
UH, WE SHOULD GO...
GOODBYE, DR. RUNEFIELD. PERHAPS WE CAN MEET AGAIN AND EXCHANGE WACKY STORIES OF PROFESSIONAL FOLLY?
JOLLY GOOD, OLD SPORT!
CABBY
WAIT FOR ME!

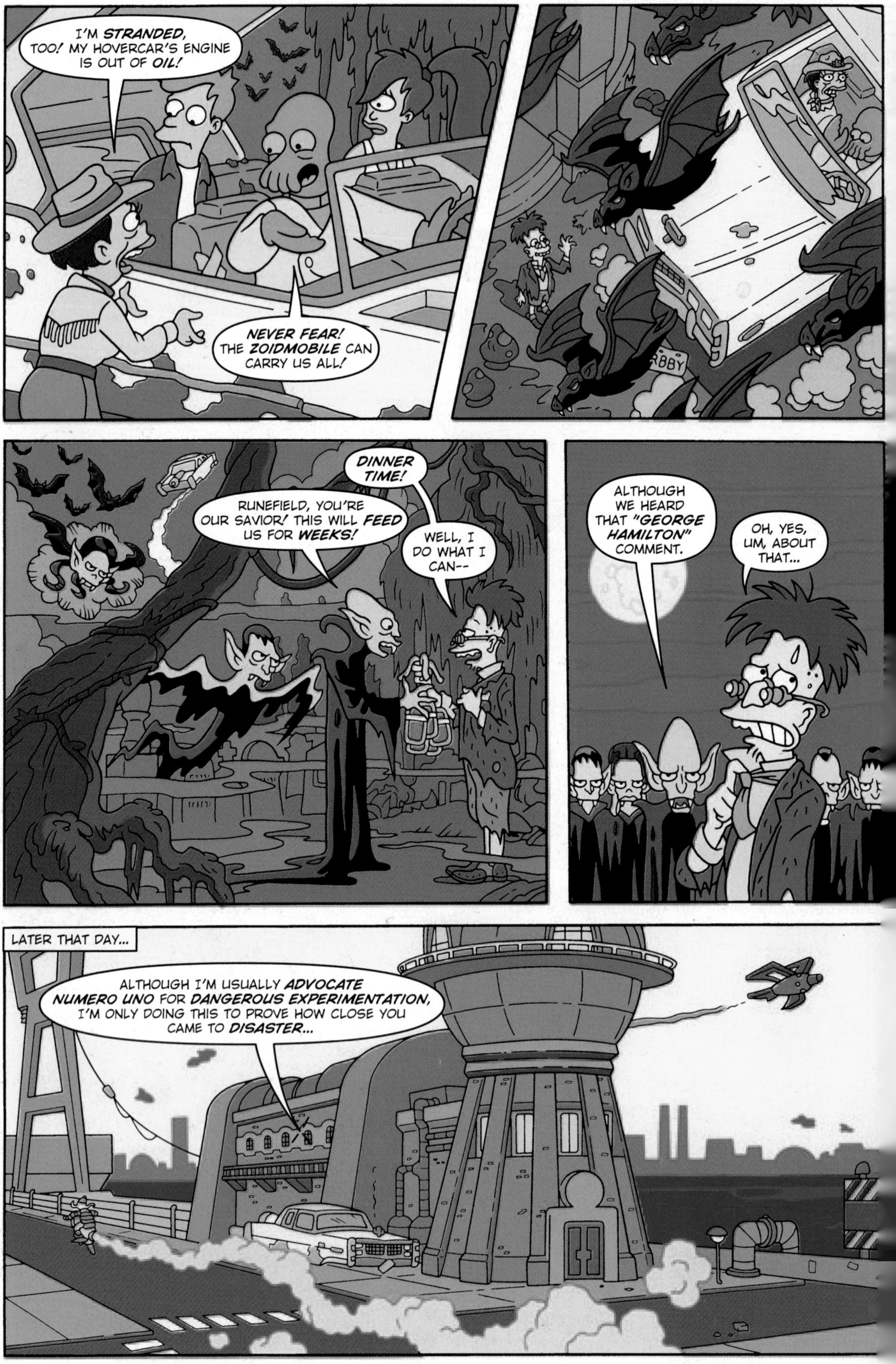
I'M STRANDED, TOO! MY HOVERCAR'S ENGINE IS OUT OF OIL!
NEVER FEAR! THE ZOIDMOBILE CAN CARRY US ALL!
RBBY
DINNER TIME!
RUNEFIELD, YOU'RE OUR SAVIOR! THIS WILL FEED US FOR WEEKS!
WELL, I DO WHAT I CAN--
ALTHOUGH WE HEARD THAT "GEORGE HAMILTON" COMMENT.
OH, YES, UM, ABOUT THAT...
LATER THAT DAY...
ALTHOUGH I'M USUALLY ADVOCATE NUMERO UNO FOR DANGEROUS EXPERIMENTATION, I'M ONLY DOING THIS TO PROVE HOW CLOSE YOU CAME TO DISASTER...

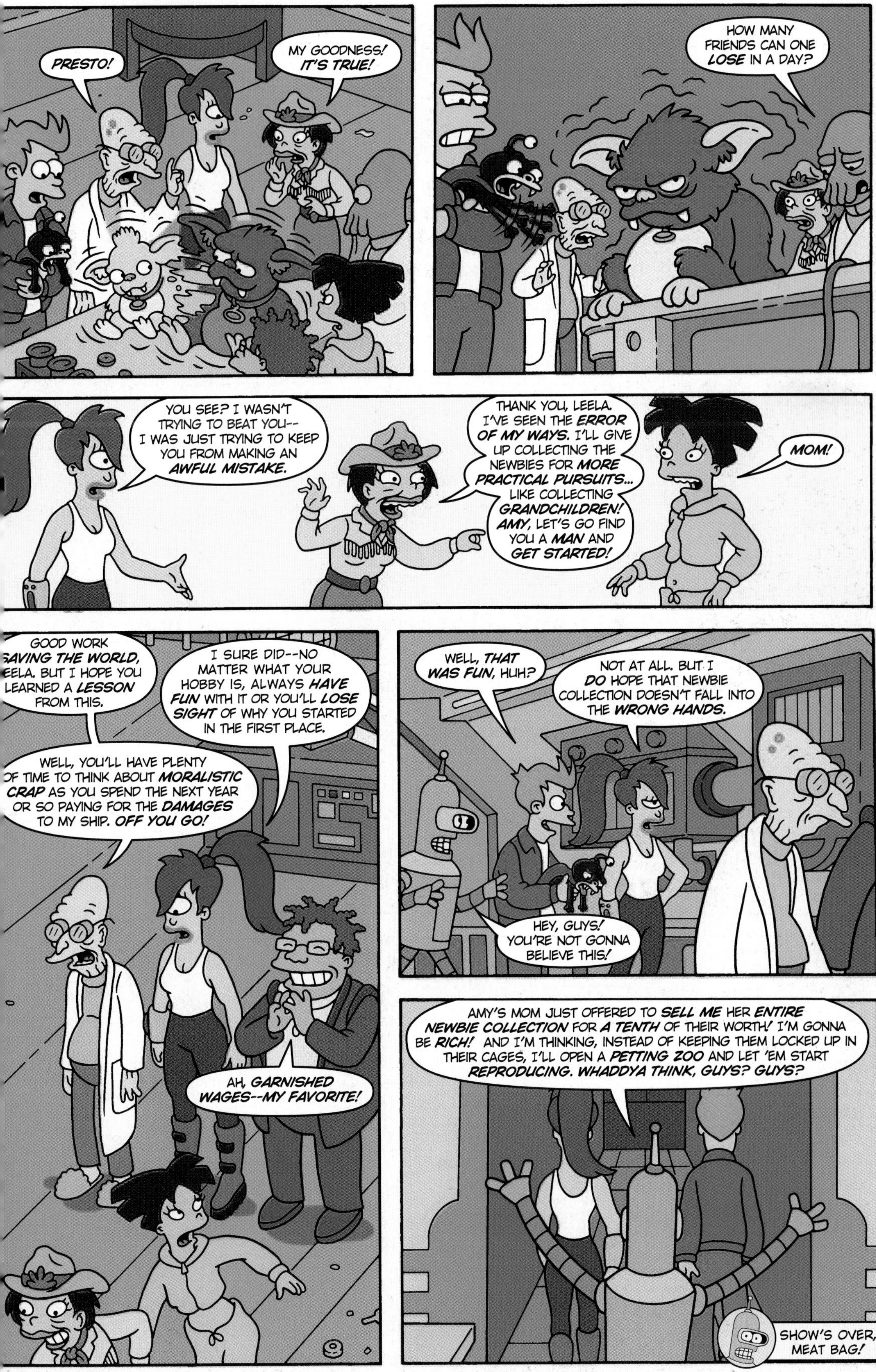
PRESTO!
MY GOODNESS! IT'S TRUE!
HOW MANY FRIENDS CAN ONE LOSE IN A DAY?
YOU SEE? I WASN'T TRYING TO BEAT YOU-- I WAS JUST TRYING TO KEEP YOU FROM MAKING AN AWFUL MISTAKE.
THANK YOU, LEELA. I'VE SEEN THE ERROR OF MY WAYS. I'LL GIVE UP COLLECTING THE NEWBIES FOR MORE PRACTICAL PURSUITS... LIKE COLLECTING GRANDCHILDREN! AMY, LET'S GO FIND YOU A MAN AND GET STARTED!
MOM!
GOOD WORK SAVING THE WORLD, LEELA. BUT I HOPE YOU LEARNED A LESSON FROM THIS.
I SURE DID--NO MATTER WHAT YOUR HOBBY IS, ALWAYS HAVE FUN WITH IT OR YOU'LL LOSE SIGHT OF WHY YOU STARTED IN THE FIRST PLACE.
WELL, YOU'LL HAVE PLENTY OF TIME TO THINK ABOUT MORALISTIC CRAP AS YOU SPEND THE NEXT YEAR OR SO PAYING FOR THE DAMAGES TO MY SHIP. OFF YOU GO!
AH, GARNISHED WAGES--MY FAVORITE!
WELL, THAT WAS FUN, HUH?
NOT AT ALL. BUT I DO HOPE THAT NEWBIE COLLECTION DOESN'T FALL INTO THE WRONG HANDS.
HEY, GUYS! YOU'RE NOT GONNA BELIEVE THIS!
AMY'S MOM JUST OFFERED TO SELL ME HER ENTIRE NEWBIE COLLECTION FOR A TENTH OF THEIR WORTH! I'M GONNA BE RICH! AND I'M THINKING, INSTEAD OF KEEPING THEM LOCKED UP IN THEIR CAGES, I'LL OPEN A PETTING ZOO AND LET 'EM START REPRODUCING. WHADDYA THINK, GUYS? GUYS?
SHOW'S OVER, MEAT BAG!

KiDS!

EVER WANTED TO OWN A CELEBRITY HEAD-IN-A-JAR?

NOW YOU CAN!!!

I'M HILARIOUS AND TALK IN A FUNNY VOICE! OWN ME, KIDS!!!
GILBERT GOTTFRIED

We've saved too many celebrities' heads! Our over-zealous ways mean the deal of a lifetime FOR YOU!

Boys and Girls, has it always been your dream to own the head of one of today's most popular celebrities? To have them at your beck and call for your own personal entertainment at any time?

NOW'S YOUR CHANCE!

The Head Museum of New New York has too many heads in stock and some heads must go! Our lack of shelf space means hours of fun for you and your friends! And, oh boy, are these heads priced to move!

ANY CELEBRITY LISTED FOR ONLY $1.98!!!

EXCITING AND TALENTED CELEBRITIES INCLUDE:

TOM GREEN | ROSEANNE | MINI ME | DAVID DUCHOVNY | MATT GROENING

MANY MORE TO CHOOSE FROM, INCLUDING:

- David Lee Roth
- Vanilla Ice
- Joan Rivers
- The Olsen Twins
- Carrot Top
- Melanie Griffith
- Adam West
- RuPaul
- Chuck Norris
- Any cast member of "The View"
- Any cast member of "The Real World"
- Flavor Flav
- Any Wayans Brother
- Dr. Laura Schlesinger
- Terry Bradshaw
- Maury Povich
- Calista Flockhart

YES, THEY ARE ENTERTAINING, BUT THEY HAVE PRACTICAL USES TOO, SUCH AS

Doorstop	Paper weight	Decorative Decanter
Fish bowl	Poker buddy	Trash receptacle
Marble jar	Burglar alarm	Hat rack

...OR WHATEVER YOUR HEART DESIRES! IT WILL BE **YOUR HEAD** -- YOU CAN DO WHAT YOU WANT WITH IT!"

I NEVER THOUGHT I COULD OWN THE HEAD OF ARSENIO HALL. BUT THEN I SAW THIS AD, SENT MY $1.98, AND NOW IT'S "WOOF WOOF WOOF" EVERY NIGHT AT MY HOUSE!
FOR GOD'S SAKE, KID...I CAN'T "GET BUSY" ANYMORE! I NEED SLEEP, LITTLE HOMIE!

Rush coupon now for your own celebrity head and Head Museum catalogue! Try for 10 days, risk-free! If not completely satisfied, we will fully refund your money!*

MAIL TODAY!

Head Museum of New New York
36 N. Xlyroklx St., Suite 5.176
New New York, NY 10101.71453

Dear Sirs:
Please rush my chosen **Head-In-Jar** to me.
I am enclosing **$1.98** in full for each head ordered.

Celebrity Head(s) ______
Total Number of Heads ______
Name______
Address______
City______ State__ Planet______
Galaxy______ Zip______

*Sending head back not necessary for refund. In fact, no refund will be sent if merchandise is returned. We mean it. Do what you want with the head, just don't give it back to us!

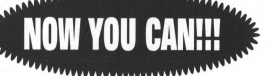

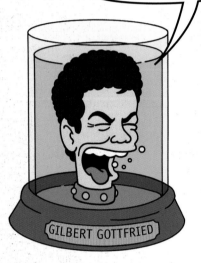

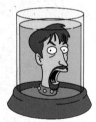

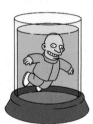

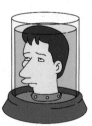

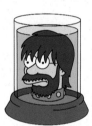

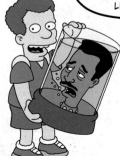

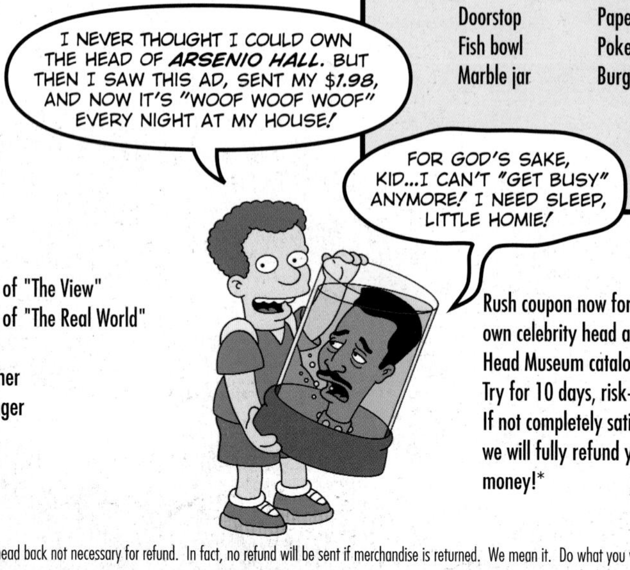

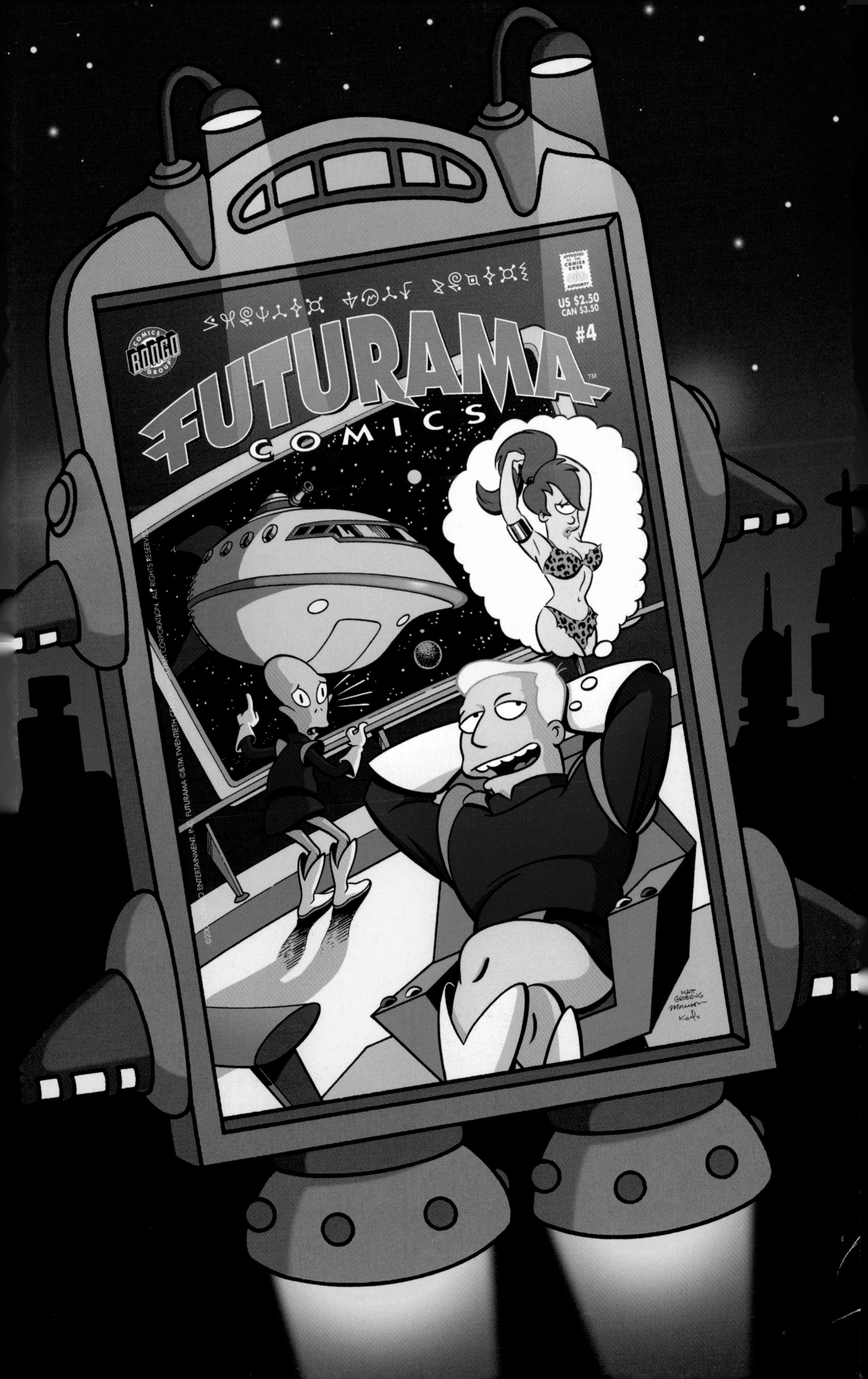

BONGO COMICS GROUP
FUTURAMA™
COMICS
APPROVED BY THE COMICS CODE AUTHORITY
US $2.50
CAN $3.50
#4
MATT GROENING

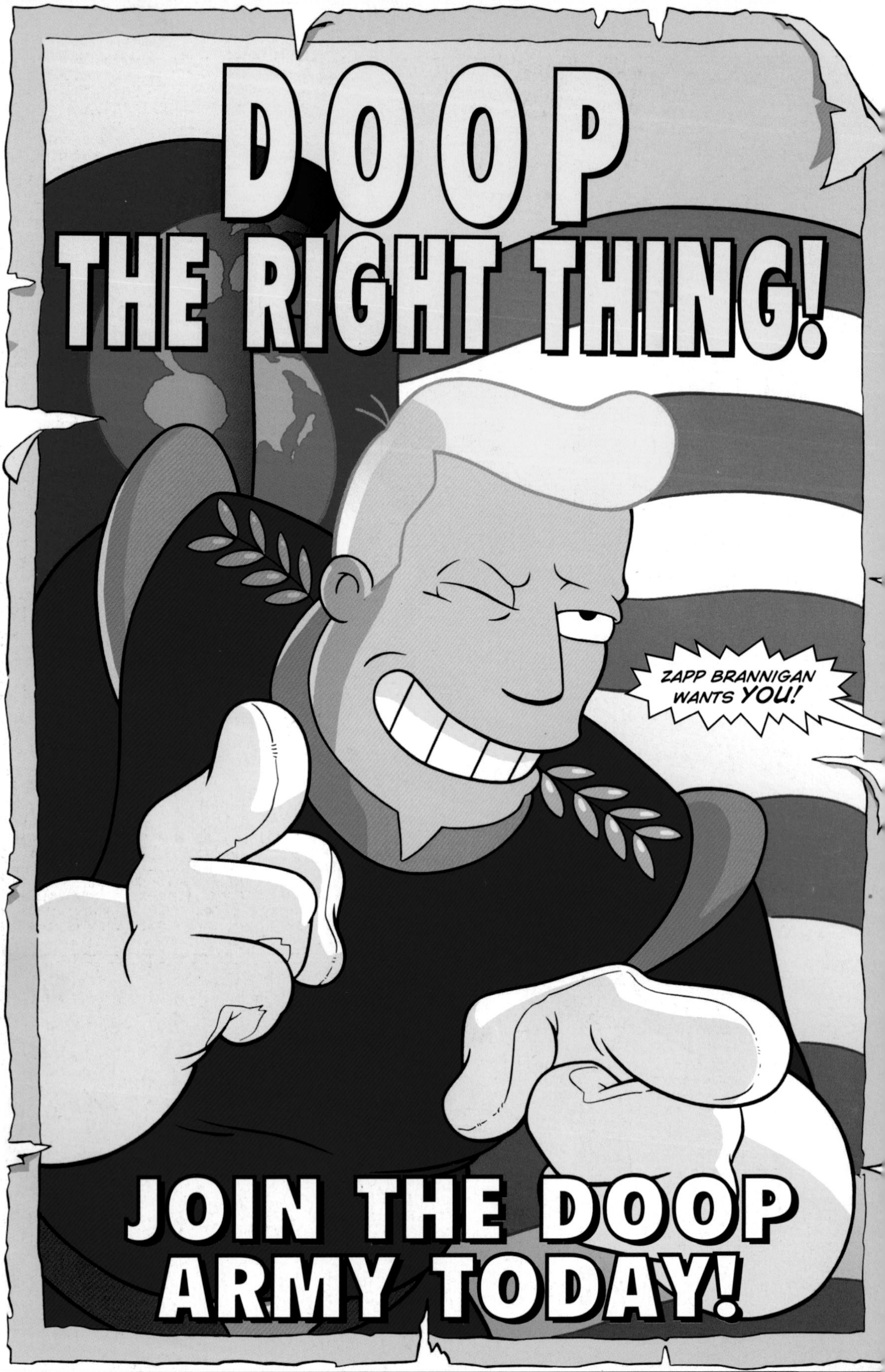
DOOP
THE RIGHT THING!
ZAPP BRANNIGAN WANTS YOU!
JOIN THE DOOP ARMY TODAY!

SCRIPT	PENCILS	INKS	LETTERS	COLORS	EDITS	ART SUPERVISION	JUNGLE LORD
ERIC ROGERS	PAM COOKE	PHYLLIS NOVIN	KAREN BATES	DAVE STEWART	BILL MORRISON	NATHAN KANE	MATT GROENIN

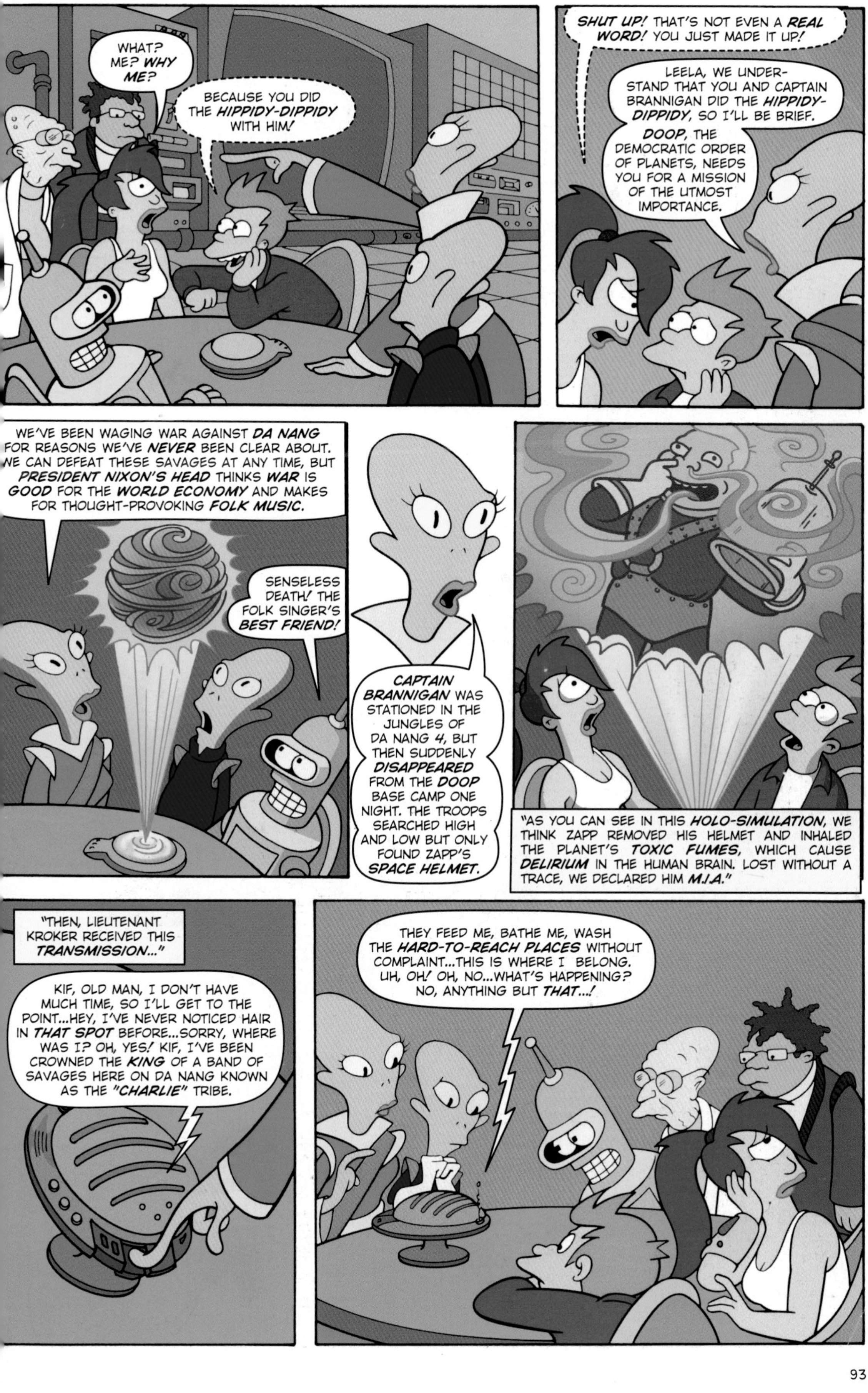

WHAT? ME? WHY ME?
BECAUSE YOU DID THE HIPPIDY-DIPPIDY WITH HIM!
SHUT UP! THAT'S NOT EVEN A REAL WORD! YOU JUST MADE IT UP!
LEELA, WE UNDERSTAND THAT YOU AND CAPTAIN BRANNIGAN DID THE HIPPIDY-DIPPIDY, SO I'LL BE BRIEF.
DOOP, THE DEMOCRATIC ORDER OF PLANETS, NEEDS YOU FOR A MISSION OF THE UTMOST IMPORTANCE.
WE'VE BEEN WAGING WAR AGAINST DA NANG FOR REASONS WE'VE NEVER BEEN CLEAR ABOUT. WE CAN DEFEAT THESE SAVAGES AT ANY TIME, BUT PRESIDENT NIXON'S HEAD THINKS WAR IS GOOD FOR THE WORLD ECONOMY AND MAKES FOR THOUGHT-PROVOKING FOLK MUSIC.
SENSELESS DEATH! THE FOLK SINGER'S BEST FRIEND!
CAPTAIN BRANNIGAN WAS STATIONED IN THE JUNGLES OF DA NANG 4, BUT THEN SUDDENLY DISAPPEARED FROM THE DOOP BASE CAMP ONE NIGHT. THE TROOPS SEARCHED HIGH AND LOW BUT ONLY FOUND ZAPP'S SPACE HELMET.
"AS YOU CAN SEE IN THIS HOLO-SIMULATION, WE THINK ZAPP REMOVED HIS HELMET AND INHALED THE PLANET'S TOXIC FUMES, WHICH CAUSE DELIRIUM IN THE HUMAN BRAIN. LOST WITHOUT A TRACE, WE DECLARED HIM M.I.A."
"THEN, LIEUTENANT KROKER RECEIVED THIS TRANSMISSION..."
KIF, OLD MAN, I DON'T HAVE MUCH TIME, SO I'LL GET TO THE POINT...HEY, I'VE NEVER NOTICED HAIR IN THAT SPOT BEFORE...SORRY, WHERE WAS I? OH, YES! KIF, I'VE BEEN CROWNED THE KING OF A BAND OF SAVAGES HERE ON DA NANG KNOWN AS THE "CHARLIE" TRIBE.
THEY FEED ME, BATHE ME, WASH THE HARD-TO-REACH PLACES WITHOUT COMPLAINT...THIS IS WHERE I BELONG. UH, OH! OH, NO...WHAT'S HAPPENING? NO, ANYTHING BUT THAT...!

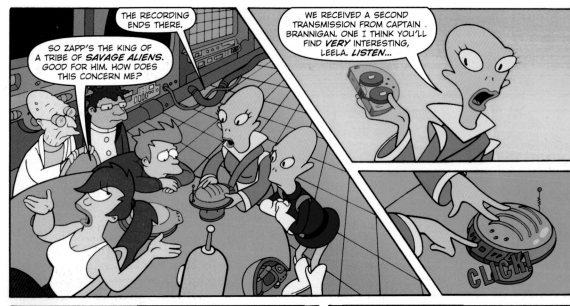

THE RECORDING ENDS THERE.

SO ZAPP'S THE KING OF A TRIBE OF *SAVAGE ALIENS.* GOOD FOR HIM. HOW DOES THIS CONCERN ME?

WE RECEIVED A SECOND TRANSMISSION FROM CAPTAIN BRANNIGAN. ONE I THINK YOU'LL FIND *VERY* INTERESTING, LEELA. *LISTEN...*

CLICK!

KIF, IT'S ME AGAIN. SORRY ABOUT THAT *FIRST* TAPE. I WAS HAVING MY NIGHTLY *BODY DIP TREATMENT,* AND THE MUD STARTED CONGEALING IN MY *VARIOUS ORIFICES.*

KIF, AS MY TRUEST FRIEND AND CONFIDANT, I NEED *ONE LAST FAVOR* BEFORE WE PART WAYS, FOREVER.

A KING NEEDS A QUEEN. A *ONE-EYED QUEEN* TO BE PRECISE...*LEELA!*

BRING HER TO ME HERE ON DA NANG 4, AND I PROMISE YOU'LL NEVER HEAR FROM ME AGAIN. ONCE YOU'VE ARRIVED AND MY SPIES REPORT TO ME THAT YOU HAVE LEELA, I'LL SEND YOU THE *SECRET COORDINATES* TO MY VILLAGE. GO I MUST, OLD MAN. CONRAD SAYS IT'S TIME FOR MY *12 O'CLOCK HIGH COLONIC.* UNTIL WE MEET AGAIN...

FORGET IT! THERE'S *NO WAY IN HELL* THAT I'M GOING NEAR ZAPP BRANNIGAN, LET ALONE BE HIS *JUNGLE QUEEN!*

LEELA, WE ONLY WANT TO USE YOU AS A *DECOY* TO UNCOVER ZAPP'S WHEREABOUTS. CAPTAIN BRANNIGAN KNOWS THE *DOOP'S BATTLE PLANS.* HE COULD GIVE AWAY SECRETS AND TRAIN AN ARMY OF SAVAGES TO ATTACK *OUR* FORCES, WHICH COULD *TURN THE TIDE* OF THE WAR!

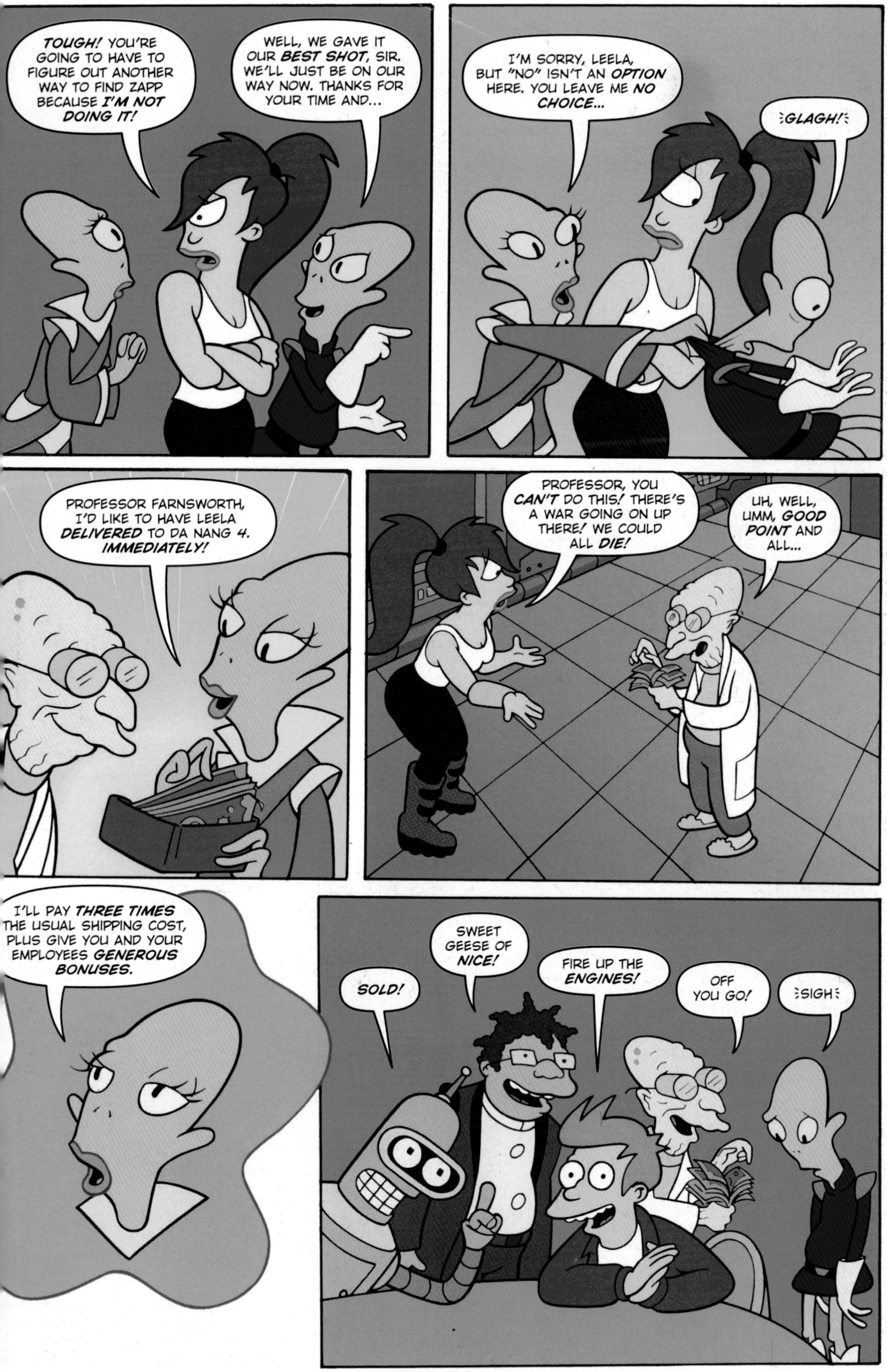
TOUGH! YOU'RE GOING TO HAVE TO FIGURE OUT ANOTHER WAY TO FIND ZAPP BECAUSE I'M NOT DOING IT!
WELL, WE GAVE IT OUR BEST SHOT, SIR. WE'LL JUST BE ON OUR WAY NOW. THANKS FOR YOUR TIME AND...
I'M SORRY, LEELA, BUT "NO" ISN'T AN OPTION HERE. YOU LEAVE ME NO CHOICE...
GLAGH!
PROFESSOR FARNSWORTH, I'D LIKE TO HAVE LEELA DELIVERED TO DA NANG 4. IMMEDIATELY!
PROFESSOR, YOU CAN'T DO THIS! THERE'S A WAR GOING ON UP THERE! WE COULD ALL DIE!
UH, WELL, UMM, GOOD POINT AND ALL...
I'LL PAY THREE TIMES THE USUAL SHIPPING COST, PLUS GIVE YOU AND YOUR EMPLOYEES GENEROUS BONUSES.
SOLD!
SWEET GEESE OF NICE!
FIRE UP THE ENGINES!
OFF YOU GO!
SIGH

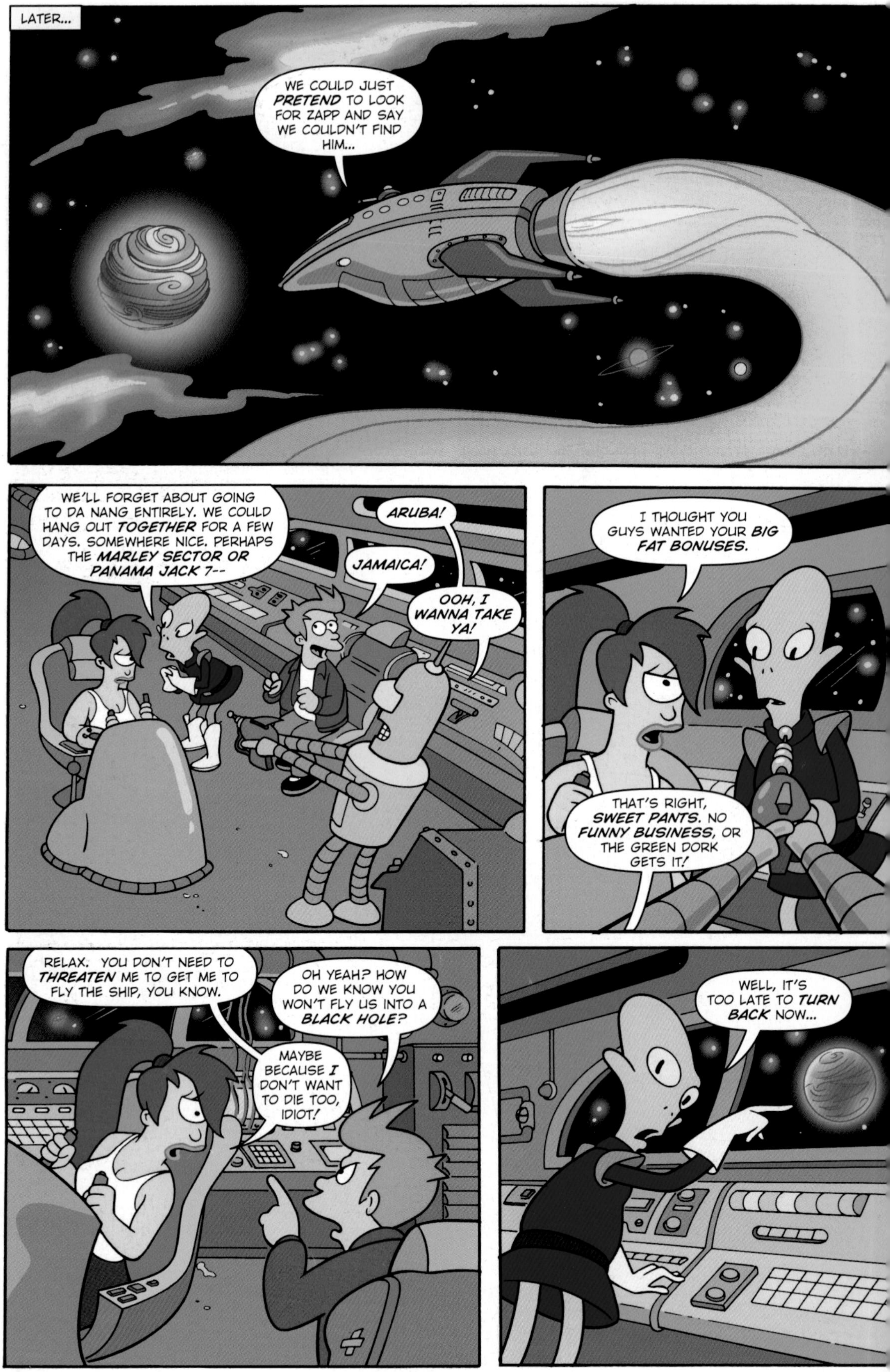
LATER...
WE COULD JUST PRETEND TO LOOK FOR ZAPP AND SAY WE COULDN'T FIND HIM...
WE'LL FORGET ABOUT GOING TO DA NANG ENTIRELY. WE COULD HANG OUT TOGETHER FOR A FEW DAYS. SOMEWHERE NICE. PERHAPS THE MARLEY SECTOR OR PANAMA JACK 7--
ARUBA!
JAMAICA!
OOH, I WANNA TAKE YA!
I THOUGHT YOU GUYS WANTED YOUR BIG FAT BONUSES.
THAT'S RIGHT, SWEET PANTS. NO FUNNY BUSINESS, OR THE GREEN DORK GETS IT!
RELAX. YOU DON'T NEED TO THREATEN ME TO GET ME TO FLY THE SHIP, YOU KNOW.
OH YEAH? HOW DO WE KNOW YOU WON'T FLY US INTO A BLACK HOLE?
MAYBE BECAUSE I DON'T WANT TO DIE TOO, IDIOT!
WELL, IT'S TOO LATE TO TURN BACK NOW...

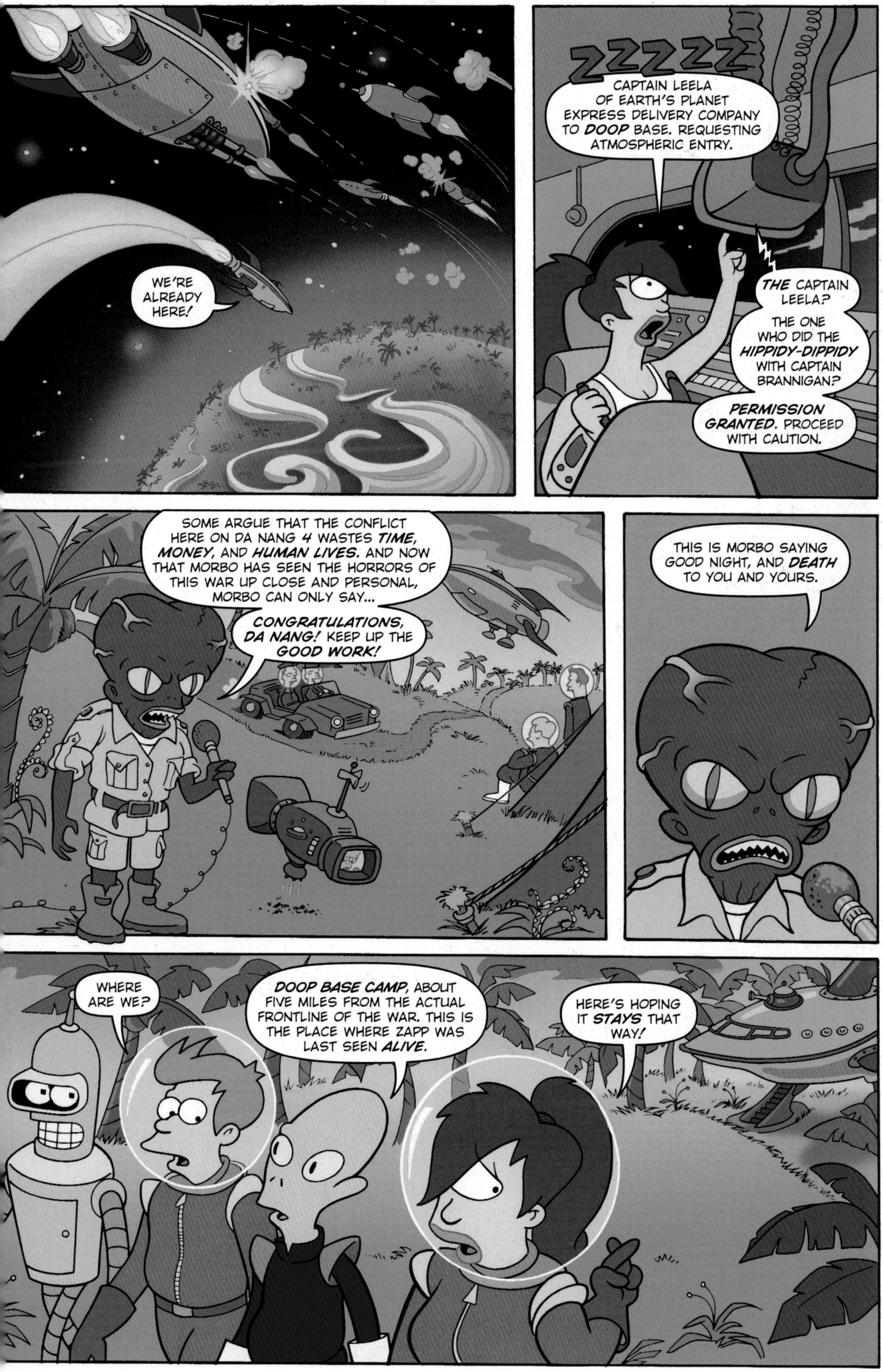
WE'RE ALREADY HERE!
ZZZZZZ
CAPTAIN LEELA OF EARTH'S PLANET EXPRESS DELIVERY COMPANY TO DOOP BASE. REQUESTING ATMOSPHERIC ENTRY.
THE CAPTAIN LEELA?
THE ONE WHO DID THE HIPPIDY-DIPPIDY WITH CAPTAIN BRANNIGAN?
PERMISSION GRANTED. PROCEED WITH CAUTION.
SOME ARGUE THAT THE CONFLICT HERE ON DA NANG 4 WASTES TIME, MONEY, AND HUMAN LIVES. AND NOW THAT MORBO HAS SEEN THE HORRORS OF THIS WAR UP CLOSE AND PERSONAL, MORBO CAN ONLY SAY...
CONGRATULATIONS, DA NANG! KEEP UP THE GOOD WORK!
THIS IS MORBO SAYING GOOD NIGHT, AND DEATH TO YOU AND YOURS.
WHERE ARE WE?
DOOP BASE CAMP, ABOUT FIVE MILES FROM THE ACTUAL FRONTLINE OF THE WAR. THIS IS THE PLACE WHERE ZAPP WAS LAST SEEN ALIVE.
HERE'S HOPING IT STAYS THAT WAY!

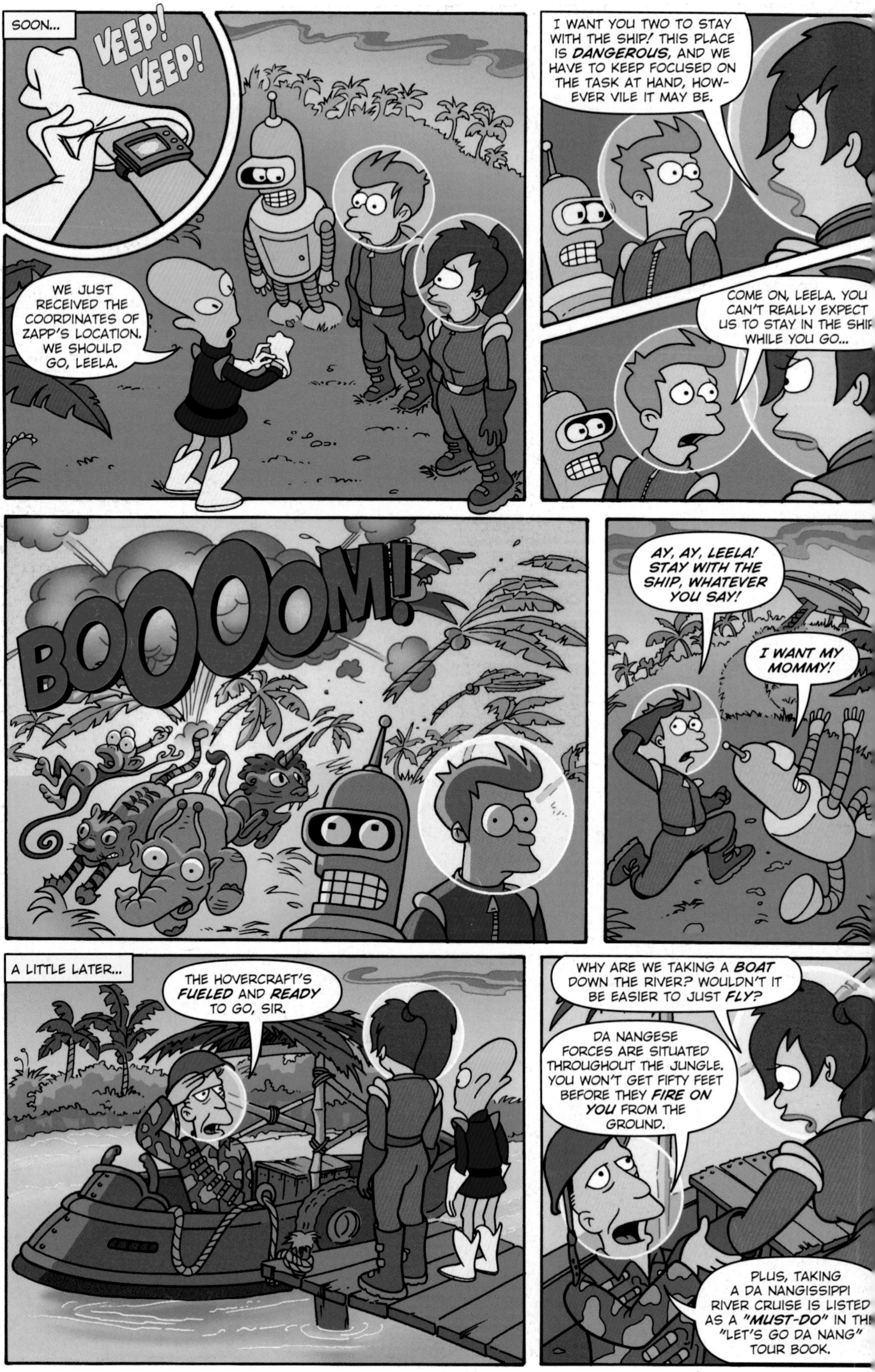
SOON...
VEEP! VEEP!
WE JUST RECEIVED THE COORDINATES OF ZAPP'S LOCATION. WE SHOULD GO, LEELA.
I WANT YOU TWO TO STAY WITH THE SHIP! THIS PLACE IS DANGEROUS, AND WE HAVE TO KEEP FOCUSED ON THE TASK AT HAND, HOWEVER VILE IT MAY BE.
COME ON, LEELA. YOU CAN'T REALLY EXPECT US TO STAY IN THE SHIP WHILE YOU GO...
BOOOOOM!
AY, AY, LEELA! STAY WITH THE SHIP, WHATEVER YOU SAY!
I WANT MY MOMMY!
A LITTLE LATER...
THE HOVERCRAFT'S FUELED AND READY TO GO, SIR.
WHY ARE WE TAKING A BOAT DOWN THE RIVER? WOULDN'T IT BE EASIER TO JUST FLY?
DA NANGESE FORCES ARE SITUATED THROUGHOUT THE JUNGLE. YOU WON'T GET FIFTY FEET BEFORE THEY FIRE ON YOU FROM THE GROUND.
PLUS, TAKING A DA NANGISSIPPI RIVER CRUISE IS LISTED AS A "MUST-DO" IN THE "LET'S GO DA NANG" TOUR BOOK.

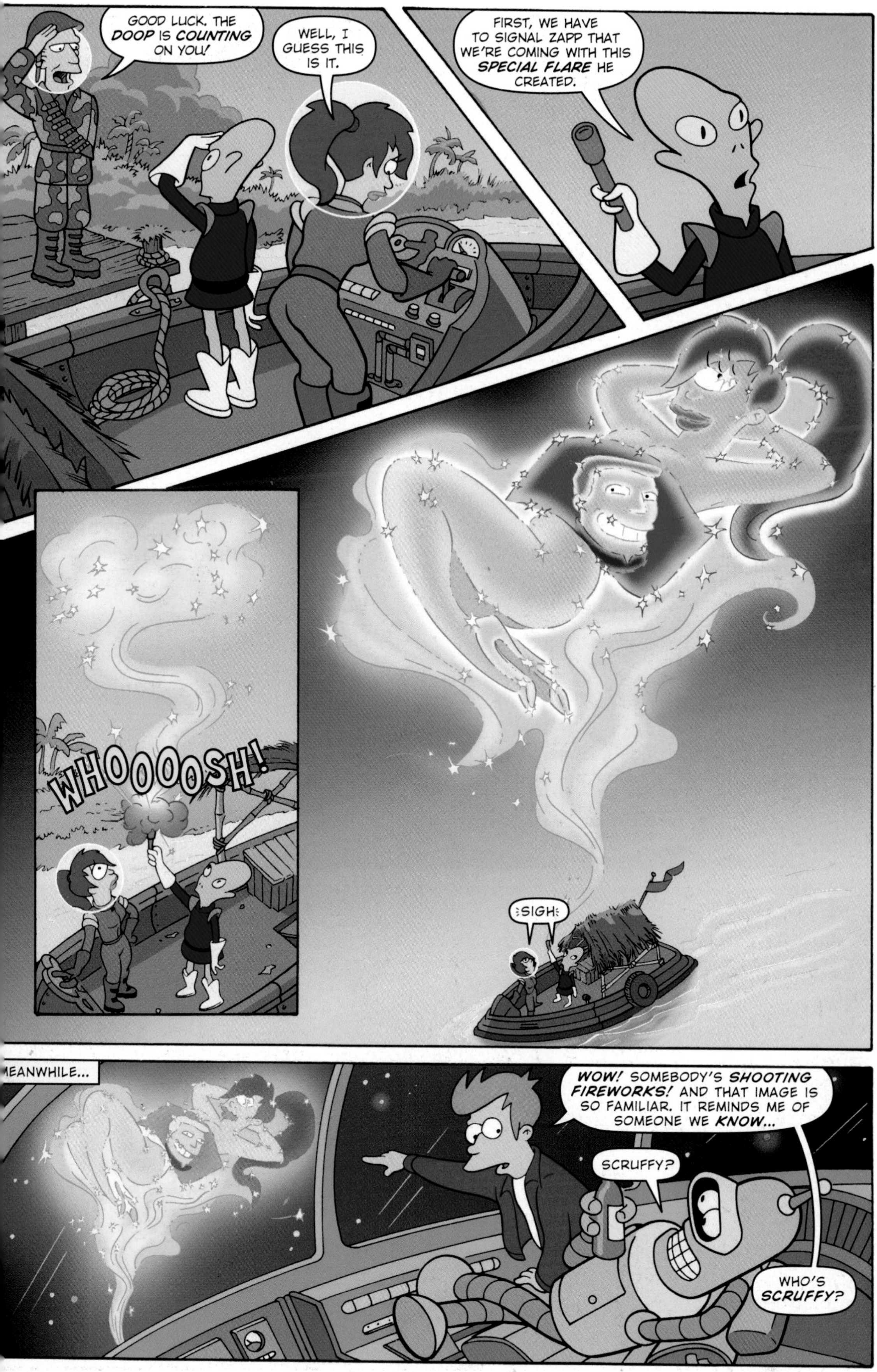

GOOD LUCK. THE DOOP IS COUNTING ON YOU!
WELL, I GUESS THIS IS IT.
FIRST, WE HAVE TO SIGNAL ZAPP THAT WE'RE COMING WITH THIS SPECIAL FLARE HE CREATED.
WHOOOOSH!
SIGH
MEANWHILE...
WOW! SOMEBODY'S SHOOTING FIREWORKS! AND THAT IMAGE IS SO FAMILIAR. IT REMINDS ME OF SOMEONE WE KNOW...
SCRUFFY?
WHO'S SCRUFFY?

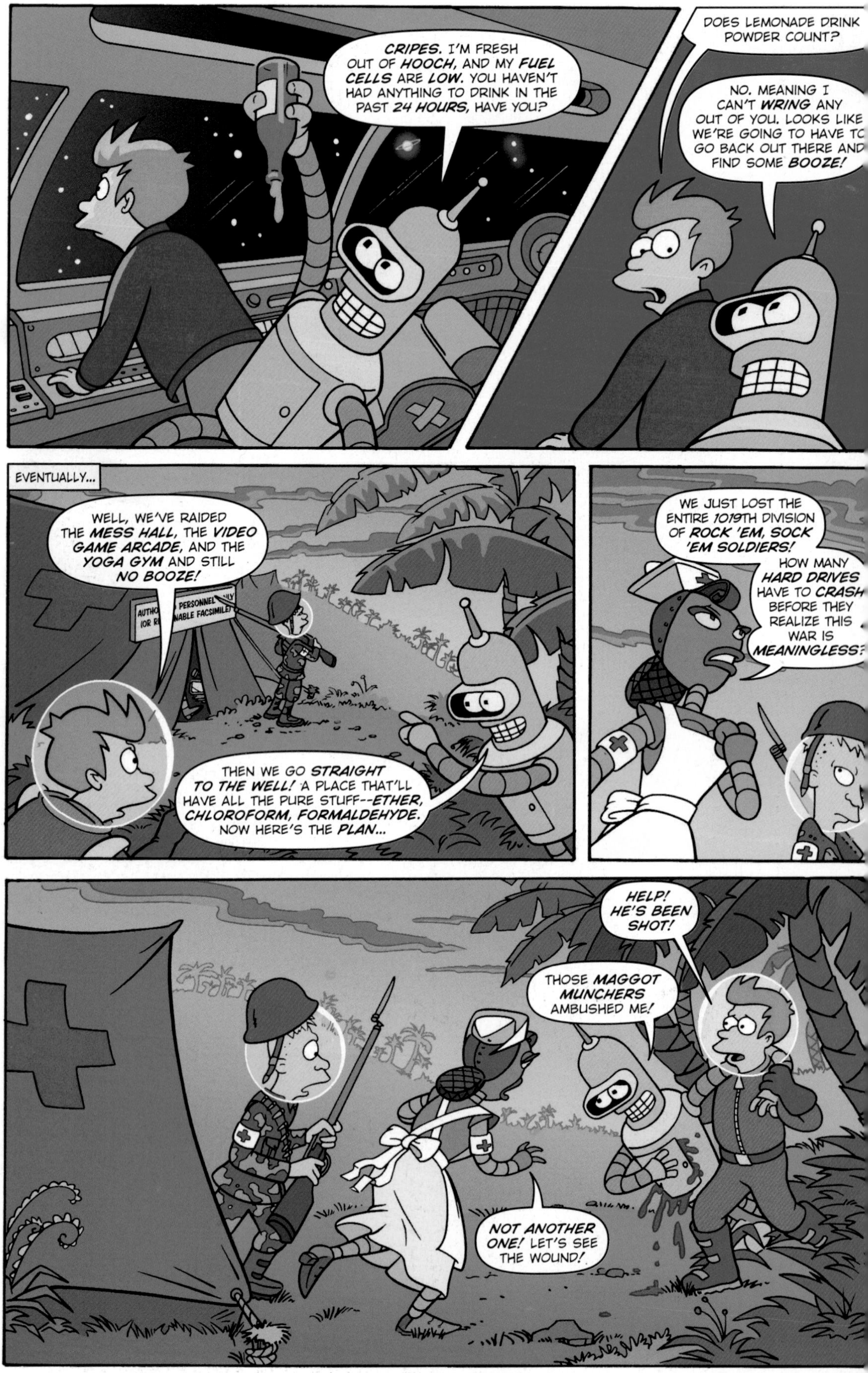
CRIPES. I'M FRESH OUT OF HOOCH, AND MY FUEL CELLS ARE LOW. YOU HAVEN'T HAD ANYTHING TO DRINK IN THE PAST 24 HOURS, HAVE YOU?
DOES LEMONADE DRINK POWDER COUNT?
NO. MEANING I CAN'T WRING ANY OUT OF YOU. LOOKS LIKE WE'RE GOING TO HAVE TO GO BACK OUT THERE AND FIND SOME BOOZE!
EVENTUALLY...
WELL, WE'VE RAIDED THE MESS HALL, THE VIDEO GAME ARCADE, AND THE YOGA GYM AND STILL NO BOOZE!
THEN WE GO STRAIGHT TO THE WELL! A PLACE THAT'LL HAVE ALL THE PURE STUFF--ETHER, CHLOROFORM, FORMALDEHYDE. NOW HERE'S THE PLAN...
WE JUST LOST THE ENTIRE 1019TH DIVISION OF ROCK 'EM, SOCK 'EM SOLDIERS!
HOW MANY HARD DRIVES HAVE TO CRASH BEFORE THEY REALIZE THIS WAR IS MEANINGLESS?
HELP! HE'S BEEN SHOT!
THOSE MAGGOT MUNCHERS AMBUSHED ME!
NOT ANOTHER ONE! LET'S SEE THE WOUND!

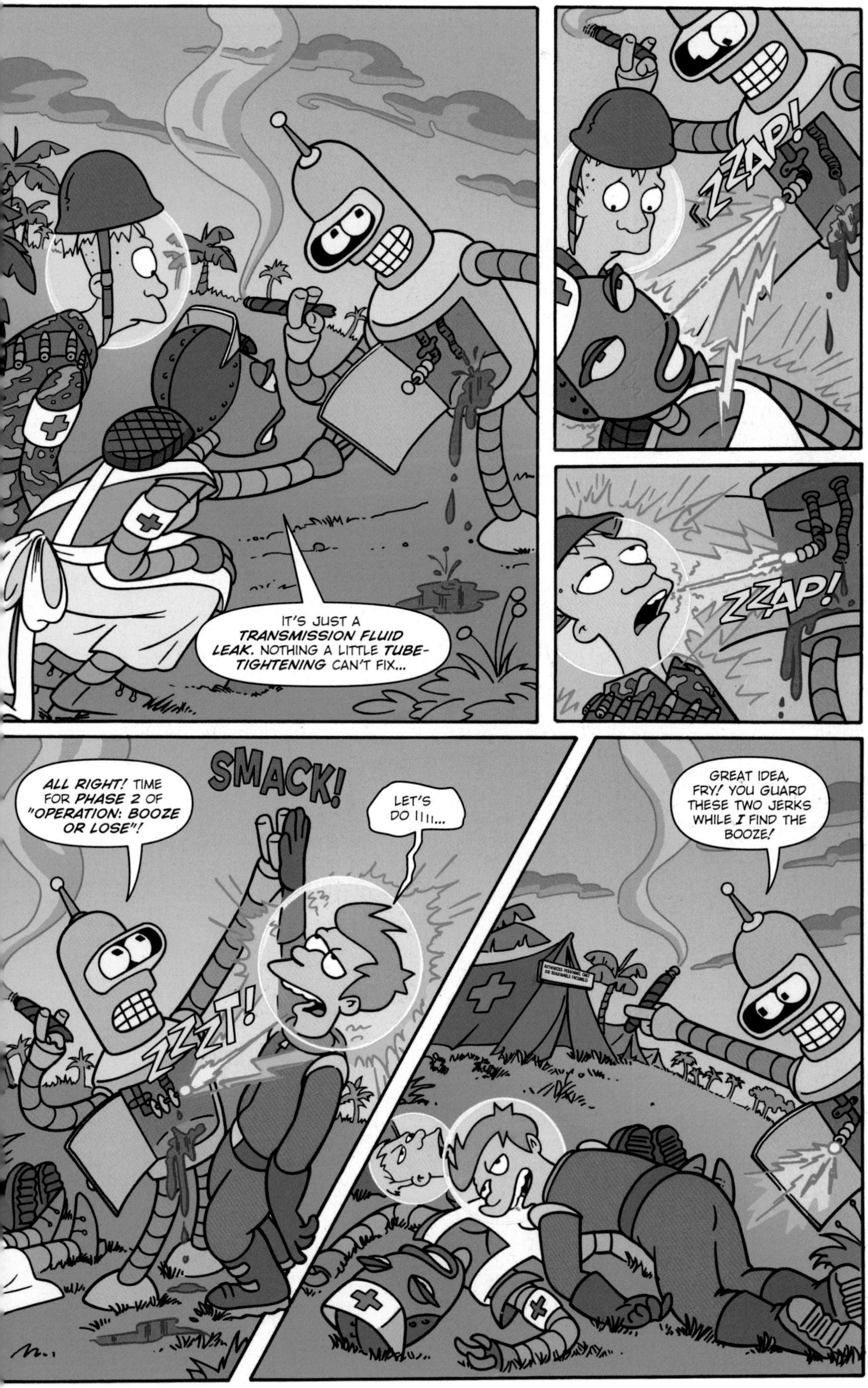
IT'S JUST A TRANSMISSION FLUID LEAK. NOTHING A LITTLE TUBE-TIGHTENING CAN'T FIX...
ZZAP!
ZZAP!
ALL RIGHT! TIME FOR PHASE 2 OF "OPERATION: BOOZE OR LOSE"!
SMACK!
LET'S DO IIII...
ZZZT!
GREAT IDEA, FRY! YOU GUARD THESE TWO JERKS WHILE I FIND THE BOOZE!

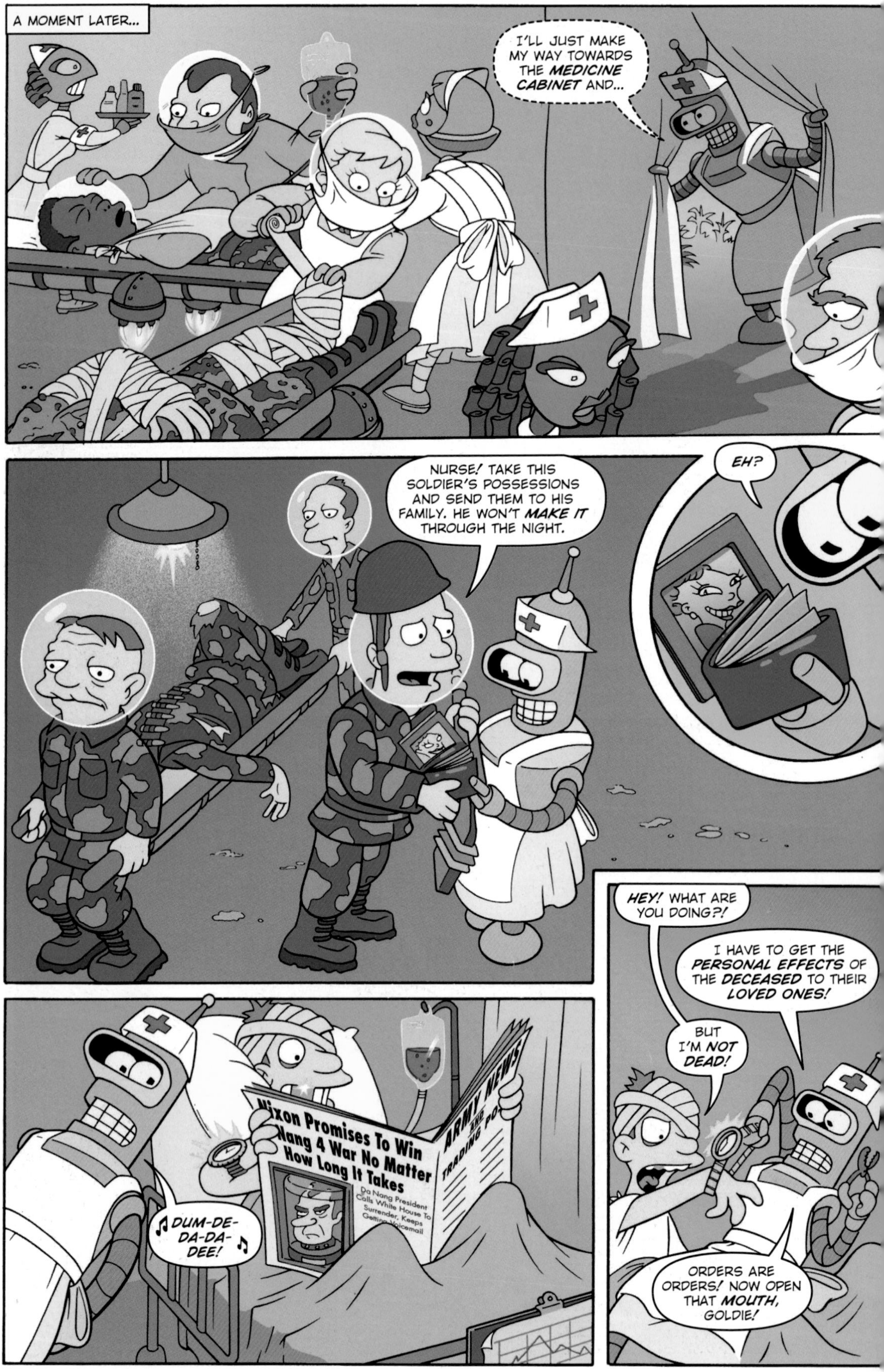

A MOMENT LATER...
I'LL JUST MAKE MY WAY TOWARDS THE MEDICINE CABINET AND...
NURSE! TAKE THIS SOLDIER'S POSSESSIONS AND SEND THEM TO HIS FAMILY. HE WON'T MAKE IT THROUGH THE NIGHT.
EH?
ARMY NEWS
Nixon Promises To Win Nang 4 War No Matter How Long It Takes
Da Nang President Calls White House To Surrender, Keeps Getting Voicemail
♪ DUM-DE-DA-DA-DEE! ♪
HEY! WHAT ARE YOU DOING?!
I HAVE TO GET THE PERSONAL EFFECTS OF THE DECEASED TO THEIR LOVED ONES!
BUT I'M NOT DEAD!
ORDERS ARE ORDERS! NOW OPEN THAT MOUTH, GOLDIE!

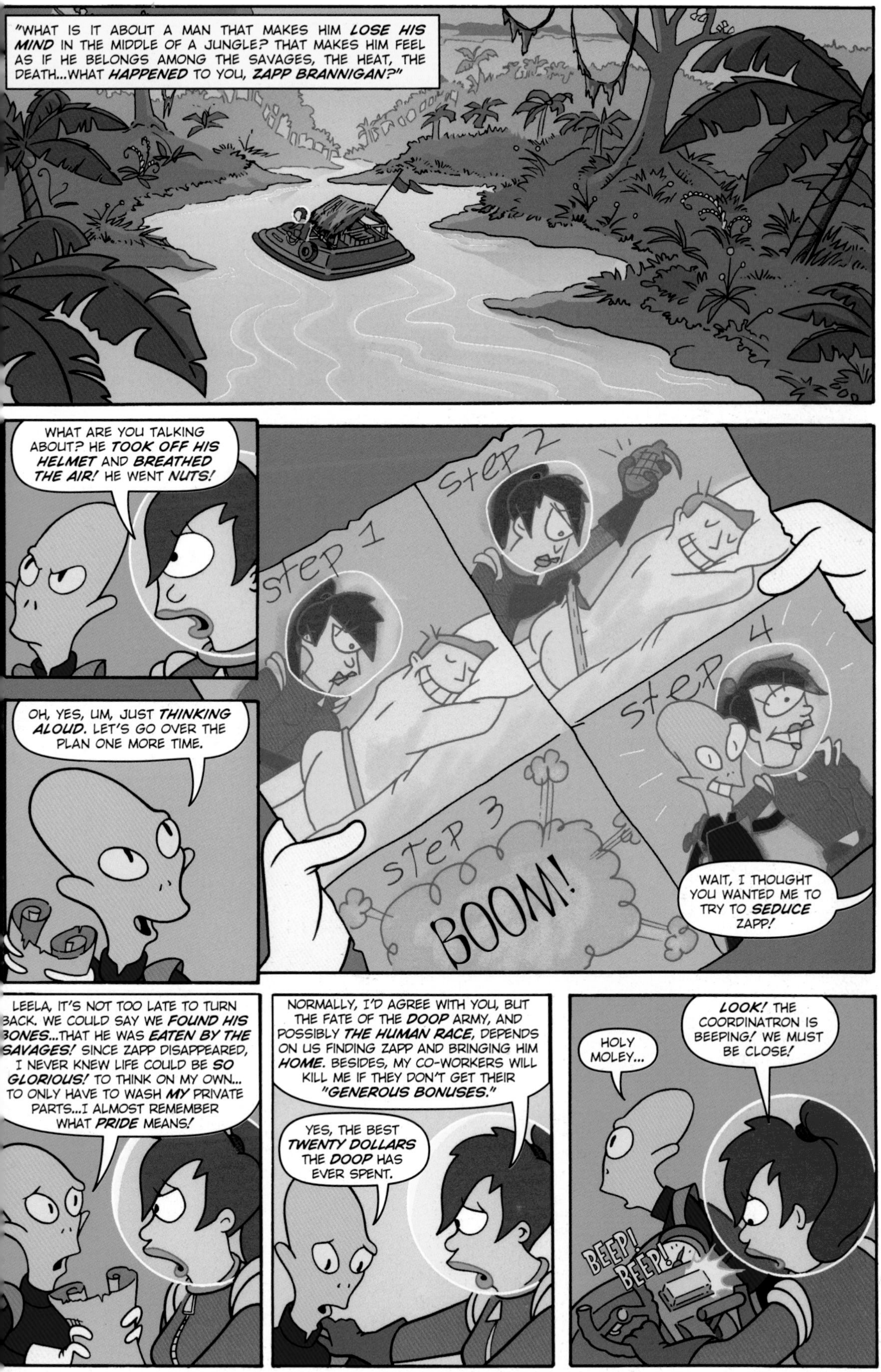
"WHAT IS IT ABOUT A MAN THAT MAKES HIM LOSE HIS MIND IN THE MIDDLE OF A JUNGLE? THAT MAKES HIM FEEL AS IF HE BELONGS AMONG THE SAVAGES, THE HEAT, THE DEATH...WHAT HAPPENED TO YOU, ZAPP BRANNIGAN?"
WHAT ARE YOU TALKING ABOUT? HE TOOK OFF HIS HELMET AND BREATHED THE AIR! HE WENT NUTS!
OH, YES, UM, JUST THINKING ALOUD. LET'S GO OVER THE PLAN ONE MORE TIME.
STEP 1
STEP 2
STEP 3
BOOM!
STEP 4
WAIT, I THOUGHT YOU WANTED ME TO TRY TO SEDUCE ZAPP!
LEELA, IT'S NOT TOO LATE TO TURN BACK. WE COULD SAY WE FOUND HIS BONES...THAT HE WAS EATEN BY THE SAVAGES! SINCE ZAPP DISAPPEARED, I NEVER KNEW LIFE COULD BE SO GLORIOUS! TO THINK ON MY OWN... TO ONLY HAVE TO WASH MY PRIVATE PARTS...I ALMOST REMEMBER WHAT PRIDE MEANS!
NORMALLY, I'D AGREE WITH YOU, BUT THE FATE OF THE DOOP ARMY, AND POSSIBLY THE HUMAN RACE, DEPENDS ON US FINDING ZAPP AND BRINGING HIM HOME. BESIDES, MY CO-WORKERS WILL KILL ME IF THEY DON'T GET THEIR "GENEROUS BONUSES."
YES, THE BEST TWENTY DOLLARS THE DOOP HAS EVER SPENT.
HOLY MOLEY...
LOOK! THE COORDINATRON IS BEEPING! WE MUST BE CLOSE!
BEEP! BEEP!

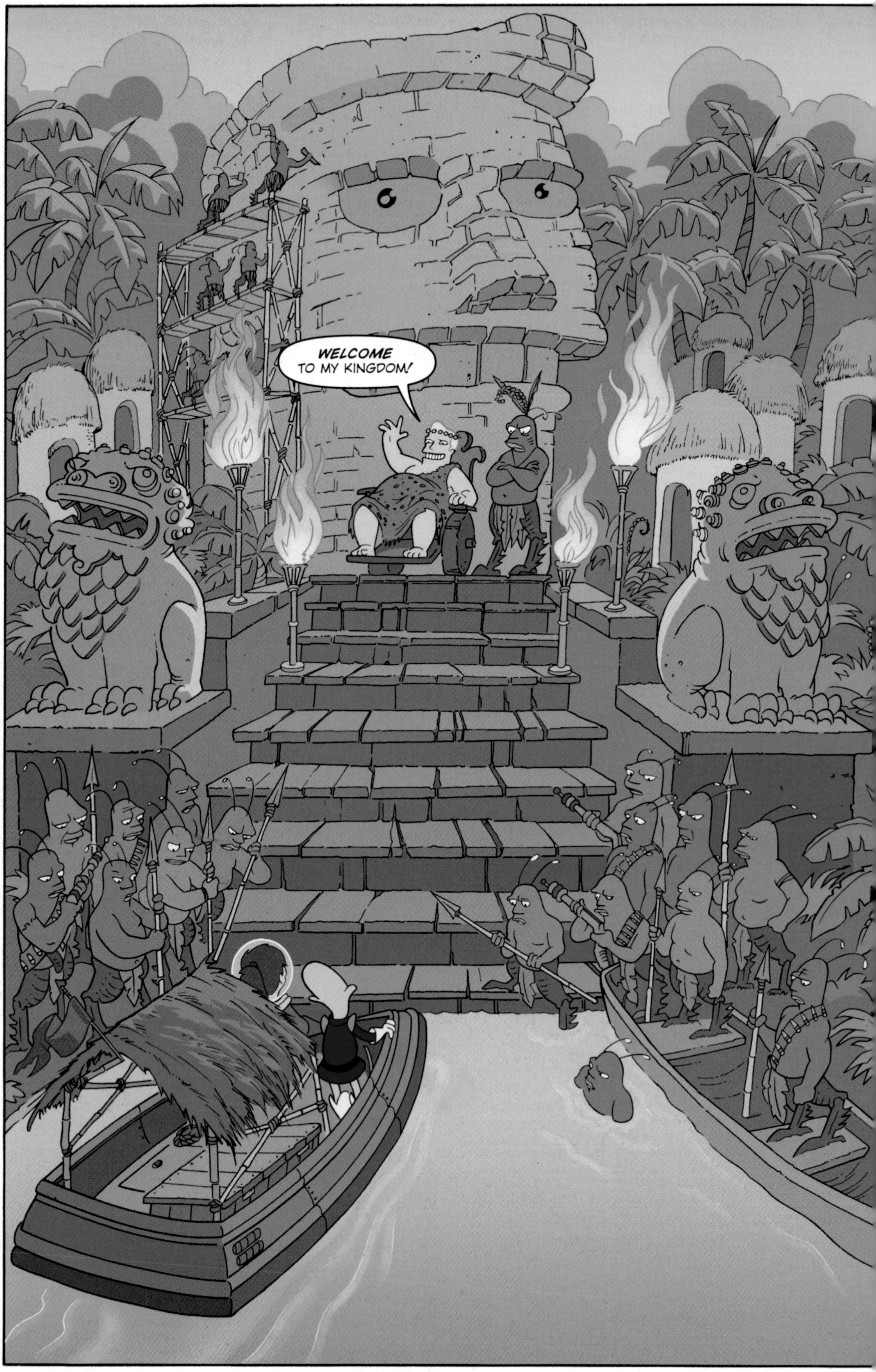
WELCOME TO MY KINGDOM!

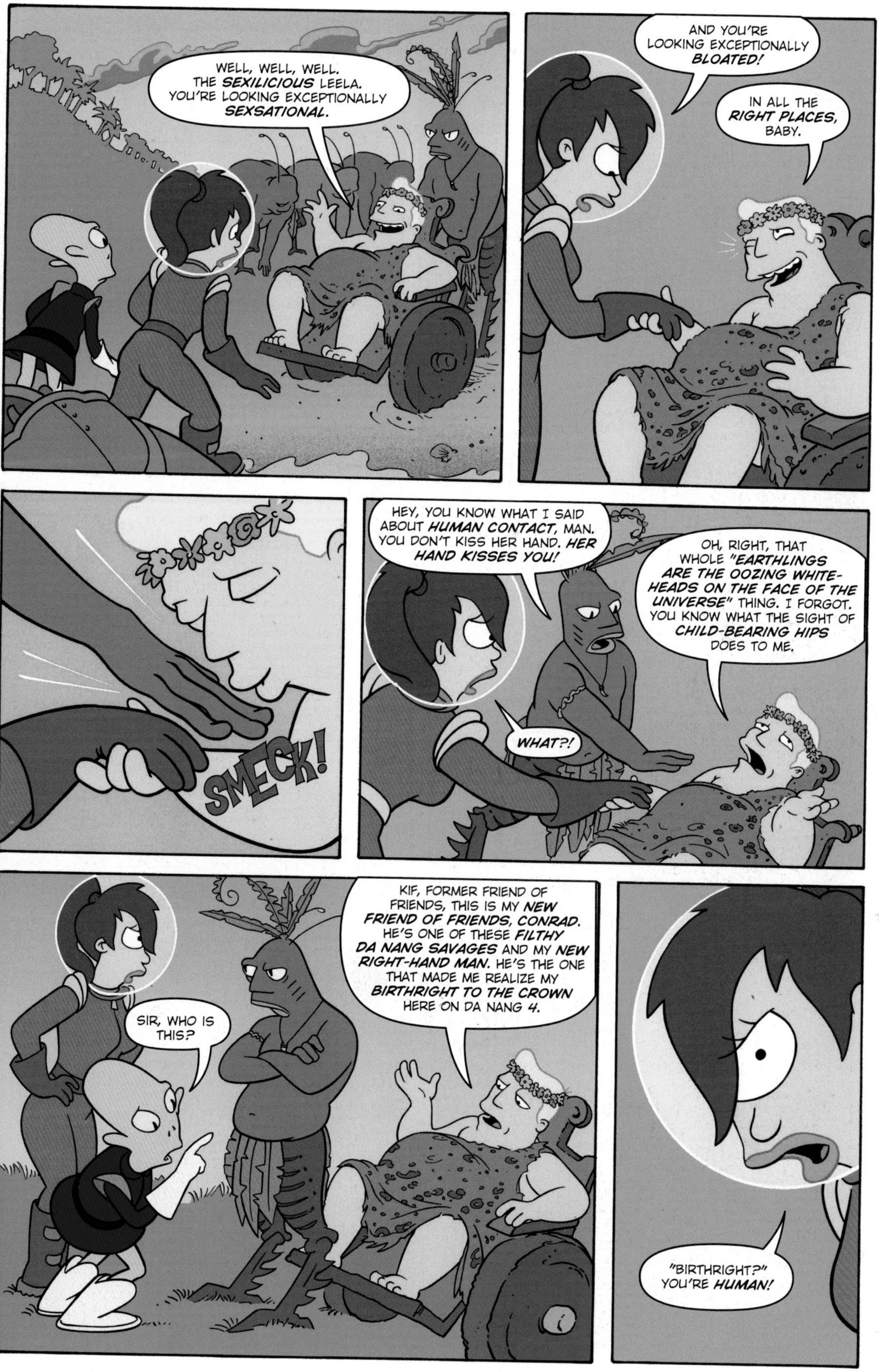

WELL, WELL, WELL. THE SEXILICIOUS LEELA. YOU'RE LOOKING EXCEPTIONALLY SEXSATIONAL.
AND YOU'RE LOOKING EXCEPTIONALLY BLOATED!
IN ALL THE RIGHT PLACES, BABY.
SMECK!
HEY, YOU KNOW WHAT I SAID ABOUT HUMAN CONTACT, MAN. YOU DON'T KISS HER HAND. HER HAND KISSES YOU!
OH, RIGHT, THAT WHOLE "EARTHLINGS ARE THE OOZING WHITE-HEADS ON THE FACE OF THE UNIVERSE" THING. I FORGOT. YOU KNOW WHAT THE SIGHT OF CHILD-BEARING HIPS DOES TO ME.
WHAT?!
SIR, WHO IS THIS?
KIF, FORMER FRIEND OF FRIENDS, THIS IS MY NEW FRIEND OF FRIENDS, CONRAD. HE'S ONE OF THESE FILTHY DA NANG SAVAGES AND MY NEW RIGHT-HAND MAN. HE'S THE ONE THAT MADE ME REALIZE MY BIRTHRIGHT TO THE CROWN HERE ON DA NANG 4.
"BIRTHRIGHT?" YOU'RE HUMAN!

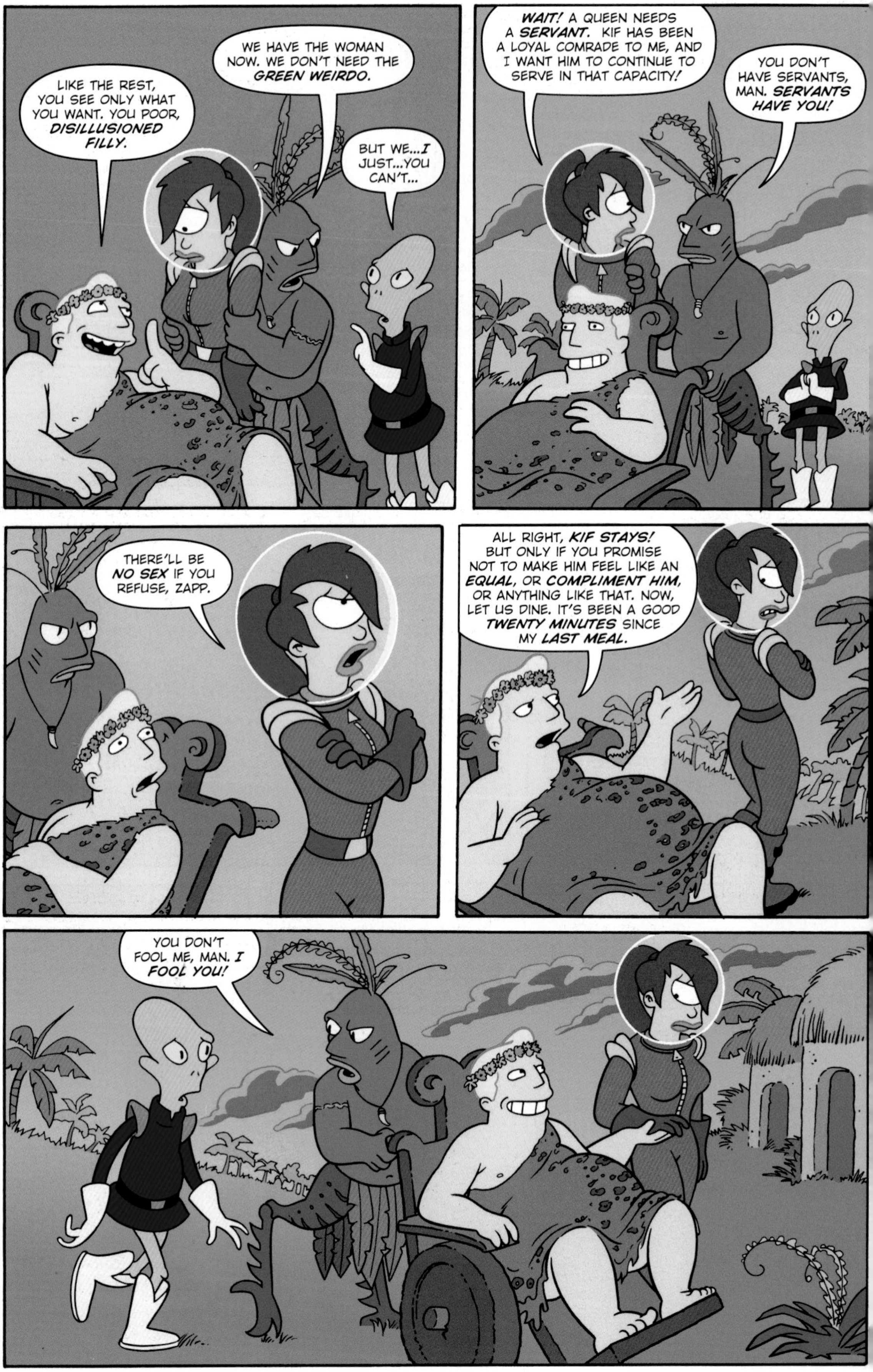
LIKE THE REST, YOU SEE ONLY WHAT YOU WANT. YOU POOR, DISILLUSIONED FILLY.
WE HAVE THE WOMAN NOW. WE DON'T NEED THE GREEN WEIRDO.
BUT WE...I JUST...YOU CAN'T...
WAIT! A QUEEN NEEDS A SERVANT. KIF HAS BEEN A LOYAL COMRADE TO ME, AND I WANT HIM TO CONTINUE TO SERVE IN THAT CAPACITY!
YOU DON'T HAVE SERVANTS, MAN. SERVANTS HAVE YOU!
THERE'LL BE NO SEX IF YOU REFUSE, ZAPP.
ALL RIGHT, KIF STAYS! BUT ONLY IF YOU PROMISE NOT TO MAKE HIM FEEL LIKE AN EQUAL, OR COMPLIMENT HIM, OR ANYTHING LIKE THAT. NOW, LET US DINE. IT'S BEEN A GOOD TWENTY MINUTES SINCE MY LAST MEAL.
YOU DON'T FOOL ME, MAN. I FOOL YOU!

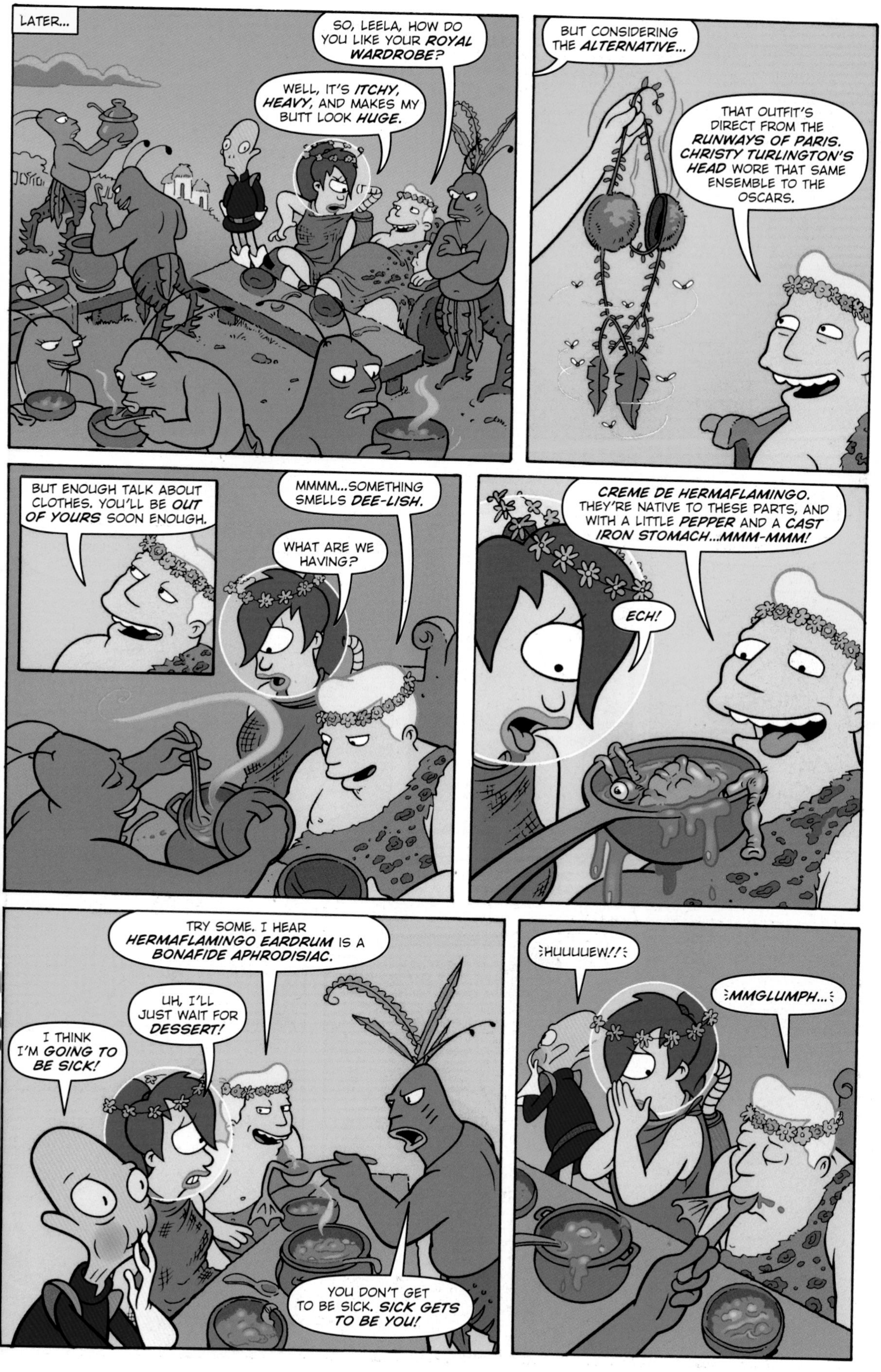
LATER...
SO, LEELA, HOW DO YOU LIKE YOUR ROYAL WARDROBE?
WELL, IT'S ITCHY, HEAVY, AND MAKES MY BUTT LOOK HUGE.
BUT CONSIDERING THE ALTERNATIVE...
THAT OUTFIT'S DIRECT FROM THE RUNWAYS OF PARIS. CHRISTY TURLINGTON'S HEAD WORE THAT SAME ENSEMBLE TO THE OSCARS.
BUT ENOUGH TALK ABOUT CLOTHES. YOU'LL BE OUT OF YOURS SOON ENOUGH.
MMMM...SOMETHING SMELLS DEE-LISH.
WHAT ARE WE HAVING?
CREME DE HERMAFLAMINGO. THEY'RE NATIVE TO THESE PARTS, AND WITH A LITTLE PEPPER AND A CAST IRON STOMACH...MMM-MMM!
ECH!
TRY SOME. I HEAR HERMAFLAMINGO EARDRUM IS A BONAFIDE APHRODISIAC.
UH, I'LL JUST WAIT FOR DESSERT!
I THINK I'M GOING TO BE SICK!
YOU DON'T GET TO BE SICK. SICK GETS TO BE YOU!
HUUUUEW!!
MMGLUMPH...

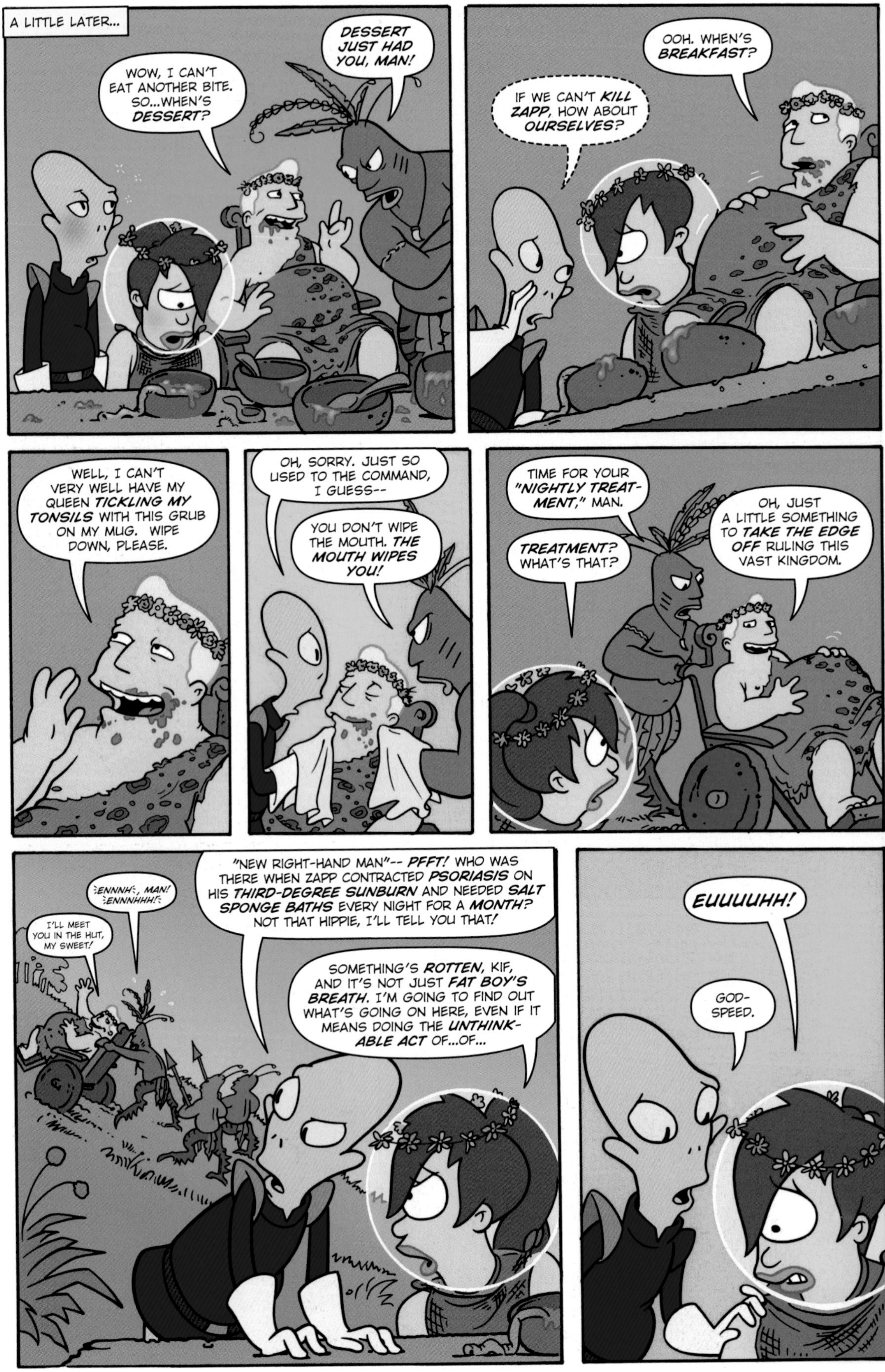
A LITTLE LATER...
WOW, I CAN'T EAT ANOTHER BITE. SO...WHEN'S *DESSERT?*
DESSERT JUST HAD YOU, MAN!
IF WE CAN'T *KILL ZAPP*, HOW ABOUT *OURSELVES?*
OOH. WHEN'S *BREAKFAST?*
WELL, I CAN'T VERY WELL HAVE MY QUEEN *TICKLING MY TONSILS* WITH THIS GRUB ON MY MUG. WIPE DOWN, PLEASE.
OH, SORRY. JUST SO USED TO THE COMMAND, I GUESS--
YOU DON'T WIPE THE MOUTH. *THE MOUTH WIPES YOU!*
TIME FOR YOUR *"NIGHTLY TREATMENT,"* MAN.
TREATMENT? WHAT'S THAT?
OH, JUST A LITTLE SOMETHING TO *TAKE THE EDGE OFF* RULING THIS VAST KINGDOM.
I'LL MEET YOU IN THE HUT, MY SWEET!
ENNNH, MAN! ENNNHHH!*
"NEW RIGHT-HAND MAN"-- *PFFT!* WHO WAS THERE WHEN ZAPP CONTRACTED *PSORIASIS* ON HIS *THIRD-DEGREE SUNBURN* AND NEEDED *SALT SPONGE BATHS* EVERY NIGHT FOR A *MONTH?* NOT THAT HIPPIE, I'LL TELL YOU THAT!
SOMETHING'S *ROTTEN*, KIF, AND IT'S NOT JUST *FAT BOY'S BREATH*. I'M GOING TO FIND OUT WHAT'S GOING ON HERE, EVEN IF IT MEANS DOING THE *UNTHINKABLE ACT* OF...OF...
EUUUUHH!
GOD-SPEED.

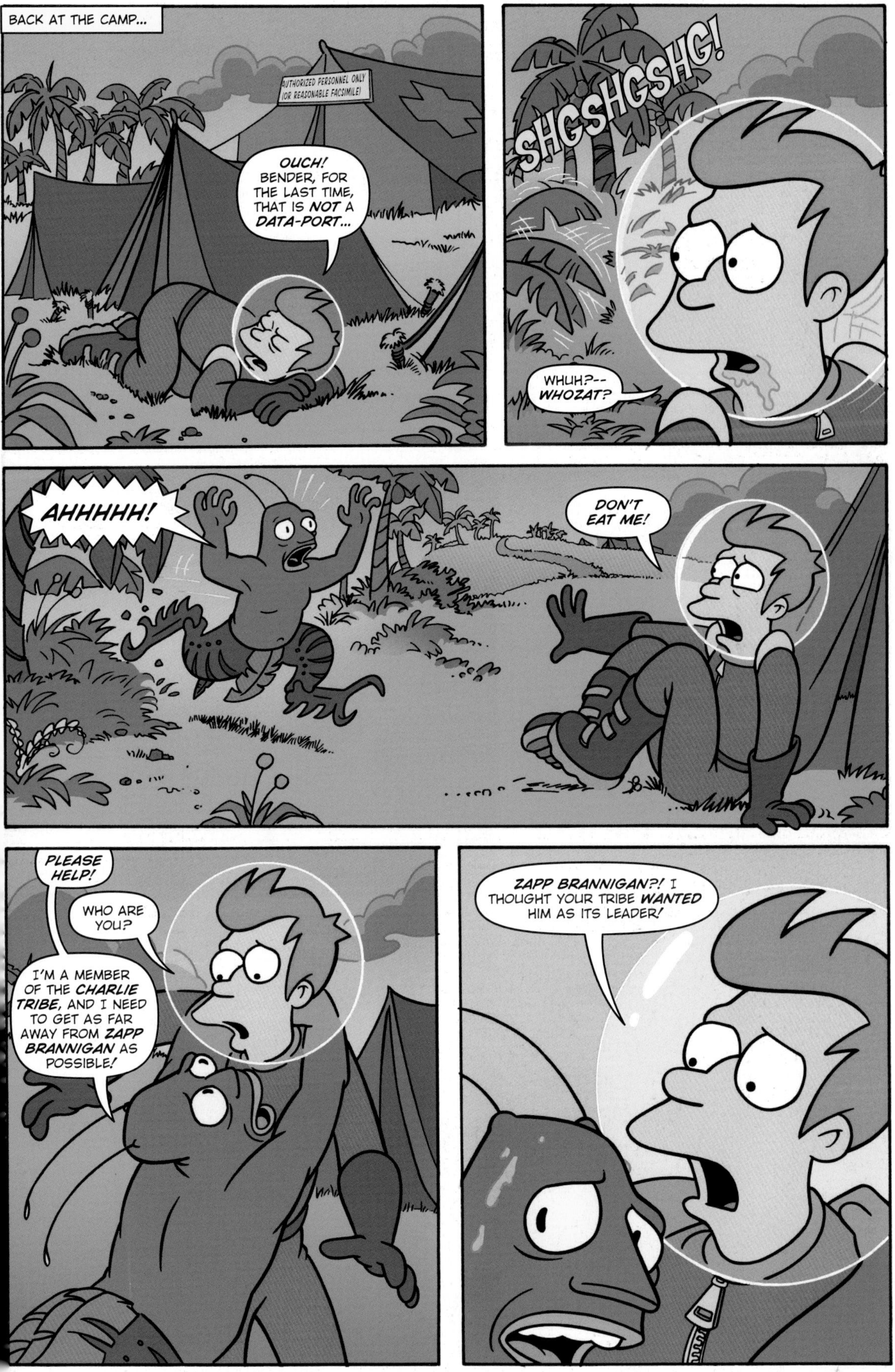
BACK AT THE CAMP...
AUTHORIZED PERSONNEL ONLY (OR REASONABLE FACSIMILE)
OUCH! BENDER, FOR THE LAST TIME, THAT IS NOT A DATA-PORT...
SHGSHGSHG!
WHUH?-- WHOZAT?
AHHHHH!
DON'T EAT ME!
PLEASE HELP!
WHO ARE YOU?
I'M A MEMBER OF THE CHARLIE TRIBE, AND I NEED TO GET AS FAR AWAY FROM ZAPP BRANNIGAN AS POSSIBLE!
ZAPP BRANNIGAN?! I THOUGHT YOUR TRIBE WANTED HIM AS ITS LEADER!

NEVER! HE *THINKS* HE'S THE KING OF OUR TRIBE, BUT WE'RE ONLY *USING HIM* FOR A *SNEAK ATTACK* ON THE *DOOP!*

I TELL YOU THIS BECAUSE I'LL *SHOOT MYSELF* IF I HAVE TO SERVE HIS *PUP-TENT WEARING BUTT* ANOTHER MINUTE!

AUTHORIZED PERSONNEL ONLY (OR REASONABLE FACSIMILE)

FRY, LET ME HELP THIS POOR, WOUNDED, *HOPEFULLY WEALTHY* SOLDIER!

HE'S PART OF ZAPP'S *TRIBE!*

GOT ANY *MONEY?*

NO.

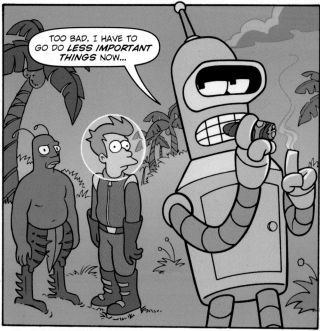

TOO BAD. I HAVE TO GO DO *LESS IMPORTANT THINGS* NOW...

WAIT, BENDER! THE *DOOP'S* BEING *SET UP!* THEY NEED OUR *HELP!*

WOW, REALLY? LET ME THINK... *NOPE. NOT INTERESTED.* I'M GOING BACK TO THE SHIP TO *REFUEL MY CELLS.*

BUT *YOU* HAVE A GOOD TIME WITH THAT *"RISKING YOUR LIFE"* THING.

MOR-FIEND BRAND PAIN REDUCER THE ADDICT'S CHOICE

AS USUAL, IT'S UP TO *ME* TO SAVE THE UNIVERSE. *TAKE ME TO YOUR LEADER!*

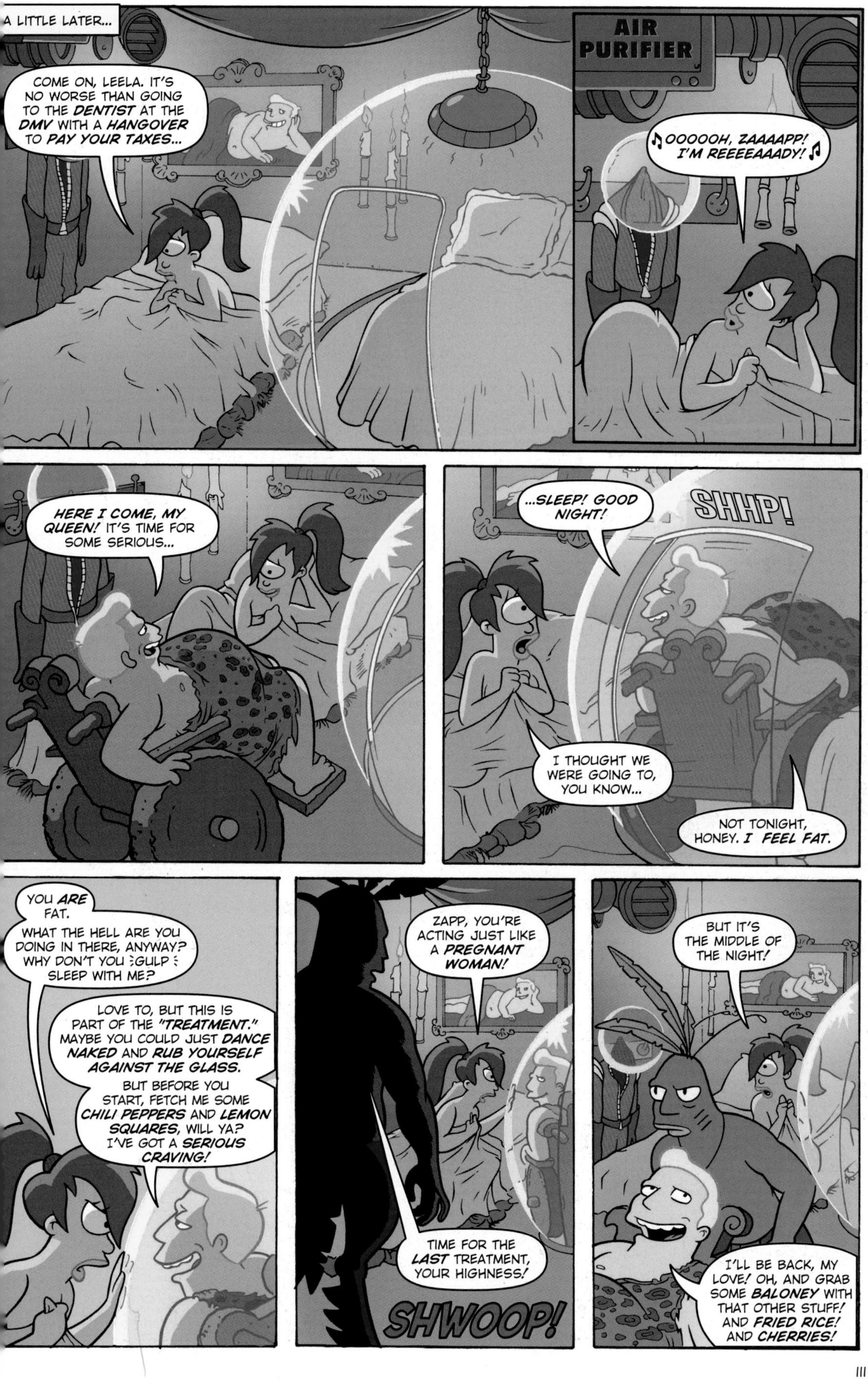
A LITTLE LATER...
COME ON, LEELA. IT'S NO WORSE THAN GOING TO THE DENTIST AT THE DMV WITH A HANGOVER TO PAY YOUR TAXES...
AIR PURIFIER
♫ OOOOOH, ZAAAAPP! I'M REEEEAAADY! ♫
HERE I COME, MY QUEEN! IT'S TIME FOR SOME SERIOUS...
...SLEEP! GOOD NIGHT!
SHHP!
I THOUGHT WE WERE GOING TO, YOU KNOW...
NOT TONIGHT, HONEY. I FEEL FAT.
YOU ARE FAT.
WHAT THE HELL ARE YOU DOING IN THERE, ANYWAY? WHY DON'T YOU ⁝GULP⁝ SLEEP WITH ME?
LOVE TO, BUT THIS IS PART OF THE "TREATMENT." MAYBE YOU COULD JUST DANCE NAKED AND RUB YOURSELF AGAINST THE GLASS.
BUT BEFORE YOU START, FETCH ME SOME CHILI PEPPERS AND LEMON SQUARES, WILL YA? I'VE GOT A SERIOUS CRAVING!
ZAPP, YOU'RE ACTING JUST LIKE A PREGNANT WOMAN!
TIME FOR THE LAST TREATMENT, YOUR HIGHNESS!
SHWOOP!
BUT IT'S THE MIDDLE OF THE NIGHT!
I'LL BE BACK, MY LOVE! OH, AND GRAB SOME BALONEY WITH THAT OTHER STUFF! AND FRIED RICE! AND CHERRIES!

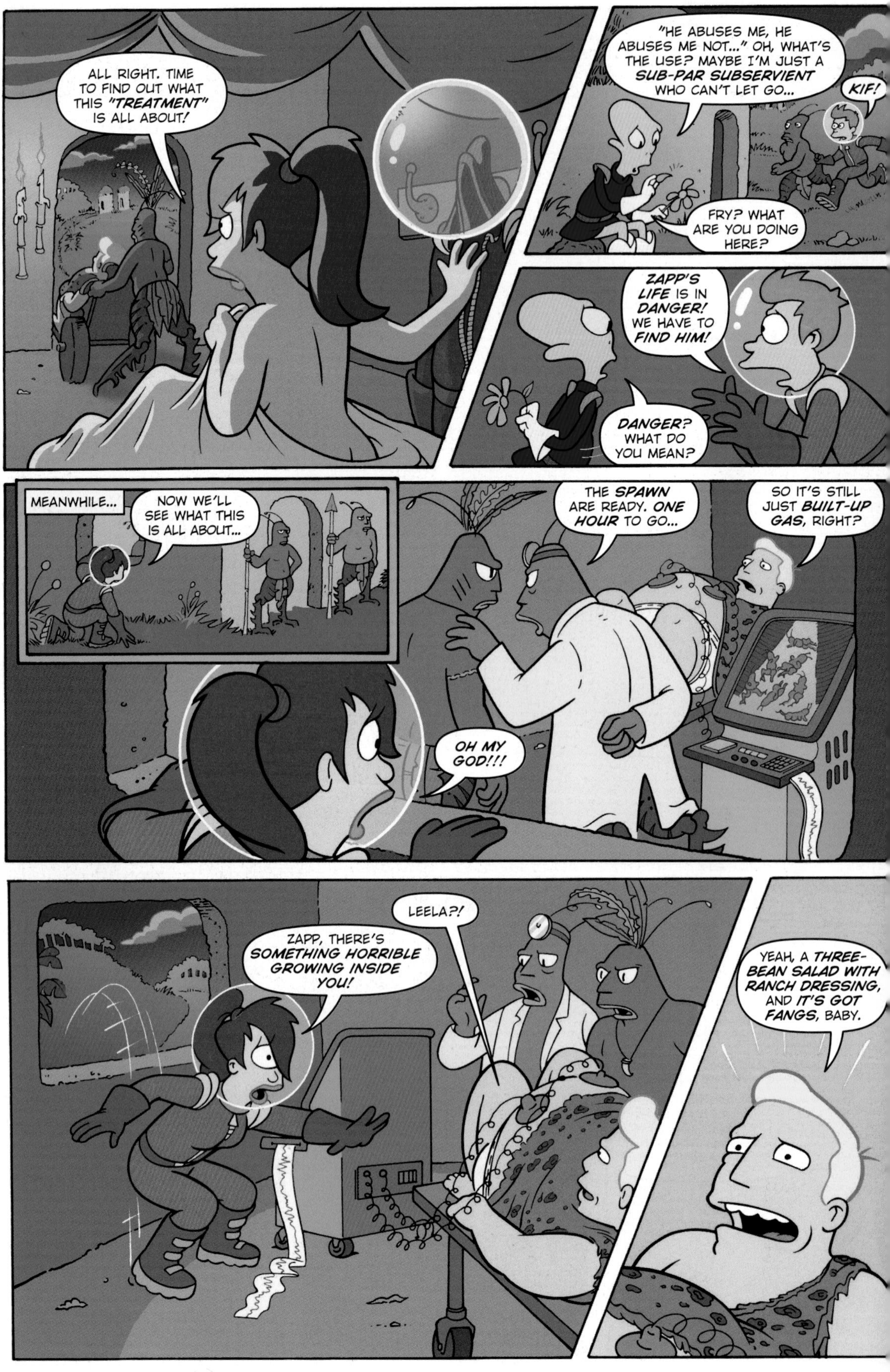
ALL RIGHT. TIME TO FIND OUT WHAT THIS "TREATMENT" IS ALL ABOUT!
"HE ABUSES ME, HE ABUSES ME NOT..." OH, WHAT'S THE USE? MAYBE I'M JUST A SUB-PAR SUBSERVIENT WHO CAN'T LET GO...
KIF!
FRY? WHAT ARE YOU DOING HERE?
ZAPP'S LIFE IS IN DANGER! WE HAVE TO FIND HIM!
DANGER? WHAT DO YOU MEAN?
MEANWHILE...
NOW WE'LL SEE WHAT THIS IS ALL ABOUT...
THE SPAWN ARE READY. ONE HOUR TO GO...
SO IT'S STILL JUST BUILT-UP GAS, RIGHT?
OH MY GOD!!!
LEELA?!
ZAPP, THERE'S SOMETHING HORRIBLE GROWING INSIDE YOU!
YEAH, A THREE-BEAN SALAD WITH RANCH DRESSING, AND IT'S GOT FANGS, BABY.

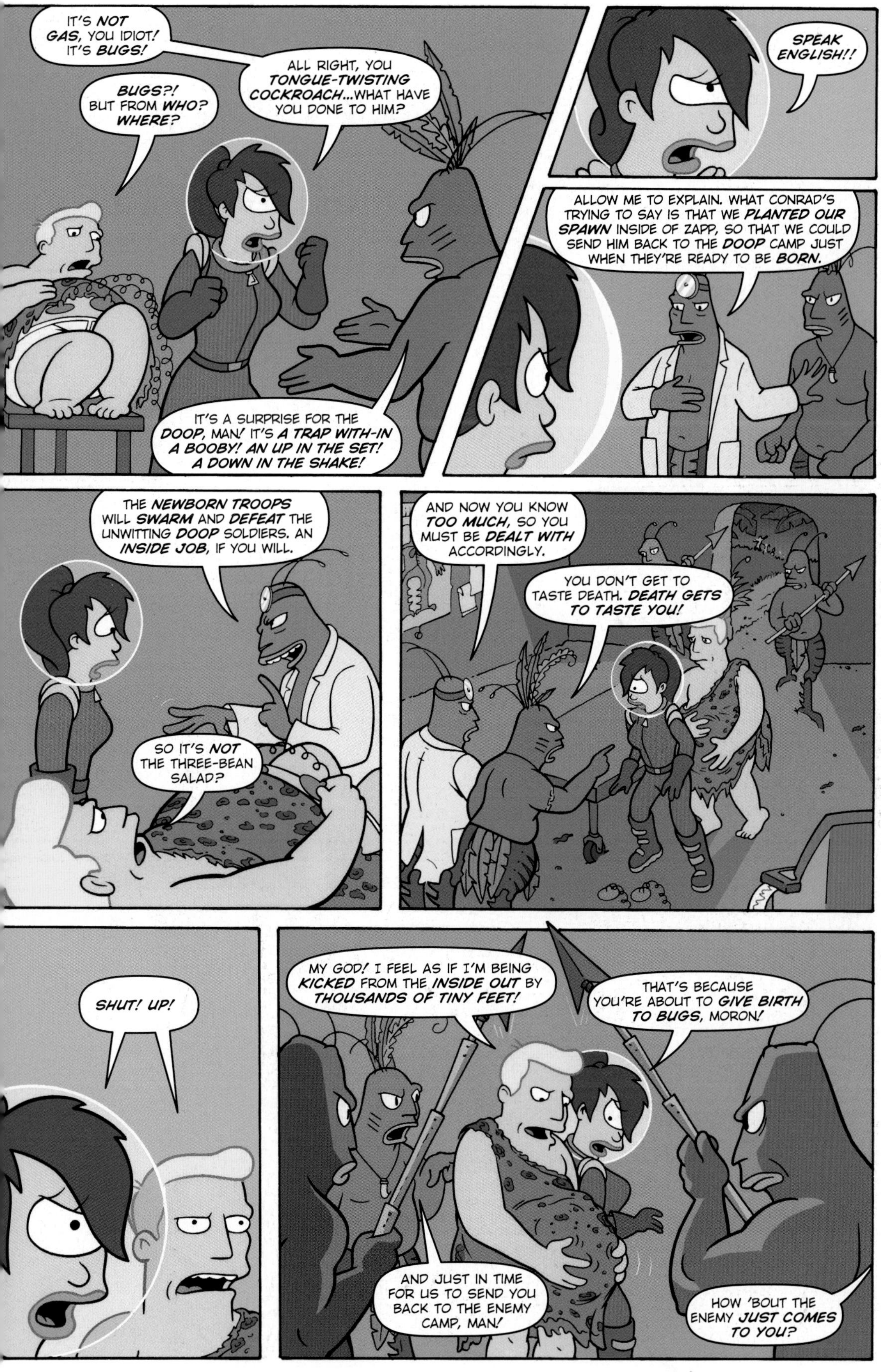
IT'S NOT GAS, YOU IDIOT! IT'S BUGS!
BUGS?! BUT FROM WHO? WHERE?
ALL RIGHT, YOU TONGUE-TWISTING COCKROACH...WHAT HAVE YOU DONE TO HIM?
IT'S A SURPRISE FOR THE DOOP, MAN! IT'S A TRAP WITH-IN A BOOBY! AN UP IN THE SET! A DOWN IN THE SHAKE!
SPEAK ENGLISH!!
ALLOW ME TO EXPLAIN. WHAT CONRAD'S TRYING TO SAY IS THAT WE PLANTED OUR SPAWN INSIDE OF ZAPP, SO THAT WE COULD SEND HIM BACK TO THE DOOP CAMP JUST WHEN THEY'RE READY TO BE BORN.
THE NEWBORN TROOPS WILL SWARM AND DEFEAT THE UNWITTING DOOP SOLDIERS. AN INSIDE JOB, IF YOU WILL.
SO IT'S NOT THE THREE-BEAN SALAD?
AND NOW YOU KNOW TOO MUCH, SO YOU MUST BE DEALT WITH ACCORDINGLY.
YOU DON'T GET TO TASTE DEATH. DEATH GETS TO TASTE YOU!
SHUT! UP!
MY GOD! I FEEL AS IF I'M BEING KICKED FROM THE INSIDE OUT BY THOUSANDS OF TINY FEET!
THAT'S BECAUSE YOU'RE ABOUT TO GIVE BIRTH TO BUGS, MORON!
AND JUST IN TIME FOR US TO SEND YOU BACK TO THE ENEMY CAMP, MAN!
HOW 'BOUT THE ENEMY JUST COMES TO YOU?

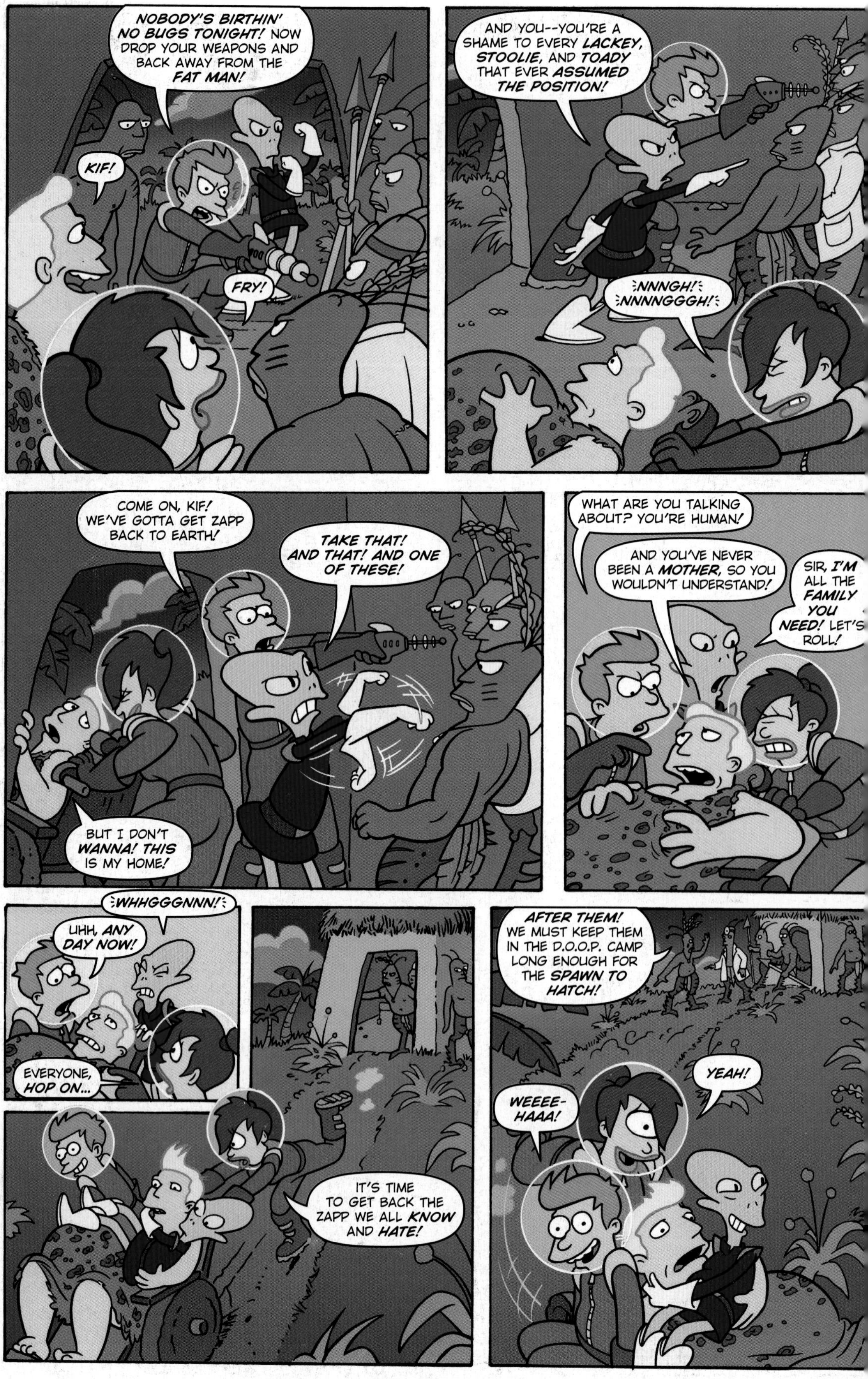
NOBODY'S BIRTHIN' NO BUGS TONIGHT! NOW DROP YOUR WEAPONS AND BACK AWAY FROM THE FAT MAN!
KIF!
FRY!
AND YOU--YOU'RE A SHAME TO EVERY LACKEY, STOOLIE, AND TOADY THAT EVER ASSUMED THE POSITION!
NNNGH! NNNNGGGH!
COME ON, KIF! WE'VE GOTTA GET ZAPP BACK TO EARTH!
TAKE THAT! AND THAT! AND ONE OF THESE!
BUT I DON'T WANNA! THIS IS MY HOME!
WHAT ARE YOU TALKING ABOUT? YOU'RE HUMAN!
AND YOU'VE NEVER BEEN A MOTHER, SO YOU WOULDN'T UNDERSTAND!
SIR, I'M ALL THE FAMILY YOU NEED! LET'S ROLL!
WHHGGGNNN!
UHH, ANY DAY NOW!
EVERYONE, HOP ON...
IT'S TIME TO GET BACK THE ZAPP WE ALL KNOW AND HATE!
AFTER THEM! WE MUST KEEP THEM IN THE D.O.O.P. CAMP LONG ENOUGH FOR THE SPAWN TO HATCH!
YEAH!
WEEEE-HAAA!

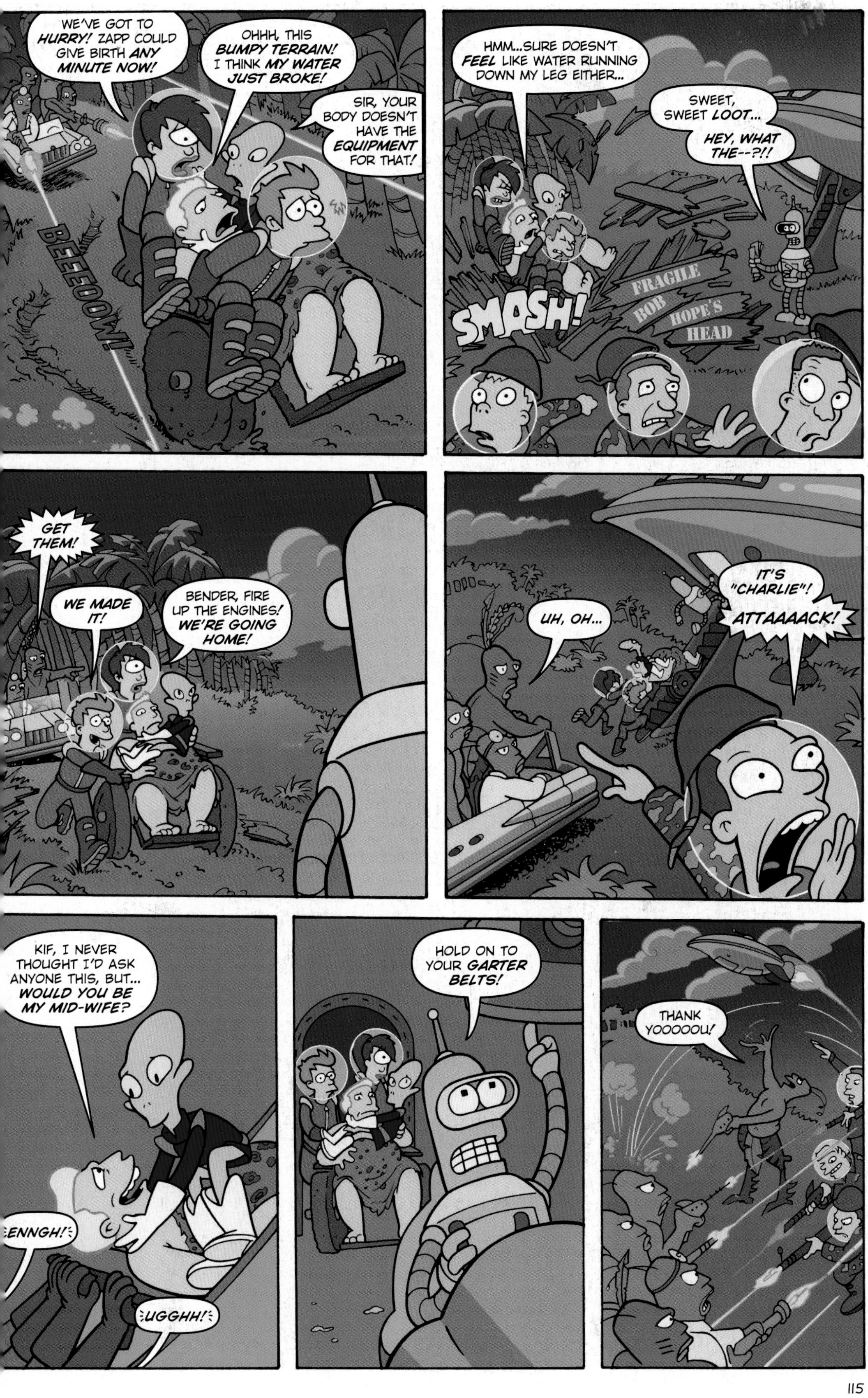
WE'VE GOT TO HURRY! ZAPP COULD GIVE BIRTH ANY MINUTE NOW!
OHHH, THIS BUMPY TERRAIN! I THINK MY WATER JUST BROKE!
SIR, YOUR BODY DOESN'T HAVE THE EQUIPMENT FOR THAT!
BEEEOOW!
HMM...SURE DOESN'T FEEL LIKE WATER RUNNING DOWN MY LEG EITHER...
SWEET, SWEET LOOT...
HEY, WHAT THE--?!!
SMASH!
FRAGILE
BOB HOPE'S HEAD
GET THEM!
WE MADE IT!
BENDER, FIRE UP THE ENGINES! WE'RE GOING HOME!
UH, OH...
IT'S "CHARLIE"!
ATTAAAACK!
KIF, I NEVER THOUGHT I'D ASK ANYONE THIS, BUT... WOULD YOU BE MY MID-WIFE?
ENNGH!
UGGHH!
HOLD ON TO YOUR GARTER BELTS!
THANK YOOOOOU!

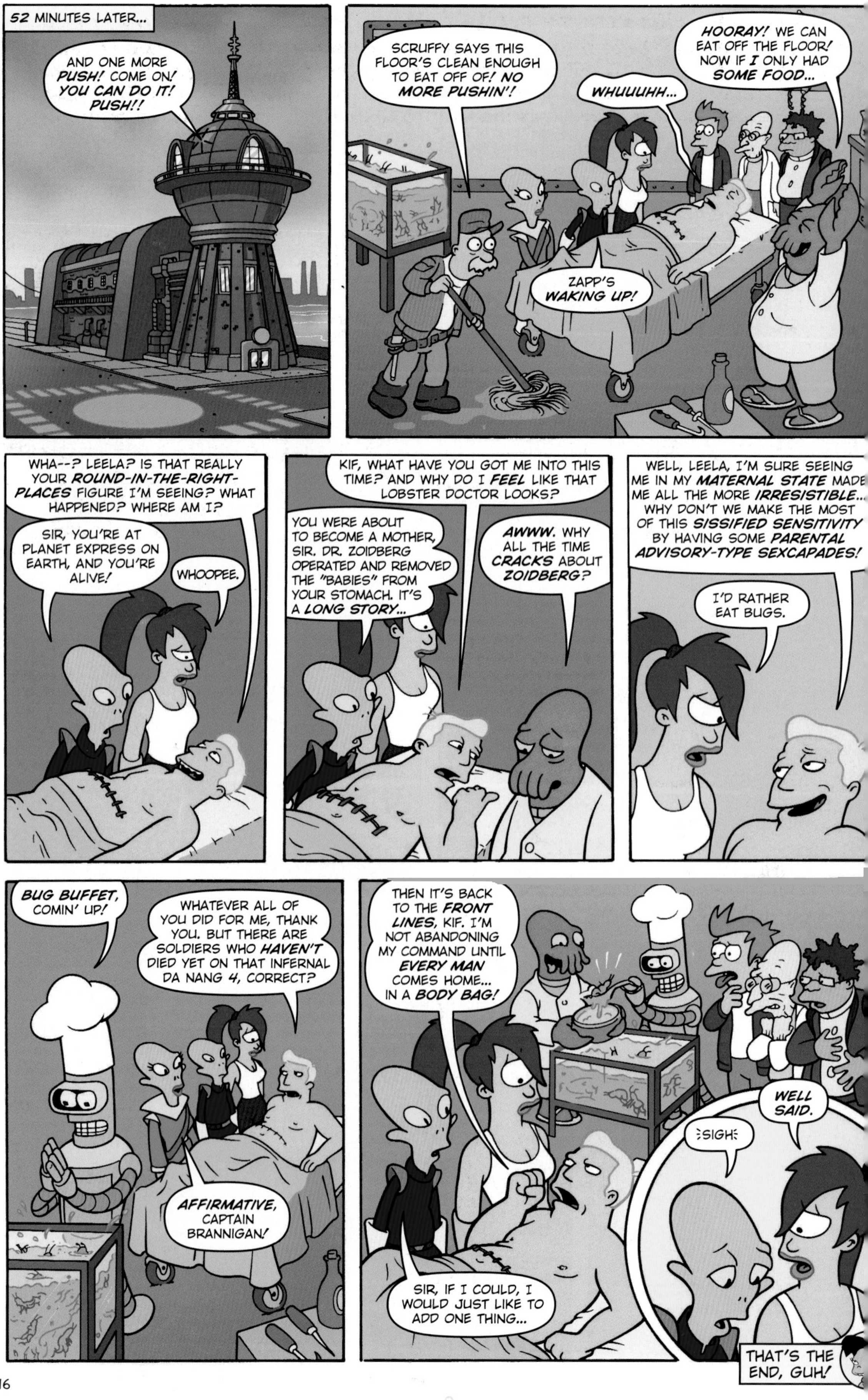

52 MINUTES LATER...
AND ONE MORE PUSH! COME ON! YOU CAN DO IT! PUSH!!
SCRUFFY SAYS THIS FLOOR'S CLEAN ENOUGH TO EAT OFF OF! NO MORE PUSHIN'!
WHUUUHH...
HOORAY! WE CAN EAT OFF THE FLOOR! NOW IF I ONLY HAD SOME FOOD...
ZAPP'S WAKING UP!
WHA--? LEELA? IS THAT REALLY YOUR ROUND-IN-THE-RIGHT-PLACES FIGURE I'M SEEING? WHAT HAPPENED? WHERE AM I?
SIR, YOU'RE AT PLANET EXPRESS ON EARTH, AND YOU'RE ALIVE!
WHOOPEE.
KIF, WHAT HAVE YOU GOT ME INTO THIS TIME? AND WHY DO I FEEL LIKE THAT LOBSTER DOCTOR LOOKS?
YOU WERE ABOUT TO BECOME A MOTHER, SIR. DR. ZOIDBERG OPERATED AND REMOVED THE "BABIES" FROM YOUR STOMACH. IT'S A LONG STORY...
AWWW. WHY ALL THE TIME CRACKS ABOUT ZOIDBERG?
WELL, LEELA, I'M SURE SEEING ME IN MY MATERNAL STATE MADE ME ALL THE MORE IRRESISTIBLE... WHY DON'T WE MAKE THE MOST OF THIS SISSIFIED SENSITIVITY BY HAVING SOME PARENTAL ADVISORY-TYPE SEXCAPADES!
I'D RATHER EAT BUGS.
BUG BUFFET, COMIN' UP!
WHATEVER ALL OF YOU DID FOR ME, THANK YOU. BUT THERE ARE SOLDIERS WHO HAVEN'T DIED YET ON THAT INFERNAL DA NANG 4, CORRECT?
AFFIRMATIVE, CAPTAIN BRANNIGAN!
THEN IT'S BACK TO THE FRONT LINES, KIF. I'M NOT ABANDONING MY COMMAND UNTIL EVERY MAN COMES HOME... IN A BODY BAG!
WELL SAID.
SIR, IF I COULD, I WOULD JUST LIKE TO ADD ONE THING...
:SIGH:
THAT'S THE END, GUH!

Philip J. Fry didn't become everyone's favorite animated space adventurer overnight. Creating the look of Fry and the other characters on Futurama took Matt Groening and his crack team of artists over 2 years from conception to animated life. The experiments along the way weren't always perfect, but the final product was well worth the long, sweaty hours of pencil-pushing! Bongo proudly presents an inside look at...

THE FRY THAT TIME FORGOT

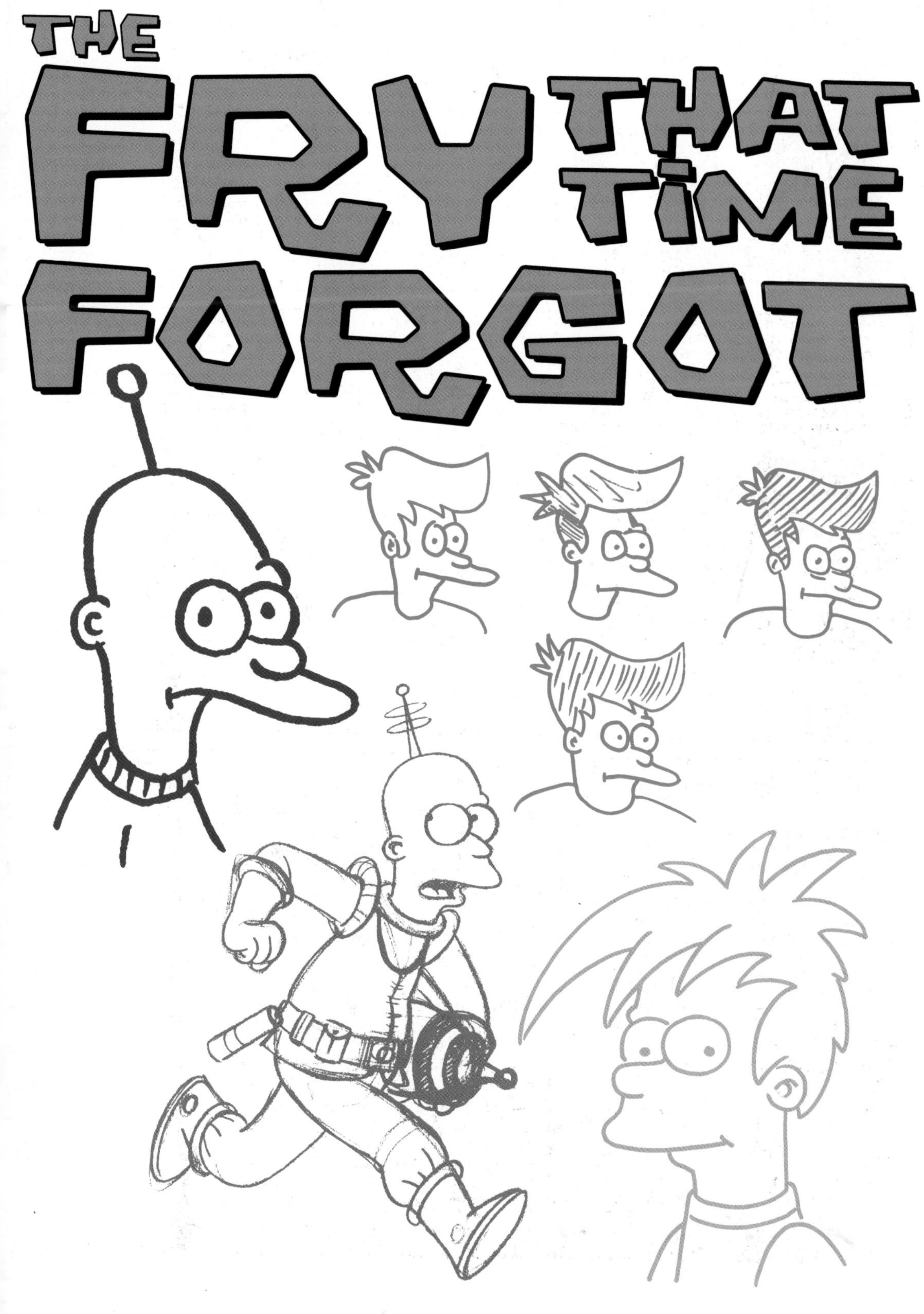

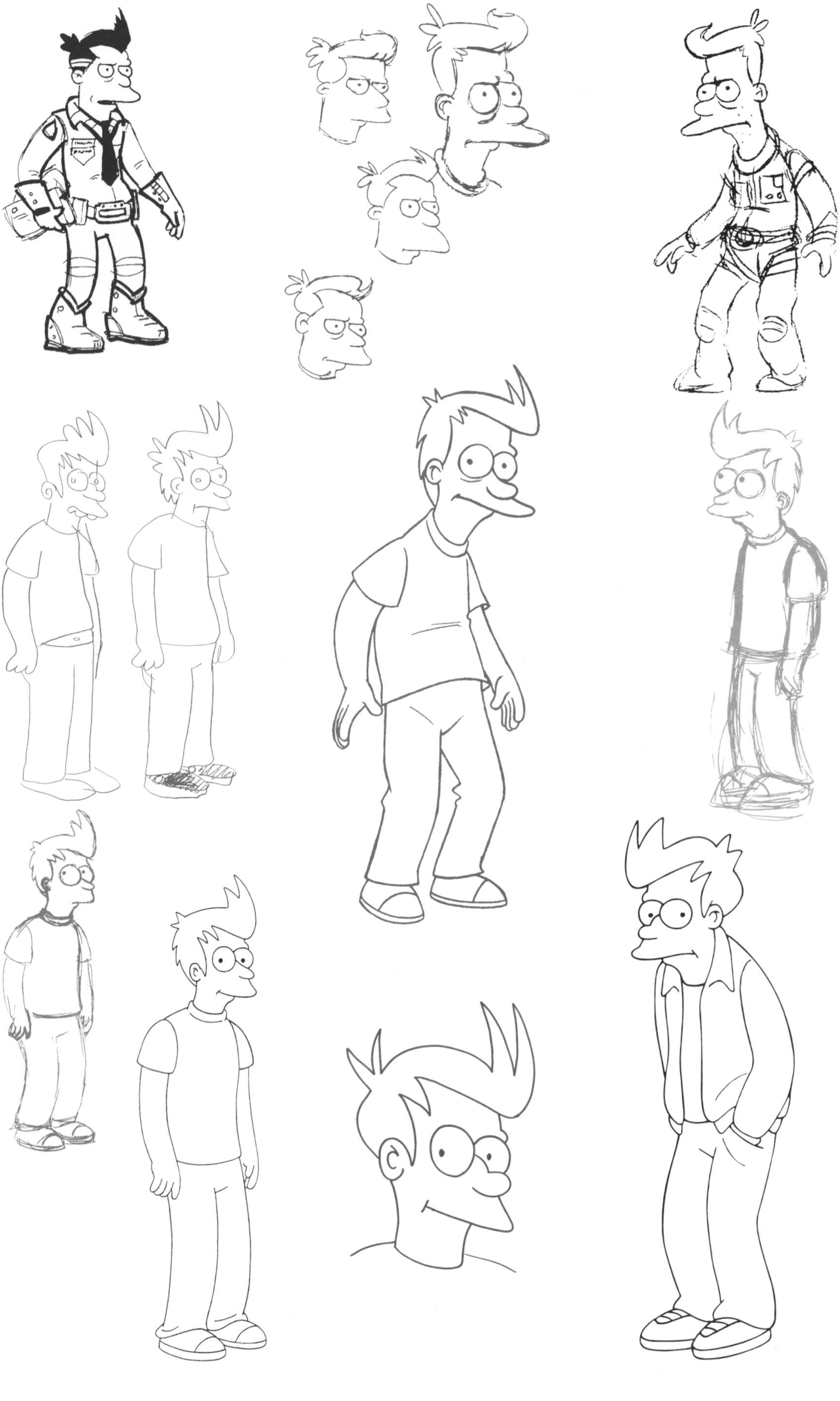

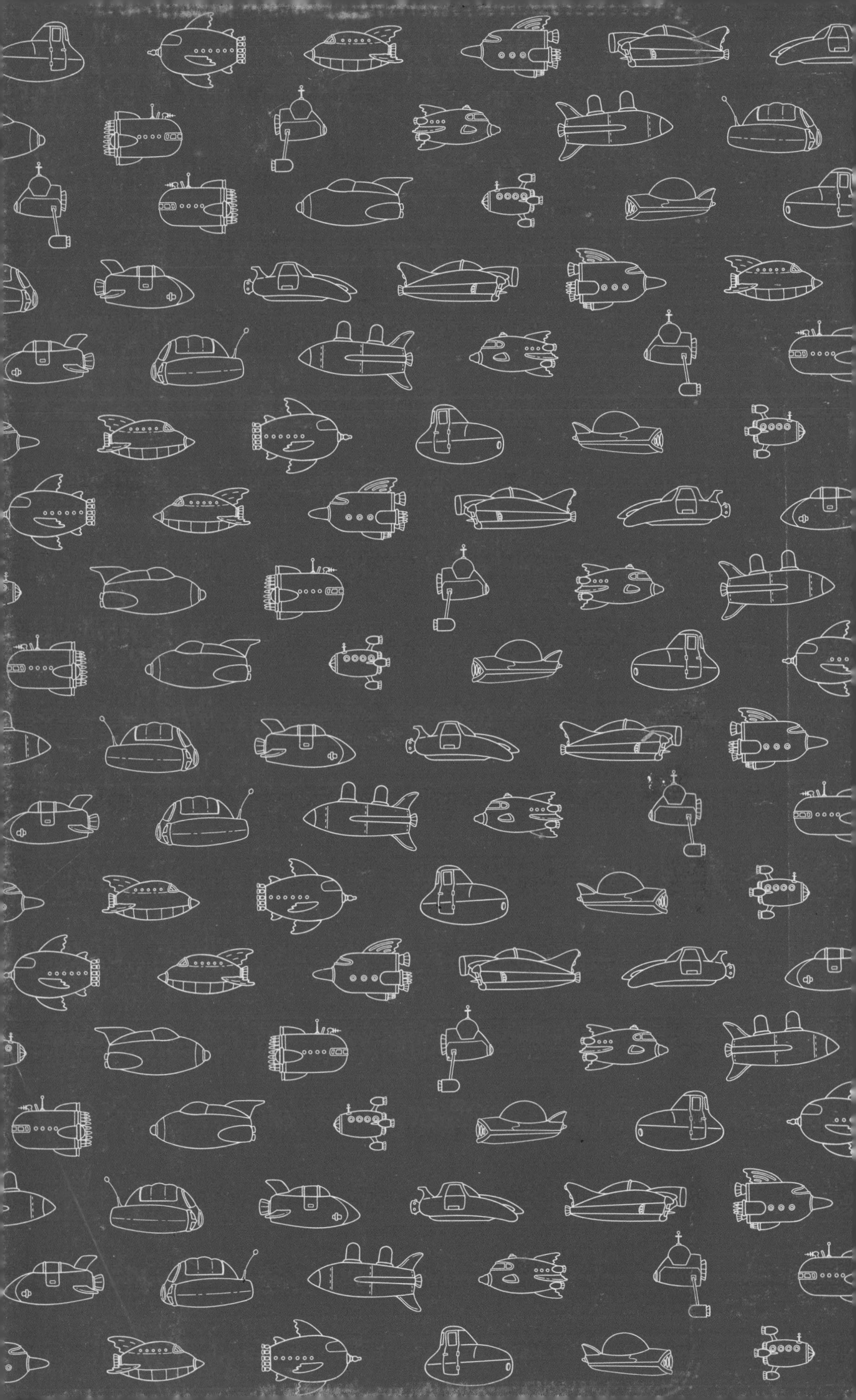